JOSE FERRATER MORA has been professor of philosophy at Bryn Mawr College since 1949. A graduate of the University of Barcelona, he has lived in France, Cuba, and Chile. Mr. Ferrater Mora is the author of twelve books, among which are a study of Ortega y Gasset and a study of Miguel de Unamuno. He is best known for his *Dictionary of Philosophy*, a widely used reference work.

José Ferrater Mora

MAN AT THE CROSSROADS

Translated from the Spanish by Willard R. Trask

GREENWOOD PRESS, PUBLISHERS
NEW YORK   1968

Preface to the American Edition

When the original Spanish edition of the present book was published in 1952, I had hoped that it could be translated into English. After all, the book was written in the United States, and in the very same place at which this preface is being written. The Beacon Press has realized this hope. I am happy to express to the Press, and in particular to its Director, Mr. Thomas A. Bledsoe, my sincere gratitude. I also wish to extend my acknowledgments to Mr. Willard R. Trask, who is too well known as a translator to need my praise; and to President Katharine E. McBride, of Bryn Mawr College, who has helped in various ways to make the present edition possible.

The fact that the book was written in the United States is not irrelevant for the understanding of its contents. As early as 1945, I had planned this work. Much travel and research had paved the way for writing it, but it is my experience of American life superimposed upon my European background that has given the book its specific character: its "optimistic realism," or perhaps its "realistic optimism." These expressions sound commonsensical enough to be frowned upon by both incorrigible dreamers and sophisticated prophets of doom. But it is not my fault if common sense is often truer to life than apocalyptic fantasy. It is my contention throughout the book that threats to mankind are more serious today than they ever have been, for they include the threat of self-extermination. But it is also my contention that hopes for the improvement of the whole of mankind have never been brighter than they are now. I am not willing therefore to prognosticate the ruin of mankind or to forecast for tomorrow a paradisiacal planet. Between hell and heaven there is still room for all.

The American edition contains a number of changes in respect to the original Spanish edition. Some of the changes are major ones: they include a rewriting of the first chapter, substantial alterations in a number of pages, and the addition of some

long notes at the end of the last two chapters. These notes are
intended to treat of problems whose importance was not commonly acknowledged at the time the book was written. I do
not think that the world begins anew every day, as newspaper
editors and radio and television broadcasters tend to make us
believe. But I think that when major events occur, and major
problems arise, they should be analyzed. Some of the changes
are minor ones: they include the rephrasing of some sentences,
and modifications in the bibliographical notes. This edition contains also a complete subject and name index.

Each chapter of the book is followed by its own series of notes.
They are not mere footnotes which have been relegated to the
end in order to free the text from them and make it more read-
able. They have their own character, and can be read as a continuation of the chapter. They are commentaries on the problems discussed, fuller treatment of certain interesting questions,
clarifications of doubtful points. Hence they are printed in the
same type as the rest of the book. Under these conditions, it has
not mattered that some of the notes are rather long; the only consideration has been that they should not prove tedious.

The last note in each series is bibliographical. It provides the
necessary references for the authors or books cited in the corresponding chapter. It must be borne in mind that many of the
books mentioned are secondary sources. The primary sources
have also been taken into account, but it has not always seemed
advisable to cite them. For example, texts from the Stoics and
from Plotinus have been mentioned in the notes to chapters 2
and 3, but direct references to Christian texts—the majority of
which are surely familiar to the reader—have been almost entirely omitted. The case is the same with the bibliographical data
for chapters 7 and 11. The author has not forgotten the principal writers of the periods he was describing, especially the
philosophical writers, of whom his knowledge is least inadequate.
But except when he has dealt with a specific passage from such a
writer (for example, that from Locke in the last note to chapter
8), he has omitted references. Mustering texts to illustrate the
various conceptions studied would not only have been cumber-

some, but would have been inappropriate to the nature of this book. Thus, Descartes is discussed, and Luther, Montaigne, Machiavelli are mentioned, but no texts of theirs are cited. Moreover, some important names do not appear at all, but this does not mean that they have not been taken into consideration. Hence the bibliographical and illustrative material may appear to have been arbitrarily selected. The author asks that this be imputed not only to his ignorance, but also to his plan.

JOSÉ FERRATER MORA

Bryn Mawr, Pennsylvania
March, 1957

PART I. *Philosophy, Anxiety, and Renewal*

1. The Question Proposed

The question.–Two ways of answering it.–The beginning of the crisis: philosophy.–Socrates in a concentration camp.–The wise man as a type.–Philosophy as science and philosophy as life.–The philosopher and other
men.–The anonymous power, or historical phenomena as
geological phenomena.–Answers to the question.

The problems to be raised in this book are manifold, but all of
them will be found to revolve around one question: Is it possible
to integrate our steadily enlarging societies—and ultimately the
whole of human society—in forms of higher material and spiritual life?

This question we shall answer in the affirmative. Against those
who delight in painting a gloomy future, we maintain that the
future looks comparatively bright. But the author, though fundamentally an optimist, is under no illusion: he knows that, today
more than ever, mankind is at a crossroads, and that the road to
reconstruction runs close beside the road to ruin. Hence he has
not yielded to the temptation to substitute dreams for facts, or
to ignore the ambivalent character of all great human phenomena.

Now, before we come to discuss the present human situation,
a long history must be unfolded. In Part II of this book, then,
we shall treat of the modern period and of the various crises that
it underwent before reaching the great—and, in our view, fruitful—crisis of contemporary society. Why, then, must we yet pre-
cede this treatment by an historical analysis of the problems that
rose to confront ancient man in the "West," particularly during
the period when his world was beginning to break up?

We must do so because, in the same sense in which we cannot
understand past forms of life without relating them to contemporary problems, so it is equally impossible to understand our

3

own problems fully without the perspective provided by the examination of a comparatively distant past. Needless to say, this cannot be merely any past; it must be one in which we find situations similar to our own. But this condition is fulfilled precisely by the ancient world, and especially by that world in its final phase. To be sure, not even the final phase of the ancient world is *altogether* comparable to the development of the modern world. The differences between them are in many respects irreconcilable. But some striking similarities between them justify our subjecting both to detailed examination. Hence it may be seen that there is inevitably a close relationship between the two parts of this book. As we describe the ancient world, we shall constantly have the contemporary world in mind. As we examine the present, we shall try to illumine it by the knowledge we have gained of the more remote past. The resulting historical study will be complex; perhaps it will as well be illuminating.

Such, then, is our question. It is time to see how it was answered.

It should be noted that the question did not present itself in ancient times in the same way that it does now; what men asked themselves was whether, and how, they could react to a phenomenon that emerged as a terrifying fact, more geological than historical: the formation of a "Universal State."

The question became more and more disturbing, and especially during the phase in which the Hellenistic-Roman world perished and the Occidental-Christian world was born. For a number of centuries, man was in danger of remaining helpless before an historical process that no one seemed to be setting in motion, that seemed to belong to everyone and to no one, in which everyone was embraced and no one included, a process of nature rather than of history, an immense and anonymous State. It can be understood to mean various things: a great empire or a huge political organization; a type of society that pretends to usurp all of man's functions; perhaps nothing other than the feeling—justified or not—that the historical horizon is blocked and that there is no way of escape.

It is not easy to determine when this process started. Unlike a physical phenomenon, an historical process does not begin at a particular point in time. Yet, even at the risk of incurring the objection that our description embraces too long a period, we shall make the beginning of a consciousness that a crisis was approaching coincide with the beginnings of philosophy. The process in question began when certain individuals felt themselves exiled from their native society, and sought for something to fill the consequent void in their minds. Thus Greek philosophy, which technically was an objective investigation of reality, could, from the human point of view, be considered as a form of life which was instigated by solitude. To say this is not to relativize thought. Human thought has two aspects: on the one hand, it denotes or connotes—or both at once—a reality; on the other, it expresses a human attitude. These two aspects of thought are, indeed, inseparable. But we shall be concerned primarily with thought as a human activity and, therefore, as a "subjective belief" in certain supposedly immutable principles.

I have often asked myself what Socrates would have done today in the horror of a concentration camp. True to himself, he would not have rebelled. Rebellion is a reaction of the man who still believes in the efficacy of society. Nor would he have asked for help. He would have descended into himself, slowly and serenely; he would have sought in reason—in his own reason—strength enough to resist the horrors by which he was surrounded. In so doing, he would have distinguished himself from the rest of men; he would have gained a tragic greatness. He would have become, as in fact he became, an example of the human type that was known in Greece as the *sóphos*, the "sage" or "wiseman." Socrates was not the first exemplification of this species in the history of the West, but he was the first who exemplified it with incomparable maturity. He was, indeed, the wiseman who is not wise simply because he knows many things, but because he knows only one important thing: that reason is one and permeates the whole of reality.

If the Greek sage discovered reason, however, it was because he needed it. It has been said that philosophy arose as an attempt to replace a world of beliefs that had evaporated. Such an attempt can be made only when man feels himself existentially alone. This is why anxiety and philosophy can be associated. For by the term "anxiety" we do not mean a vague feeling of concern. We mean, rather, an extremely concrete fact—the fact that, during certain moments, a man feels that he is segregated from society, unable to fit into it, yet at the same time believing neither that he is above it, as a model for all existence, nor that he is below it, as a passive and resigned portion of nature.

Philosophy can be, then, understood in two ways. From one viewpoint, it is a science elaborated by professional philosophers, a result of a reflective activity that, in principle, could be exercised by any rational being. From another viewpoint, it is a mode of being of human existence. Now if, in order to determine what a philosophy *says* we must abide by the first conception, in order to know what a philosophy *means*, we shall do well to keep the second in mind. It is the conception that we shall emphasize throughout this book. "Philosophy" will primarily be understood as "philosophic life," a life that usually emerges between the moment in which man feels himself still alone and the moment in which he has already renewed himself.

The emergence of such a life does not happen at any random instant. A certain combination of circumstances is presupposed. In the ancient world it was the "schism in the body social"—to use Toynbee's vocabulary—that precipitated the process that we plan to describe: the "schism in the soul." It was a long process. From the fourth century B.C. to the "banishment" of the "last philosopher" by Justinian in 529 A.D., a historical development took place in a *crescendo* so well harmonized that it resembles not only a symphony, but even a classical symphony. Two melodies are perceptible in this symphony: one is the termination of the ancient Greek world; the other, the termination of the Imperial Roman world. Since, however, a common theme underlies these two melodies, it is necessary to delineate it. Tentatively, we may say that our task consists in determining to what degree the anxiety originally felt by some philosophers disseminated through a considerable mass of men. Thus we have accorded to philosophers an attention seemingly out of proportion to the role that they played in history. But the importance of a man's role in history is not measured solely by the changes that he introduces in society; it can also be measured by his capacity to mirror such changes. Marx has said that philosophers have confined themselves to explaining the world, but that what is needed is to change it. He did not sufficiently take into account the fact that philosophical contemplation is not only a passive activity. It would be unjust, then, to be too critical of the philosophers because of their inability to govern society or to build pyramids—especially since some of them have provided the intellectual instruments that are prerequisites for performing these operations.

A certain number of men—and the philosophers more clearly than anyone else—formulated the question that everyone was trying to solve. During a period of several centuries, very different groups were in essentially the same situation. Many of them had one primary aim: to resist. Many others relied on action or on hope. But all of them found themselves placed in a frightening world, over which they could exercise no power. In the world of Antiquity, a moment arrived when man could not even exercise the power of confidently asking the augurs what his destiny was. Destiny was still consulted, but the answer vouchsafed was believed only because it was adverse. "All auguries for these forty days have been inauspicious; and that proves that we may place trust in them." For by now destiny was in the hands neither of men nor of gods. It was in the hands of an anonymous, vague, and featureless force. The arena of history saw the appearance of a "Universal State," created by men, but as imposing and ineluctable as a phenomenon of nature. In the last analysis, it did not even need to assume the figure of a State; and, perhaps for that reason, the word "society" would be more apt than "Universal State." Our basic theme is, then, that at certain moments great historical phenomena are *like* great geological cataclysms; nobody and nothing can stop them. At such times man feels that he is lost; his personal life hardly counts in the face of such elemental impulses of "History-Nature." And even those who have succeeded in imposing themselves, in "directing" events, the "Caesars," are no more than the crest of the great wave. Man has lost his old freedom without having gained any new kind of freedom. His choice has been reduced to its minimum; like the Word to which Faust referred, it is nothing but noise and smoke clouding the dome of heaven.

What can man do at such times? It has been said that man thinks and acts to the full only when the sword is at his throat. This is not at all certain if we take into account the many oc-

casions on which, in such situations, men have perished by the
sword. But taking the notion *cum grano salis,* we can agree that
it is in such moments that the incomparable faculty of human
invention reveals itself with singular force. For the time at which
there appears to be no alternative to despair is the time in which
most deeply men dig the pit from which the roots of hope will
draw nourishment. In any case, man can do whatever he pleases
except remain paralyzed. A number of the things he has done
will be related in the following pages. As we shall see, some men
tried to resist, in the various ways in which resistance is possible: through scorn, indifference, renunciation, or flight. These
were the philosophers. Others lived in a world quivering with
innumerable visions, some consecrated by tradition, some blown
on the winds of prophecy. They were the futurists. Others tried
to ride the wave of the time. These were the powerful, the imi-
tators (or the servants) of Caesar. Others set out to destroy
society, without having any new society in view. These were the
"barbarians." Still others dimly foresaw a new kingdom, which,
though not of this world in its beginning, ended by changing the
world. These were the Christians. It was these voices, apparently discordant, but in fact profoundly akin, which, for a period
of several centuries, composed the melody of "universal history."

Notes

In this and other chapters we have touched upon difficult
problems in the sociology of knowledge. In fact, one of the
basic questions discussed—whether certain philosophic doctrines
can be interpreted as "human reactions to a historical situation"
—depends upon the results of such a sociology. To admit
this does not imply adherence to a radical historicism. In his
The Open Society and Its Enemies, London, Vol. II (1945), 205
ff., K. R. Popper has sharply criticized the so-called historicism
of the sociology of knowledge (especially that implied in the
works of Karl Mannheim and Max Scheler) by showing that
the defenders of such a "science" pay no attention to the "objectivity of scientific method." We think, however, that the
"objectivity of scientific method" demands that all the charac-

teristics of reality be considered. One of these characteristics is the "human aspect" of knowledge.

It has often been asked whether philosophy appeared as a novelty characteristic of Western life, or as a reaction against all novelties, as a manifestation of nostalgia. Probably, at its birth, philosophy followed a twofold path. On the one hand, it was a thinking response to a new historical situation; on the other hand, it was a wish to reconstruct a mythical and legendary past. In the former case philosophy was conceived as a rational system; in the latter case philosophy was considered as a new form of mythical thinking. It is difficult to disentangle what belongs to each one of the above concepts of philosophy in the systems of the Presocratics. It is quite probable that each system of Presocratic philosophy contains *logos* as much as it contains *mythos*. In some respects, for instance, Heraclitus was a traditionalist; the rise of the masses did more than preoccupy him —it disgusted him. But at the same time we can find in his ideas some violent attacks on what Gilbert Murray and E. R. Dodds have called "the Inherited Conglomerate." The sophists belonged to the Greek "age of Enlightenment." But the *Anonymus Iamblichi* contains injunctions of a clearly "regressive" character. The poets followed the same twofold path as the philosophers. There is, in fact, an inextricable mixture of reason and tradition in the works of Pindar, or Sophocles or Aristophanes. We can conclude that rational thinking and mythical thinking are equally alive in classic Greek philosophy and even in the whole of classic Greek civilization. It is a well-known fact that Plato tried to blend these two apparently contradictory ingredients. Plato's aim in this respect, however, was not only philosophical, but also political. He thought that a delicate balance between reason and myth was needed in order to succeed in reforming—or rather "counterreforming"—society (see on this point, E. R. Dodds, *The Greeks and the Irrational*, Berkeley and Los Angeles [1951], chapters VI and VII).

The expression "end of the ancient world," which is frequently used in Part I of this book, does not necessarily imply our having taken any definite position in regard to the flexible dividing line between the ancient world and the medieval world or the Western Christian world. Until recently, Christianity was commonly regarded as representing the chief dividing line. This thesis was seriously shaken when it was realized that Christianity had also been an important factor in the development of the ancient world. Then too, as it was discovered to what an extent the "barbarian invasions" had failed to alter many important elements of Antiquity, a more precise boundary was sought. In his posthumous book *Mahomet et Charlemagne* (Paris [1937]; English translation, *Mohammed and Charlemagne*, New York [1939]), Henri Pirenne pointed out that what we call the "ancient world" is defined by the Mediterranean littoral (Pirenne's thesis goes back to 1922, in an article under the above title published in the *Revue belge de Philologie et d'Histoire*, I [1922], 77-86). Hence the end of ancient civilization coincides with the rupture of Mediterranean unity. This rupture took place when the ancient world was split by the Islamic invasion. Pirenne's views have been developed by Ernst Kornemann in his *Weltgeschichte des Mittelmeer-Raumes von Philipp von Makedonien bis Muhammed*, München, 2 vols. (1948). To be sure, Kornemann devotes considerably less attention than did Pirenne to the littoral aspect of this civilization, and includes in it, with convincing arguments, the Near Eastern and Middle Eastern worlds. If we adhere to Toynbee's postulate that a "civilization" deserves this name only when it can be self-sufficient, "Iranism" must, then be incorporated with "Hellenism" and "Romanism"; all three were aspects of a single culture and influenced one another reciprocally. This doctrine is now gaining deserved favor among historians. Now, since our analysis does not belong to historiography, we are not obliged to involve ourselves in these questions except in so far as we need certain concrete references to explain the expression "end of the ancient world." We believe that the expression is equally admissible if we take the epoch of Constantine as the dividing line or if we regard the year 711 as the point of rupture.

To José Ortega y Gasset I owe the suggestion that philosophy may have arisen to fill the void left by beliefs. See his essay "Notes on Thinking—Its Creation of the World and Its Creation of God" in *Concord and Liberty*, New York (1946), 49-82, a translation of "Apuntes sobre el pensamiento. Su teurgia y su demiurgia," first published in *Logos*, Buenos Aires, Vol. I, No. 1 (1944) and included in the latest edition of his *Obras completas*, 6 vols., 1946-47 (hereafter cited as *O.C.*), Madrid, Vol. V (1947), pp. 517-546.–The expressions "Universal State," "schism in the body social," and "schism in the soul" occur in Toynbee, *A Study of History.*, V and VI (1939), as well as in the abridgment of the *Study* by D. C. Somervell, New York (1947), 371-530.–The quotation concerning the inauspicious auguries is from Ibsen, *Emperor and Galilean*, II, 5 (translated by William Archer in *The Collected Works of Henrik Ibsen*, Vol. V, New York [1907]). Cf. in this connection Calderón's verses: "¡Qué pocas veces el hado / que dice desdichas miente . . . !" ("Ah! few the times when Fate, / telling disaster, lies") (*La vida es sueño*, II, xi).–The pressure of what we have called "History-Nature" was clearly perceived by certain ancient writers; it seems, for example, that Seneca had in mind the situation we have attempted to describe, when he said (*De clementia*, III, xxiv, 5) that to kill great multitudes and indiscriminately is a power proper to fire and disaster—*multos quidem occidere et indiscretos incendi ac ruinae potentia est.* When cruelty reaches excessive proportions, it seems incredible that it is the work of men.

2. Cynics and Stoics

Lucidity.–Cynicism as a way of life.–The Cynic school. –Cynic extremism.–Suppression of action: Cynic immobility and Christian immobility.–Contempt for conventions.–The Cynic as "bastard."–Cynicism and nihilism.

Resistance.–The Stoic school.–Physics, Logic, Ethics.–The Stoic as mediator.–Knowledge and cure.–Stoic ethics.–The problem of happiness: the two kinds of happiness.–Increase and diminution of life.–The inner dwelling.–Freedom for resistance.–Indifference to "things." –Impassibility: life without anger and without hate.– Compassion and apathy.–The problem of self-sufficiency. –Life in retreat.–The refuge of the "self" and the "exit" into nature.–Aspiration and quietism.–The Stoic illusion.–Disinterestedness without compassion.–The failure of Stoicism.

One of the recourses that man discovers in order to live, without falling into complete despair, in the "concentration camp" that society from time to time becomes, is lucidity. Such, in any case, was the surmise of three types of sages who stood out in the struggle between the schools—Cynics, Stoics, and Platonists. All three transformed a way of thinking into an ideal of life. The same tendency was followed by some other philosophers: the Epicureans and the Sceptics. We dismiss them from our account, however, because some of the dominant characteristics that we shall encounter in the first three are merely repeated, though less markedly, in the others.

Let us begin with the Cynic. He is not only a man who holds a particular philosophic doctrine. In his account of the opinions of Antisthenes, Diogenes Laërtius speaks of an *enstasis biou*, of a way of life. It is not an ordinary way of life, but one pursued in a spirit of constant dedication. To be sure, Socrates had already considered philosophy as an *enstasis biou*. In discerning the possibility that society might strangle itself, either through overorganization or through anarchy, Socrates made a major discovery: that, under society, there is always *man*—man as an individual entity and at the same time as a representative of all human beings. Thenceforth man became, for many philosophers, the being who not only has problems, but who *is* a problem. Such a discovery was not trivial. Moreover, it could only be made by someone who had felt in his life a "void" that was not automatically filled by the society around him. Hence, from the time of Socrates, man was often defined as what remains after all adjustments between the individual and society have been unsuccessfully attempted. A human being, so many thought, cannot be reduced to a "social animal." Socrates himself did not express these thoughts clearly, but he lived, and died, in strict accordance with them. The Cynics, on the other hand, made no mystery of their philosophy of human existence. Preceded by a series of economic upheavals, by the formation of a socially uprooted proletarian mass, the Cynics built, on the basis of Socrates' discoveries, an outspokenly antisocial ideology. So there is nothing extraordinary in the fact that it is more befitting to regard Cynicism as a human reaction to a historical situation than as a phase in an abstract history of ideas.

This explains its "atmospheric" character. It is difficult to measure Cynicism by the usual pattern of philosophic systems. What, actually, did the Cynic do—from Antisthenes or Diogenes down to the last Cynic of Antiquity, the philosopher Sallust? Something very simple: he theorized a particular attitude toward life and turned the resulting doctrine into philosophico-literary productions whose most constant form of expression, especially from the second century B.C., was the "diatribe." The diatribe performed the same office as the proverbial shepherd's-crook and wallet. It allowed the Cynic to stand out from the rest of mankind and at the same time to offer himself as a model to mankind. This is why the Cynics, despite their ferocious individualism, formed a school. In a period in which, as today, groups, sects, and circles flourished and proliferated, there was in fact nothing else to do but to adopt the social form which would be most effective for all those who, without pretending to power, sought to represent something for society—a ferment, perhaps a seed. Thus our description applies equally to the Cynic type and to the Cynic school.

The school flourished at two periods. The first was the time of Diogenes. The atmosphere was charged to the point where a deluge seemed to threaten. It is the period of confusion described by Dio Chrysostom in his eighth *Discourse*. The second was four centuries later. It is the period described by Lucian of Samosata. Between the two periods, a decisive event took place: for a time, the Roman power seemed to be strong enough to stabilize society once and for all. The difference between the two periods marked the difference between two forms of Cynicisms. In Greece, Cynicism was still an intellectual attitude; it addressed itself to minorities, to those capable of going into raptures over philosophical ideas. In Rome, it was already a historical event; though not always—as is sometimes said—the philosophy of the dispossessed classes, it greatly appealed to them. The classes in power had other, more "dignified" means of facing the historical situation. In short: in Greece, Cynicism was still a theory; in Rome, it became a rule of action—a very paradoxical rule of action, for it invited men to refuse to act.

What, then, was Cynicism? If we reduce all its variants to a common denominator we can define it as "a way of facing a crisis." As a matter of fact, it faced the crisis by pushing it to an extreme. It was the philosophy of total insecurity. The world in which Cynicism arose was a world full of threats. The themes of the ancient Cynic diatribe—exile, slavery, loss of freedom— were no mere rhetorical commonplaces; they designated impending dangers. There are certain periods in which men discover that they can even cease to be men. The first and most urgent thing to do then is "to stand out." But "to stand out" does not here mean simply to preserve one's social positions. On the contrary, it means to abandon them and concentrate on an imperative most difficult to follow: to be a man. In order to comply with this imperative the Cynic even renounced action. Confronted with a society in which, as he thought, all action is futile, the Cynic decided "to suspend movement." It would, however, be mistaken to equate this decision with one that was characteristic of certain primitive Christian groups. The Cynic "suspension of movement" did not consist in remaining in the state in which one had happened to be when "one was called." The primitive Christian abstained from action out of hope, whereas the Cynic aspired to immobility out of pure desperation. This is probably the meaning which, according to Diogenes Laërtius, was contained in certain counsels of Diogenes. For Diogenes praised those who were about to marry and renounced doing so, those who intended to take a journey and did not set out, those who thought of devoting themselves to political life and did not enter it. Christian immobility was only apparent; to suspend movement was to act *as if* one did not act. Only thus could the inner movement, the infinite tension, of hope shine through. Cynic immobility, on the other hand, was real; to the Cynic, all inner tension appeared to be an illusion that should be unmasked. But since it is impossible to do absolutely nothing, all his capacity for action was concentrated in one simple, insolent, naked act: contempt.

Of society, there now seemed to be nothing left—or, at most, its mask, the conventions. Even these were not living conventions, manifestations of an intense faith; they were dead conventions, vestiges of remote golden ages. What was to be done about them? They could, for example, be accepted. This was in fact what most people did. Society thus found the solution for its problem in a way of life that had once flourished but that was now almost desiccated—"correctness." The Cynic could do nothing of the sort. His first battle cry was "Down with the conventions!" For the Cynic did not yet believe that, between this moribund society and the solitary individual, there could be anything else; he did not admit that, between complete self-consciousness and complete self-alienation there could be a middle term: charity. Outside oneself there was, in his view, only a terrifying void. Nothing could fill it; hence he must not hesitate to

abolish it. Conventions were a bond which no longer bound anything. Why, then, should he make an effort to preserve them?
Why hypocritically keep up appearances? Better to throw everything overboard, refuse to live falsely, face the crisis without
squeamishness. Here we have the essence of Cynicism. The
Cynic could be ascetic or moderately hedonistic. It made no
difference; all that he sought to do was to survive in the universal shipwreck. To the rest of mankind, he said—he screamed—
"You really believe in nothing; and it is in vain that you try to
hide it. Why struggle to preserve your empty conventions? Act
as you feel, as you are; perhaps by so doing you will achieve
the one thing for which, at bottom, you hope—to save your-
selves."

The Cynic's entire life, tense by force of relaxation, had but
one purpose—to resist through contempt, to destroy the dusty
carapace of a dead society. Thus the Cynic, as one of those who
knew him best has said, became a "bastard," an "outsider." But
we must not forget that incompatibility with the present sometimes conceals a certain affinity with the future. And in fact the
Cynic attitude seemed to foreshadow some of the attitudes—
monasticism, for example—which were characteristic of nascent
Christianity. Unlike the Christian, however, the Cynic found no
inner peace; his consciousness was always a "divided, unhappy
consciousness." But since the "divided consciousness" was both
an individual and a social phenomenon, there came a time when
it was extremely difficult to distinguish between two attitudes so
different as the cynicism of the spirit and the cynicism of power.
The confusion arose from the fact that they appeared to be two
nuances of the same will to contempt. In any case, Cynicism
operated as a refuge—a refuge *against* society, *against* man himself. The two were equally tyrannical. Now, the Cynic avoided
all tyranny. Coercion—outward or inward—was the great
enemy of what in the last analysis he sought: peace, quiet, rest.

These were difficult to attain—and all the more so within such
narrow margins. Deceived by his own self-confidence the
Cynic thought that he could easily find under the ruins of a stagnant society the necessary strength to confront the historical
situation. By dint of seeking a radical solution, the Cynic, how-

ever, ended with nothing. He had to throw off practically every-thing: knowledge, civil life, the possibility of mutual aid and even of communication. Hence Cynicism, which began as a way of life that scorned learning, had to end as a caricature of learn-ing. Like all radicalism, Cynicism gnawed its own tail. Some men, it is true, could still be Cynics; but not all men, or even a substantial number of them. And so another more popular solu-tion had to be found.

Did Stoicism provide it?

Carried by the immense tidal wave of the time, man could not always swim entirely against the stream. But there is another way of meeting the violence of a current: to resist it. This way was the Stoic solution. "Resistance" is the key term of Stoic philoso-phy. All the other terms abundantly used by the Stoics—"ten-sion," "spirit," "universal reason," "nature"—can be given a mean-ing on the basis of "resistance."

Like most philosophers of the period we are describing, the Stoics organized themselves in a school. Was it, as is often said, a school of knowledge? We doubt it, if by "knowledge" we mean only "disinterested speculation." All the members of the Stoic school were in agreement on this point. To be sure, historians of philosophy insist upon the fact that the Stoic school can be split into a certain number of stages. They point out, besides, that these stages differed not only by the respective preponderance of their Greek or Roman elements but also by the increasing significance attributed to ethical motives. In our opinion, how-ever, such differences are negligible. The Stoics devoted a great deal of attention to physics and logic and they even made some noteworthy contributions to logical theory. But Zeller long since pointed out that, in however great detail the Stoics treated the different parts of philosophy, "the true core of their system" was ethics. Physics itself, "that most divine part of philosophy," was only a preparation for ethics. This attitude, we may add, was the usual one in all the Hellenistic systems; as Émile Bréhier has writ-ten, we understand them better when we see that their primary preoccupation is educational, not speculative. Here too, then, as in Cynicism, we find a form of life. But the fact that the Stoics were also concerned, and on a considerable scale, with the theo-retical parts of philosophy proves that there was a striking difference between them and the Cynics. Unlike the Cynics, the Stoics did not scoff at all knowledge; they even undertook to "save" it.

For the Cynic, in short, knowledge was justified only if it directly and immediately sustained human life. He thought, then, that to know is only to know how to behave. Of what use, then, are logic and physics? The Stoic, on the other hand, although he likewise understood knowledge in terms of human life, rejected the despotic rule of either. Was not all despotism to be avoided? And the despotism of life was not one of the least oppressing. It is true that the Cynic, too, rejected the domination of life. But as he lost, or broke, the thread that connected living with knowing, nature with convention, he finally succumbed to the tyranny of the very life he had so forcefully denounced.

The Stoic never went so far; he never admitted either a radical break or a complete identification between human life and knowledge. The Stoic was always a mediator, an eclectic, a master in the art of salving wounds and building bridges. Hence he could not fall into what was the perpetual pitfall of the Cynic— into vice transformed into virtue by self-contempt; into license transformed into a rule of action. For Cynicism, carried to its ultimate consequences, could do anything whatever with a life that had previously been cut off from all relationships. Just as, for certain Gnostics of Antiquity, or for certain modern "illuminati," what man does can become a matter of indifference to what he is; so an entirely relaxed morality could automatically supersede the asceticism and rigid morality of Cynicism. This did not actually happen among the Cynics of Antiquity, still less among those who are mentioned in histories of philosophy. But it could have happened without their in the least ceasing to be Cynics.

This, then, is one of the reasons why the Stoic could not scoff at knowledge. Knowledge was not only an instrument, it was also a medicine. For the Stoics, to know was, in the last analysis, to cure.

We must not be deceived by the fact that the work of certain Stoics—Chrysippus and Posidonius, for example—was truly encyclopaedic. This fact does not in the least modify our position in regard to the role that *all* knowledge played for them. Let us take physics. Is it a physics, properly speaking? It looks more like a labyrinth. The fire of Heraclitus, "rational seeds," the world as a great living being, Destiny as ruler of the universe and sometimes identified with it—what do we not find when we set out to enumerate the component elements of this *imago mundi* in which common sense alternated with fantasy? The only thread that can guide us through such a labyrinth is the one we have so often mentioned before—man. *In principle,* the world and its description *should be* matters of indifference. *In fact,* the omnipresence of man makes them inescapable. Like the Platonist, the Stoic pretended to "save phenomena." But never at the price of his own existence. For the sake of individualism? It is doubtful. Does not the Stoic preach the dissolution of each in the whole, the final restitution of our being to Nature? But the radical "objectivism" of the Stoics can only be explained by the fact that it was nourished by an ethical, human attitude. Should the Universe be emptied of humanity, Stoic physics would immediately lose its meaning. Hence, unlike the "physiology" of the Ionians, or Aristotelian "physics," Stoic physics was not a principle but a consequence. The classic Greek philosophers could, as Empedocles or Democritus had done, derive their conduct from their conception of the Universe. The Stoics sought, and found, a conception of the Universe which would harmonize with their conduct. Physical knowledge, then, did not disappear, but became subordinate. The "saving" of phenomena continued, but only as a consequence of the will to save human life.

The Stoics were not, then, solely concerned with ethics. But whatever they did, they did *as if* they pretended to solve ethical problems. Their ideas about the hierarchy of philosophic disciplines fulfilled this basic condition. Let us consider the doctrine of Epictetus. The first step in philosophy, Epictetus says, is to abide by such injunctions as: "Do not lie." Next comes the demonstration of why we should not lie. And finally, the discussion of why such a demonstration really constitutes a proof. The third step is necessary because of the second, and the second because of the first. But only the first step is absolutely necessary. Hence Stoic ethics cannot be called a purely descriptive ethics. How could the term "descriptive" be applied to an ethics that based human conduct on a materially categorical imperative?

But let us leave this subject, which would take us too far, and let us resume our investigation.

Primarily, then, the Stoics cultivated ethics. But there are many types of ethics. To engage in ethical pursuits can mean seeking the norms through which certain realities are considered good, and clearing the path in order to attain such realities. Or it can mean discovering what is the Good in itself, and trying to live in accordance with it. Being mediators, the Stoics sought not to exclude from their pursuits anything that they considered morally significant. As in physics, so in ethics they devoted themselves to combining elements, to mingling materials. But at bottom they only relied upon an inflexible and unchanging injunction: "Save yourself by a continual return to yourself." As in all the ethical systems of Antiquity, in the Stoic ethical system the concept of *eudaimonía*, of happiness, played an important role. But the meaning of the term *"eudaimonía"* in the Stoic system of ethics was not the same as in most other ethical systems of Antiquity.

The word *"eudaimonía"* has two meanings. On the one hand, it can mean the feeling of euphoria that invades us from time to time and that causes us to stretch out our arms to all men and all things. When this kind of happiness prevails, life does not only reach fullness, it overflows our being and seems to flood the rest of the universe. On the other hand, *"eudaimonía"* can mean the feeling of security that permeates our being when we reduce our wishes to a minimum. The former meaning is common in culminating periods, when there is, or there seems to be, abundance of vital projects. The latter meaning is frequent in critical periods, when the only project that seems worth considering is the project of survival. It is this second meaning of *"eudaimonía"* that the Stoics emphasized. They made happiness revolve around the "self," the only place where true peace, in their opinion, was to be found. Only from oneself was it possible— or reasonable—to set out toward the world. For only once this inner dwelling-place had been explored, only once its solidity had been tested, man would be able to live in an impregnable refuge. Such a refuge might even, as Marcus Aurelius wrote, become the basis for the perpetual and almost miraculous regeneration of the human person, "the fountain of good," always ready to flow. Thus the Stoic sought happiness in the "self," in the "things that are within us." Life was the great enemy: it produced disquiet, affliction, anxiety. It was better, then, to withdraw from life, and to contemplate the world with indifference and resignation. Thanks to this retreat the Stoic even allowed himself a luxury quite uncommon in his time: freedom. It was, of course, a purely individual freedom, not a political freedom. Using a well-known phrase of Guizot's, we could even say that it was a "freedom to resist." But while according to Guizot this freedom to resist was born in a dialectical process that incessantly oscillated from anarchy to power and from power to anarchy, according to the Stoic no process and, for that matter, no movement was necessary for the production of freedom. Freedom had always its point of rest, its place of retirement; and only from there could the stultifying weight of power and the dissolving activity of anarchy be exorcised. Hence the Stoic had no need to be concerned with temporal power. And hence, in confronting it—at least during the period of the so-called "New Stoicism"—he adopted an attitude *similar* to that of the Gospels. To render unto Caesar the things that are Caesar's is, in the last analysis, the consequence of having previously regarded these things as external goods. Caesar could exercise his power over everything except one thing—the individual judgment.

Thus, for the Stoic freedom had no connection with "things." Freedom was not holding a consulship or ruling a province; it was knowledge of how the wiseman must live in order to resist. And since being wise was incompatible with being a rhetorician, a tax-gatherer, or an imperial procurator, there was nothing to do but to perform these functions—when circumstances demanded—*as if* one were not performing them. In this "as if" the Stoic found the supreme artifice of his life. Incapable of throwing everything overboard, as the Cynic did, he found himself compelled to assume a mask. He did not bear in mind that the mask frequently supersedes the face. And perhaps, if Stoicism did not achieve its final aim of becoming the *ultima religio* of the still assimilable masses of the Roman Empire, it was because it put too much confidence in the virtues of masquerade. The Stoic sought always to live in the margin. It is not surprising that he became at the end a supporter of the very society at

which he had first directed his most violent invectives. The un-
fortunate thing was that such a society did not accept his
injunctions. In fact, it accepted the injunctions of no philosophers. As happens in all periods of serious crisis, many persons
then decided to philosophize on the theme, "We are against
philosophies."

But the Stoic was not much affected by this indifference of the
world around him. He took great care to keep out of harm's way.
You can be invincible, Epictetus wrote, if you never enter a struggle in which you cannot gain the victory. This platitude was one
of the pillars of Stoic existence. By virtue of it, the Stoic could
present to other men the appearance of a suave forbearance
polished by the rigor which he had used toward himself. At the
bottom of this forbearance, however, there was impassibility.
The Stoic was forever saying that anger, violence were to be
avoided; we must not, he insisted, become irritated with others
even when we punish them, even when we separate them from
society by exile or death; though we must eliminate them, let it
be without hatred. This appears to be goodness. But it is only
indifference. The Stoic, in fact, advised treating men as if they
were things. And this advice was one of the great paradoxes of
Stoicism. For, to the Stoic, man was always "the other man"—
the one who threatened to coerce the inner and irreducible
freedom of the individual judgment. In the last analysis, then,
the Stoics could enjoy the bliss of a quiet conscience after having eliminated their fellow mortals—*sine odio, sine ira,* of course.
However, it would be unjust to arraign them too harshly; to ask
of them that, after they had renounced so many things, they
should still retain the one thing that could have tempered their
indifference—compassion.

We may conclude that Stoicism was full of contradictions. Yet
the contradictions inherent in the Stoic philosophy were basically
the result of one heroic attempt. The Stoic tried to achieve love
without compassion and, as might be expected, he had to renounce both. His attempt in its turn was the consequence of an
illusion without which he could not have maintained his impassibility, his indifference. The Stoic believed that the rest of
mankind *could,* if they would, become Stoics; if they did not,

it was because an obstacle prevented them from advancing and entering the class of the "progressives." This obstacle could not be the will; it must, then, be stupidity—the stupidity which failed to understand that only a withdrawing from the outer world could bring inner peace, that only breaking one's ties with the world could bestow tranquil rest in the bosom of Nature.

With this, we encounter a difficulty. The Stoic, although in a different way from the Cynic, appeared to be a "radical." Yet we have said that he was a mediator, an eclectic. The Stoic philosophy has even been called the "philosophy of compromise." How are the above two attitudes to be reconciled? Quite simply—by showing that the radicalism with which the Stoic withdrew into himself was more a manifestation of lack of vigor than proof of a pure will to renunciation. Certainly, the Stoic did not wish to lose himself in the gratifications of an eclectic forbearance. But, basically, this was because he feared these gratifications; he thought that he might find "life" once again looming through them. In that case, he would have to stand up and face it. But the Stoic did not want to stand up and face anything, he wanted to make sure of a place behind everything. Never, for example, did he stand up to events; at most, he hoped to submit to them without too much distress. Epictetus put it in so many words: "Do not seek to have everything that happens happen as you wish, but wish for everything to happen as it actually does happen." In support of this doctrine the Stoics employed all kinds of arguments. Man, they said, is only an actor in a drama. He cannot even introduce so much as an "ad lib." between scene and scene. All that he can do is to play his role skilfully and calmly. Nothing else matters. It matters so little that man must disregard everything that troubles him on his road toward impassibility. He must turn a deaf ear to all outer voices. What is within us is enough. Or, as Seneca wrote, in an impeccable phrase: "What suffices you is within your reach." *Ad manum est, quod sat est.*

"Life in withdrawal"—there is no better formula for the definition of Stoicism. But to withdraw is not the same as to flee. To flee means to escape from the place where one lives, in order to settle in a more pleasant or more propitious place. The Stoic did not flee. Or, if there is any reason to preserve the verb, let us say that he "fled toward himself." Avoiding the multitude (*"se ipso esse contentum*"), retreating on all fronts—these were various ways of practicing an "interiorization" which did not exclude continuing to live in society (and even governing it), but which emphasized the doctrine that social life must be practiced— once again—*as if* it were not necessary. But here a problem arose. Was the "self" indeed the final refuge? If we recollect certain Stoic texts, it seems doubtful. Let us consider a theme that is by no means merely rhetorical: voluntary departure from life, suicide. It is explained by a typical Stoic conception: the notion that life is "neutral," that it is "indifferent." The suppression of life is even recommended to man when he is suffering from intolerable pain or an incurable disease. What, then, in the last analysis, does the "self" mean? The Stoics were not chary of declarations on this point: It is not so much one's own life as the possibility of subduing it, of doing as one will with it— forcing it to mingle in society without contamination, hardening it by strictness, ending it. Hence the problem was to know "who" or "what" could master one's own life. And since the Stoics had no idea of a reality that did not follow the pattern of "things," they put forward the famous doctrine: Man's true being, his final refuge, is Nature. To live according to Nature was the cornerstone of Stoic existence. This explains why the Stoic found it comparatively easy to attain impassibility, imperturbability, apathy. How could he fail to be imperturbable who, according to Epictetus, always kept "the door open"? The Stoic had removed the final obstacle—the idea that the "self" was to be identified with his own existence. It could, then, be said of him that he was heroic—always provided that we define "heroism" as the ability to shut one's eyes in the face of "danger," of the endless perturbations introduced by life. Only when one had succeeded in lowering this heavy curtain, which completely hid the troubles of the stage, could one be said to be on the right path. The most irrefutable sign that an "aspirant" is in a state of "progress" is, according to Epictetus, the fact that he has reached a situation where he need censure no one, praise no one, not even himself. When someone heaps compliments upon him, he only smiles; when someone assails him with reproaches, he does not try to answer. Thus the Stoic passed through life like an invalid (literally: *katháper oí árrōstoi*); his sole preoccupation was to cause no trouble, either to others or to himself.

But what of the trouble that knowledge brings with it? To begin with, the knowledge whose functions are not strictly delimited by ethical utility can be abandoned with no regret. As for what knowledge remains after this elimination, it too must be exercised impassively. We should not, then, venture to maintain that the most adequate formula for the Stoic life is Spinoza's "Neither bewail nor rejoice, but understand." We are not too sure that the Stoic really wanted to understand. What he wanted was to remain quiet, safe, and, of course, impassible. The Stoic was the very opposite of Don Juan or Faust. Don Juan aspired to shed his humanity over the world, after having identified "humanity" with the "pleasure of being human." Faust aspired to bear all the brunt of experience, which, unlike the Stoic, he would do nothing to limit. But the Stoic, like a character in a desolate contemporary novel, based his security "on the power to limit experience arbitrarily." The broadcasting of one's own humanity, the non-limitation of experience, would, for the Stoic, have been the manifestation of troubled depths—*ex turbido*, as Seneca phrased it. Searching for new experiences would not even have been sin, but pure folly. Those who fail to understand this, the Stoics would have said, do not take into account the insignificance of our lives; they do not consider that we must measure our lives not only by the standard of universal history but also by that of the cosmic process. The Stoics believed that they thus could attain a more embracing vision of their own existence; as a matter of fact, they were suffering from an incomprehension of reality. For it may be that *this* little mischance which is happening to me *now* is minute and even ridiculous in the face of universal history. But this mischance is happening *to me* whereas universal history happens to "others," to the undifferentiated mass. Is this egotism? It is more nearly the acceptance of an active participation with the lives of our fellow men. The Stoics forgot, therefore, the fact that renunciation is not always an evidence of firmness; it can even be a manifestation of cowardice. Horace's *Carpe diem*, Ausonius' *Collige, virgo, rosas*, Ronsard's *Cueillez dès aujourd'hui les roses de la vie*, Garcilaso's *Coged de vuestra alegre primavera el dulce fruto*, Herrick's

Gather ye rosebuds while ye may, and other similar counsels, can be products of softness. But very often, to follow them, one must have the courage to affirm one's own will and not to let oneself be overwhelmed by anxiety. It is not always comfortable to live in the disquiet of the present. It seems better to entrust oneself to the security of the past or the imagination of the future. This is what the Stoic did; hence he was incapable of saying, like Octavio to Don Diego in Tirso's *El Burlador de Sevilla:* "There's no help in 'I was'; only 'I am' avails."

But we have not undertaken to enumerate the flaws of Stoic philosophy. Rather, we are seeking to determine to what extent the Stoic succeeded in solving the historical situation that he had confronted. In this respect, there is no doubt that the Stoic found a more effective solution than did the Cynic. The Cynic was man in crisis—and hardly anything else. The Stoic both sought something more and glimpsed something more. For example, he caught a glimpse of "universality." Beyond all rhetoric on the subject of the neutrality of life and the insignificance of the individual self in comparison with the phenomena of the universe, the Stoic perceived that there was something sound in his proposal—especially reiterated during the period of the New Stoicism—to be a "citizen of the world." This universal citizenship was in part the consequence of an old "universality" that, according to Reinhardt, had already been fostered by Posidonius. It was also the recognition of a fact: the final dissolution of the ancient ideal of the City-State. But in the end the idea of universal citizenship assumed a more concrete character. To be a citizen of the world meant to be able to move without regret from one place to another, from one society to another. For the purpose, finally, of remaining alone with oneself or of entering into intimate communion with Nature? Yes—but also in order to associate oneself with other men capable of such "withdrawals." Thus the Stoic constantly tended to congregate with other Stoics. Even more—he hoped that a day would come when the whole of humanity could become Stoic. His "retreat to himself," then, had limits. One was Nature. Another was certain fellow men with whom he imagined he could live not only according to social conventions, but also in intimate companionship.

Hence we must not be deceived by the Stoic formulas. To withdraw appears to be a proof of asceticism. Or a manifestation of pride. As if it were a certainty, requiring no proof, that man's inner self is transparent, like crystal, and not, more likely, hazy and clouded! As if the depths of the human being were a refuge and not, rather, a nest of vipers! As if the window that gives on the inner world did not most frequently show us a turbulent landscape! We must not believe that the Stoic, who knew human nature so well, was always the victim of such illusions. But here too the tendency to retreat gained the day over all others. Instead of boldly facing the historical situation and throwing everything overboard, like the Cynic; instead of plunging, as so many others were later to do, into the dark human heart and making it transparent, the Stoic preferred to find, in the depths of the self, not the particular misery of each individual, but the undifferentiated reality of Nature and the feeling of community with those who shared his belief. Thus belief in Nature as the great principle to which everything returns was not only a thesis in physics, it was also a postulate of ethics. Everything was concentrated in ethics—that is, in consolation.

It was a twofold consolation. First, that of the companionship of men like himself. Second, that of the constant support of Nature. The former was not very apparent. But the latter was everpresent. "Nature," Seneca wrote, "did not give you your brother as your own possession; as she did with other brothers, she only lent him to you. When it seemed good to her, she took him back, nor in this was she guided by your having had enough of him, but followed her own law. . . . Nature gave your brother life; to you too she gave it; she is not to be blamed for reclaiming her loan, since her terms were well known." Or, as Epictetus put it: Never say of anything, "I have lost it," but only, "I have given it back." Has your brother died? He has been given back. Has your wife died? She has been given back. And if someone takes away my house, that too has been given back, for, when all is said and done, he who gives all is the supreme "Giver," ó doús, and it is not just that he be asked for what he gives, as if it belonged to us alone. Thus life is not a possession; it is an inn. We must pass through it like travelers.

"A great and sublime movement of renunciation," we might say. But once again it turns out to be only a subterfuge. On it, the Stoic laid the foundations of his particular solution, his "creed." For, unlike the Cynic, the Stoic had a belief. Unfortunately for his historical success, the realities in which the Stoic believed (universal reason, Nature) were not sufficiently attractive to kindle the hearts of many people. To be sure, Stoic philosophy was not meant only for minorities. But neither was it meant for the great majority of people, did it seek to become a "popular" movement. Like many other men, the Stoic faced the historical situation as well as he could. Convinced of the uselessness of contempt, unconsciously seduced by the magnificence of a political power that appeared to have no limits, horrified by the energy and the simple-mindedness of the "ignorant who would storm heaven," the Stoic sought compromise everywhere, and, when he could not find it, withdrew to his refuge, to impassibility, both in order to protect himself and to show the rest of mankind—the unconscious, the fanatical, the blind—the "right way."

We have said that the foundation of the Stoic attitude was a withdrawal, a lessening of life. From this it would be only a step to say that Stoicism was a manifestation of sheer cowardice. It is a step that we should not take. In its way, Stoicism was a form of heroism. And the attraction that it has often exerted derives from that flame of heroism, which burned uninterruptedly for almost six centuries and which was rekindled by modern Neo-Stoicism. But even this type of heroism could not provide an adequate solution. For there are moments in which the salvation of life consists in a readiness to sacrifice it, to lose it in anything rather than preserving it, than protecting it, even through the supreme act in which the individual does away with himself —suicide. There could, in the long run, be a number of Stoics, indeed many Stoics—at any rate, far more Stoics than Cynics. But not all men, or even the majority of men could become Stoics. Obviously, some other "solution" was needed.

Notes

The following is the passage from the Eighth Discourse ("Diogenes, or on Virtue") of Dio Chrysostom, to which we referred in the text:

"That was the time, too, when one could hear crowds of wretched sophists around Poseidon's temple shouting and reviling one another, and their disciples, as they were called, fighting with one another, many writers reading about their stupid works, many poets reciting their poems while others applauded them, many jugglers showing their tricks, many fortune-tellers interpreting fortunes, lawyers innumerable perverting judgment, and peddlers not a few peddling whatever they happened to have." From *Dio Chrysostom, Discourses*. With an English translation by J. M. Cohoon, Vol. I, p. 381. London: William Heinemann Ltd. New York: G. P. Putnam's Sons (1932). The Loeb Classical Library.

The Stoics' eagerness to "save knowledge" is shown in many ways. One is their insistence on "dialectic" (cf. Diogenes Laërtius, VII, 47; VII, 83; cf. also the defence of logic in various passages of the *Diatribes* or *Discourses* [hereafter cited as *Dis.*] of Epictetus, for example, I, vii, viii, xvii, and especially II, xx, against the arguments of the Sceptics). To be sure, according to Epictetus, the Stoic considered it unnecessary to concern himself with the problem of the structure of the world; but this is to be understood in the light of the traditional "mixing" of the different parts of philosophy, which were not to be taught as different disciplines (Diog. Laërt., VII, 40), but as forming a "walled city ruled by reason" (*loc. cit.*). In order to know "the things that are within us," we must first inquire about the things that are *not* within us.

There is a passage in Seneca which clearly shows the Cynic's alienation from his own life. It occurs in the *De brevitate vitae*, and reads as follows: "We may argue with Socrates, doubt with Carneades, repose with Epicurus, conquer human nature with the Stoics, and transcend (*excedere*) it with the Cynics." The wiseman may do any of these things, and hence the Cynic is *also* a wiseman. But, as Epictetus said, to overcome human nature is a superhuman task. In any case, man can perform this task only if he returns to the source from which he proceeds and recognizes that God is within himself, that a sacred spirit (*sacra spiritus*) resides within him (Seneca, *Epistolae* [hereafter cited as *Ep.*], XLI; also *Ep.* XLVIII, 1 and 2); thus the good man and God differ only in the duration of their respective lives (*De Providentia*, 5). But this comparison of man with God, and this acceptance (with the reservations mentioned) of the transcendence of human nature, need not mislead us. For, in the last analysis, the divine source of man is, in turn, the *whole* of nature.

In emphasizing the *sine ira, sine odio* which the Stoic enjoins as the way to treat one's fellow man, we have not forgotten that, for Marcus Aurelius (IV, 3; also VIII, 59), rational beings "were made for one another" (cf. in addition the numerous passages in which Marcus Aurelius refers to the "community" of men; for example: II, 1; IV, 4; V, 16; VI, 7, 23, 39; VII, 13, 22, 55; IX, 23, 31, 42; XII, 20). On this point he seems to have differed markedly from Seneca. For the latter, the sage "does not compassionate, but succors." When, especially in the *Epistles to Lucilius* (for example, VII, 3 ff. and XIII, 4), Seneca preaches gentleness and mildness, he does so more from principle than from active forbearance. According to Seneca, he who cannot become a Stoic suffers all the consequences of lack of control over his own life in a world in which all manner of rebellion and violence are rife (*Ep.* IV, 8). The wiseman aspires to live for himself (*De brevitate vitae*, IV, 2); he desires to separate himself (*excerpere*) from the vulgar throng and withdraw (*recedere*) (*ibid.*, XVIII, 1). Hence we must not take too literally expressions such as those that occur in the *De clementia* (XXIII, 1), where Seneca's intention is rather to incite another to forgiveness than to make any effort to experience the feeling of clemency on his own part. Though Stoicism has a highroad, it has its byways too, which were explored individually by members of the school. In the expression of his thought Marcus Aurelius was undoubtedly less stern than Seneca or Epictetus. The differences between them also appear in another important point—their "cosmopolitanism." Seneca's was more strict and, at the same time, more "abstract" than Marcus Aurelius'. This is shown when he says (*Ep.* XXVIII, 4) that he seeks to live according to the belief that "I was not born in a corner, the wide world is my country." With this, exile becomes a mere change of place, *loci commutatio* (*Ad Helviam de consolatione*, VI, 1; cf. also *De otio*, IV, 1). Here there is no vision, such as we find in Marcus Aurelius, of the "world" as a possible extension to all mankind of the ways of life increasingly prevailing in the Roman Empire.

For Stoic reason as mediation, see especially María Zambrano, *El pensamiento vivo de Séneca,* Buenos Aires (1943). Compromise was so fundamental in Stoic philosophy that it even affected the relation of the Stoic to society. The Stoic philosopher could ultimately adopt all the conventions of society (Seneca, *Ep.* V, 2), precisely because he had freed himself from the externality that still dominated the Cynic when the latter insisted upon the need for an ostentatious shabbiness that should distinguish the philosopher from other men. To avoid "luxuriousness," said Seneca, it is not necessary to fall into "madness." Or, put in another way: one must withdraw into oneself, being careful, however, to mingle *solitudo* with *frequentia* (*De tranquilitate animi,* XVII, 3).

For an example of the conception of one's own life as an insignificant event, see Seneca, *Ad Marciam de consolatione,* XXX, 1. The theme of the "littleness of the earth" compared with the "immensity of the world" in Antiquity has been analyzed by Festugière in an article, "Les thèmes du Songe de Scipion," *Eranos,* XLIV (1946), 372 ff. We must add here that the "cosmic perspective" frequently engenders indifference and can even lead to egotism. This has been emphasized by Maurice Blondel, who points out (*L'Action,* 1893, Part I, ch. ii.) that, seen "from the viewpoint of Sirius," everything appears small and petty and nothing is left greater than love of oneself.

We shall not enter into the thorny problem of the religious character of Stoicism, at least during the Imperial period. Its religiousness has been affirmed, with reservations, by Bonhöffer in his classic *Epiktet und das Neue Testament,* Giessen (1911), 342 ff. Even if Bonhöffer's view is admitted, however, it is clear that such a religiousness is of an "immanent" character, being far more concerned with ethical problems than with religious questions. If it is true that "the whole of Stoic ethics has religious implications" (Bonhöffer, 345), this is not because of the Stoic belief in the existence of God, but because of his assumption that he had discovered a human order that was seen afterwards to coincide with the order of Providence. The distinctions established by Bonhöffer—after emphasizing the points of agreement —between Epictetus and the New Testament could be better understood in the light of the above "coincidence." Bonhöffer himself seems to adhere to this view when he brings out the

"this-worldliness" of Stoicism and its insistence upon self-sufficiency. This, he says (p. 355), constitutes "the strictest possible
opposition" between Stoicism and Christianity.

Since the Stoic could also be defined as the "outsider," there
arises the problem of the difference between him and his con-
geners in the East, especially in India. This difference cannot be
denied. As Betty Heimann shows in her article "The Outsider in
Society," *The Hibbert Journal*, XLIX (1950), 73-77, the Hellenic
and, in general, the Western conception of the man who sets himself apart from society—the *idiotes*—is never as radical as the
Hindu conception of the *Kevalin*. Even among the Platonists,
and still more among the Stoics, the man who isolates himself
does so in terms of the community in which he lives and, whether
deliberately or not, has the aim of influencing it. In the Hindu
conception, on the other hand, the separation between the
Kevalin and human society is almost absolute. When the Platonists talked of ecstatically contemplating the One, they did not
mean such an absorption into the Universal Whole as is one of
the characteristics of Hindu thought and life. In general, it may
be said that the various types of the ancient sage, even those who
were most insistent upon separation from society and the world,
are incomparably more "mundane" and "social" than the sages of
the classic East.

For the expression "way of life," Diogenes Laërtius, VI, 103.
–Information on the discussions of philologists and historians
concerning the "founder" of the Cynic school will be found in the
article "Cínicos" of the author's *Diccionario de Filosofía*, 4th.
edition, Buenos Aires (1957).–On the *diatribe*, J. Geffcken,
Kynika und Verwandtes, Heidelberg (1909), 6. Also R. Bult-
mann, *Der Stil der paulinischen Predigt und die kynisch-stoische
Diatribe*, Marburg (1910), *passim.*–On the proliferation of
"sects" and "circles" in our epoch, Max Scheler, *Die Formen des
Wissens und die Bildung*, Bonn (1925), later included in *Philoso-
phische Weltanschauung*, Bonn (1929).–For Lucian's description, the still classic book by Jacob Bernays, *Lucian und die
Kyniker*, Berlin (1879).–The themes of the Cynic diatribe are
also found among the Stoics, at least in the "New Stoicism":
death and exile—*thánatos kaí phygé*—must always be contemplated face to face, as if they were ever on the point of knocking

at the door (see Epictetus, *Encheiridion* [we shall hereafter cite the *Encheiridion* or *Manual* as *Ench.*], chap. 21.–The Cynic Diogenes' praise of those who renounced doing anything, in Diogenes Laërtius, VI, 29.–On the Cynic as *bastard*, Karl Joël, "Die Auffassung der kynischen Sokratik," II, *Archiv für Geschichte der Philosophie*, XX, Neue Folge, XIII (1907), 170.–On the Cynic's "divided consciousness," Helm, in Pauly-Wissowa, art. "Kynismus," XII, 1, col. 22.–I found the expressions "cynicism of the spirit" and "cynicism of power" in an article by Eugen Kogon, "Die Aussichten Europas," *Die Neue Rundschau*, Heft XIII (1949), 3. To the representatives of these cynicisms, the author adds, as men typical of *our* period, the "preachers" and the "illusionists of the past and the future."–For the Cynic's "negations," Helm, *art. cit.*

Stoic resistance is frequently reduced to the formula "resist and renounce" (*sustine et abstine, anékhou kaí apékhou*). The one is not possible without the other.–The reference to Zeller, in his *Geschichte*, III, 13, 206; also *ibid.*, 15 and 16. The important logical discoveries of the Stoics have been chiefly investigated by J. Łukasiewicz, I. M. Bocheński, and Benson Mates.–The reference to Bréhier, in *Chrysippe*, Paris (1910), 275. There is a new edition, with a few changes, under the title *Chrysippe et l'Ancien Stoïcisme*, Paris (1951).–For independence in the face of any despotism, Seneca, *Ep.* XXXIII, 4: *non sumus sub rege; sibi quisque se vindicat.*–On knowledge as medicine, Von Arnim III, 120 (we cite by the section numbers of Von Arnim's publication, *Stoicorum veterum fragmenta*, 3 vols, Lipsiae [1903-5]).–For the Stoic *imago mundi*, see Von Arnim, I, 97 ff.; II, 633-645. However, the Stoic "system of the world" was not entirely an arbitrary mixture of elements. *Tension—tónos—*constituted a principle capable of binding the disparate together. This concept is of the utmost importance for an understanding of Stoicism; in this connection see R. H. Hack, "La sintesi stoica. I. Tonos," *Ricerche religiose* (1925), 505-513. Chrysippus regarded *tonos* as a special form of motion; Zeno, as a force capable of connecting the parts of the whole; Cleanthes, as the propulsive force of fire (cf. M. Pohlenz, *Die Stoa*, Göttingen, I [1948], 75-76, and II [1949], 43; also Von Arnim, II, 439-462). For the "hierarchy of the parts of philosophy," see Epictetus, *Ench.* chap. 52.–For Stoic ethics as "descriptive ethics," Guido Mancini, *L'Etica stoica da Zenone a Crisippo*, Padova (1940), vii. Almost all writers on Stoicism (Paul Barth, G. Rodier, Max Pohlenz) discuss the subject.–For

the "self" as refuge and source of good, Marcus Aurelius, IV, 3.–
Guizot set forth his concept of "freedom for resistance" in several
of his books; I have commented on it in my edition and translation of his *De la peine de mort en matière politique* and *Des
conspirations et de la justice politique,* Santiago de Chile (1943).
–On Caesar's impotence before the judgment of the individual,
Epictetus, *Dis.* I, xxix, 9.–Concept of freedom, *ibid.,* IV, i, 62 ff.–
For Epictetus' platitude, *Ench.* chap. 19.–On punishing and eliminating one's fellow man without anger or hate, Seneca, *De ira,*
I, xv, 1; also Epictetus, *Dis.* III, xxii, 13, and I, xviii, 15.–On
"progress" and "progressives," Guido Mancini, *op. cit.,* especially
p. 99 (the passage from Chrysippus on the "degrees of progress,"
in *Stob. Flor.,* ed. Meineke, IV, p. 5, n. 22).–On submitting to
events, Epictetus, *Ench.* chap. 8 (trans. W. A. Oldfather, in
Epictetus: *The Discourses* . . . , *Manual, and Fragments* [Loeb
Classical Library], London: William Heinemann. New York:
G. P. Putnam's Sons [1928], II, 8), and *Dis.,* III, x, 18.–On the
external reports to which we should turn a deaf ear, Epictetus,
Dis., III, xviii, 1. Cf. also Seneca, *De tranquilitate animi,* XII,
where *auscultatio et publicorum secretorumque inquisitio* is
reckoned a vice and where it is shown that to relate and hear
multarum rerum scientia is dangerous.–On flight, withdrawal, and
contentment with oneself, Seneca, *Epist.,* VII, 1; IX, 1 ff.; XIV,
10.–Stoic apathy should not be confused with the apathy of the
Epicureans and the Sceptics. On this point, Ottmar Dittrich, *Die
Systeme der Moral. Geschichte der Ethik vom Altertum bis zur
Gegenwart,* Leipzig (1923), Vol. II, 17 ff.–On the necessity for
remaining unmoved by praise and blame, Epictetus, *Ench.* chap.
48.–The character in the contemporary novel who based his
power on the limitation of experience figures in Nathanael West's
somber story, *Miss Lonelyhearts* (chapter: "Miss Lonelyhearts
and the Fat Thumb").–On "troubled depths," Seneca, *De
clementia,* II, vi, 1.–The type of Don Juan, in the sense in which
we have used it to compare it with the Stoic, is expressed not
only in Tirso's *El Burlador de Sevilla* and Zorrilla's *Don Juan
Tenorio,* but also in Molière's *Don Juan* (especially Act I, scene
ii). Octavio's lines, in *El Burlador de Sevilla,* Act III, 76-79, ed.
A. Castro, Madrid (1937), 281.–The *locus classicus* for the formula of cosmopolitanism, in Marcus Aurelius, VI, 44 (cf. also II,
16; III, 11; IV, 4, 29; X, 15; XII, 36).–For Posidonius' "universal-
ism," Karl Reinhardt, *Posseidonios,* München (1921), 5 and 11.–

The passage from Seneca on return to Nature, in *Ad Polybium de consolatione*, X, 4 and 5. Similar ideas in *Ad Marciam de consolatione*, X, 4.–On the concept that all things belong to the supreme "Giver," Epictetus, *Ench.* chap. 11.

The preceding enumeration has omitted some references which appeared in earlier notes to this chapter: Dio Chrysostom's discourse, treatment of men as "things," Stoic reason as mediation, "cosmic perspective," etc.

3. The Platonists: Flight and Contemplation

Knowledge and salvation.–Denial of the visible.–The theoretic life.–The world of ideas: immutability and fidelity.–Man and the universe: divine reason and human reason.–"Unpopularity" of Platonism.

Plotinus and Neoplatonism.–The three types of men. –The Platonist and the common man.–Concentration of the soul upon itself.

Obverse and reverse of Platonism.–The "there above" and the "here below."–The function of the corporeal.– Dialectics of reality: scorn and praise of the world.–Justification of evil.–The visible universe, image of the intelligible universe.

The godlike life.–The soul's enemy: "consciousness." –The one source of reality.–Action and contemplation.– Platonism, the culmination of a retreat.

There were the Cynics and the Stoics. There were also the Platonists, increasing in numbers from day to day. They too formed a "school." It was a dignified school, which claimed to have extracted and distilled the essence of Greek philosophy. This noble elixir was supposed to be knowledge. But it was also a longing for salvation. In fact, for the philosophers of late Antiquity, these two ideals were inseparable. Pure knowledge did not suffice. The Platonists found the right formula (a formula that was a vicious circle): Gain knowledge in order to gain salvation—which in turn consists in knowledge. They carried this formula to its furthest consequences, refined it, made it the axis of ancient life. They were—or they thought themselves to be—the final intellectual and vital precipitate of Greek civilization in its purest form. Various juices were squeezed from the last days of Greek civilization: the most quintaessentialized of them all was Platonism.

By "Platonists" we do not mean only the strict disciples of Plato or the members of the Platonic Academy. Like the words "Cynicism" and "Stoicism," the term "Platonism" here stands for an ideal that, in principle, could be incarnated in a man ignorant of the technical details of Platonic philosophy. This ideal had far greater historical and human significance than any merely philosophical doctrine. Why, then, do we persist in describing the doctrines of these philosophers? Because through them we can clearly hear the immense murmur, the sudden jubilation, the angry cries, or the oppressive silence of the multitudes. The philosophers—like the "futurists" or the "powerful" after them— were not the only significant men of their period. But they contributed most toward illuminating it. "Platonists" in our context, then, means more than the philosophers who considered themselves followers of Plato, but less than merely contemplative men. For a man to rank as Platonist in our sense of this term, he must fulfill three conditions: he must face the historical situation by a (figurative) flight from this world, open the path to withdrawal by means of knowledge, and end in contemplation.

It is clear that not many men could fulfill these conditions. Hence there were not many Platonists—fewer than there were Cynics, far fewer than there were Stoics. The Platonists aspired to live according to reason not only with their minds but with their whole being. But in this aspiration, were they not at one with all the other philosophers? It was already a commonplace at the time to define "man" as "a being endowed with reason." But in this definition the term "reason" has a very broad meaning. It designates that "common sense" which make it possible for men, as Heraclitus had said, to dwell in the "collective" world of "reality" instead of living in the "individual" realm of "dreams." It was not this meaning, however, that our Platonists gave to the term "reason." For them, reason transcended even nature, so that to become a rational being implied a conversion that placed

man at the furthest limit of the human universe. The possession
of reason was supposed then to demand a great effort. Few persons could make it. It was not by chance, therefore, that the Platonists were a minority; for them, to be only a few was of the very
"essence" of Platonism. To become a Cynic or a Stoic was not an
easy task; to perform it required a great and sometimes a painful
effort, but once this effort had been made, the rest followed almost of itself. The Platonist, on the contrary, had to exert himself
unceasingly. He had—we shall later see with what reservations
—continually to deny the existence of the visible world, and to
do so without being sustained either by the Cynic contempt—
which presupposed an immense self-confidence—or by the Stoic
fondness for nature. "Denial" is, indeed, one of the key terms of
Platonism. But some other terms are also important in order to
understand the "Platonic attitude": "knowledge," "flight," "contemplation." Among these terms "flight" is of particular interest
to us at the moment, because it designates the Platonist's spontaneous reaction to the historical situation. We can even begin
with a formula: "The Platonist faced life by fleeing from it."

Why did the Platonist reach such a decision? First of all, for
exactly the same reason that led the Cynics and the Stoics to
adopt their respective attitudes of contempt and resistance—because the Platonists felt the heavy oppression of a world in crisis,
where society, instead of being conceived as the common meeting ground for all men, was seen as the arena in which all kinds
of struggles took place. Faced with such a world, the Platonists
determined to find in it a narrow and well-protected path: the
path of theory. Hence the expression that has been coined to
describe the Platonic attitude: the "theoretic life," the *vita beata*.
Now, if becoming a Platonist was a difficult task, it had its com-
pensations. And the chief of them was the discovery that there
was a reality in which a philosopher could truly believe, because
it appeared to provide him with more gratifications than any
other reality. Solitary as the Platonist wished to live, he never
lived in as complete isolation as the Cynic or the Stoic did.
Once the false affections and the mere semblances had been eliminated, in the depths of the Platonist's soul we always find a reality. To be sure, it is an "icy" reality: the "reality" of ideas, the

intelligible world. But if anyone pointed out to the Platonist that such a "reality" was too abstract, he had his answer ready: Intelligible reality, he declared, is the only reality that keeps faith; there is no danger that it will change into appearance. It is a truly "loyal" reality. And this is more than can be expected at a time when man cannot risk fickle friendships. Thus the Platonist can be defined as a man willing to live in the icy but immutable world of ideas. Everything—even nature—changes. Ideas do not change; they are immutable by definition. As a matter of fact, the Platonists did not scorn other realities. But their ultimate aim was always communion with the intelligible world. Only of that world could be predicated what some mystics have predicated as the least doubtful among the attributes of God: fidelity.

It would seem that what had once been the variegated tapestry of Hellenic beliefs lost with Platonism its last trace of color. Only negations remained: a man must avoid all futile curiosity, every gratuitous opinion, all "unnecessary" knowledge. Only one thing mattered: to discover the essence of things. And not only for the sake of knowing them, but to help things toward their own "revelation" of themselves. For things are always revealed through man, who is like a lyre that allows the cosmos to play on it and who can transmit the enchanting music of the Universe. Thus the Platonist, at least provisionally, accomplished two notoriously difficult tasks: first, taking refuge in reason; second, making himself the most effective instrument for the penetration of the entire cosmos by reason. For the Platonist, man was the natural intermediary between supreme Unity and complete Multiplicity, the organ through which the Universe performed the gigantic operation of returning to itself. Hence, despite all its weaknesses, human reason was the living reflection of divine reason, capable not only of understanding but also of symbolizing the entire course of the Universe.

Clearly, the above attitude could not become popular. And this unpopularity was not only due to the difficulty that most men experience when they try to put into practice this return to one's self which is assumed to parallel a like movement of return to itself on the part of the Universe. For it takes more than effort to affirm the primacy of contemplation, it requires a special and quite uncommon type of belief: the belief that the contemplation of things suffices to create them, or, better, to re-create them. Yet, according to the Platonist, this was the "mission" of man, at least of some men: man's task was to create—to "create in contemplation"; to live a "theoretic life," ashamed of its terrestrial afflictions, scorning everything except to reap the harvest of whatever intelligibles it might contain.

There was a branch of Platonism in which this attitude attained its purest development: the Neoplatonic School, and, within it, Plotinus.

We are under no illusion that we can cram the Neoplatonists into a few definitions. Neoplatonism was a complex movement; in addition, its greatest representative, Plotinus, was a towering figure, the creator of an intellectual fabric of the utmost intricacy. Yet it is possible to treat Neoplatonism as we have treated the other philosophical currents of declining Antiquity: to interpret some of its most conspicuous "technical" characteristics in the light of a particular human attitude.

This attitude is a very curious one, considerably more difficult to describe than the Stoic and the Cynic attitudes. We described the latter by emphasizing diverse separate injunctions, which it was not impossible to reduce to tolerable unity. The Platonic attitude, on the contrary, presents us with the appearance of a harmonious whole that seems irreducible to its component elements. Yet its apparent unity is soon seen to have two aspects. One is the aforesaid denial of the visible, and the flight to the intelligible. The other is the transfiguration of the visible, the assumption that seeing things from the point of view of the intelligible, suffices to render them faithful and eternal.

Let us outline the essential characteristics of the first aspect.

According to Plotinus, Man—"within" whom is the soul—is in most cases an intermediate being. And this in two senses: because of his mediocrity, and because of his situation between God—the supreme Unity— and the subhuman creation (III, ii, 8). The two senses fuse into one: man is almost always mediocre and intermediate because of his inability to live outside of society, to understand that the happiness that society offers is precarious (I, iv, 16). Fortunately, the mediocre type of man, though superabundant, is not the only existing type. In a passage in which we can uncover not only the metaphysics but also the sociology of

Neoplatonism, Plotinus says that there are three kinds of men: the sensual men, birds skimming close to the ground, unable to rise to great heights despite the fact that nature has given them "wings"; the reasonable men, who put the pleasurable below the good; and the truly godlike creatures, whose keen sight makes them alone able to see the eternal light, who can rise above the clouds and from there look down upon everything here below— who are, then, able to pass through this world like men returning from long wanderings (V, ix, 1, 2). Now, however much Plotinus may assume that in principle Nature gave wings to all men and that therefore *all men are Platonists by nature*, the fact remains that the power of flight is not the same as the act of flying. Hence there is in Plotinism a certain tendency toward selection, which relegates most men to the uncultivated majority and reserves to the rest the exquisite feeling of belonging to a supremely enlightened minority. This was equivalent to a division into "classes," but on a basis that had little to do with social standing. Like the Stoic sage, the Platonic sage was not concerned with wealth and poverty; he did not seek equality, still less did he suppose that the rich and the powerful were superior to the rest of mankind. Wealth and power, he proclaimed, were not to be taken seriously (II, ix, 9). But here Plotinus went even further than the Stoics. In the last analysis, he believed, the Stoics differed from other men only in the content of their desires. Both were lost and dissipated—the common man in pleasure, the Stoic in Nature. Hence the "Olympian" eye—for once, the cliché is unavoidable—with which the Platonist looked upon all the pretended wealth of other men—of the sensualists, the resigned, the powerful. The Stoics, for example, were indifferent to government. But not one of them refused to rule, provided he could show that he did rule *as if* he did not. Plotinus would not tolerate this subterfuge. "Superior men," he said, should not rule (III, ii, 9); they should leave great human concerns to those who take them seriously instead of realizing that they are mere games (III, ii, 15). The anxieties of the multitude can become a drama. But it is not a "true drama" (III, ii, 17). Thus, if the life of man is a role on the stage—as the Stoics insisted—it is only so superficially (III, ii, 15). To be sure, on one occasion Plotinus asserted that the superior soul exercises more sovereignty than other souls (III, i, 8). But this was a metaphor, used to emphasize the supremacy of the intelligible reality. In fact, when a man joins the small minority that ever flies above the wretched city of men, he discovers that all rule is useless. Hence the "superior" man should not rule nor search the world for miscellaneous knowledge. He must withdraw and concentrate, in order to find in the depths of himself a spark of light that is one and the same with the divine light. The *genuinely* liberated soul does not pry curiously into things; its sole quest is to reduce itself to pure unity (I, iii, 4). Only then can it remain motionless, and within itself (I, i, 9). Hence "isolation" is the necessary condition for the soul's purifying itself and attaining to what essentially constitutes it: conformity with itself (VI, ix, 2). It is a far more important conformity than mere resemblance to Nature, which, Plotinus said, adds nothing to happiness (III, ii, 6) and may even disturb it. The first conclusion to be drawn is, then, clear: the soul must forsake everything in order to undertake a flight to the intelligible world, break every kind of tie in order that it may finally find itself soaring above this lower world, alone, one, and free.

All this would appear to suffice in order to bring our investigation to an end. The dearest speculations of the Neoplatonists—their endless discussions of the One, of Spirit, of the World-Soul—can be understood in the light of the conclusions so far reached. We could, then, conclude by stating that Neoplatonism consists in a series of variations on one theme: the flight of the soul from the sensible world. To be a Platonist, then, would mean: (1) to be terrified by the magnitude of this world's problems; (2) to seek salvation in the world of ideas; (3) to free one's soul from terrestrial bonds; and (4) to devote oneself to contemplating the intelligible realm, with complete contempt for, and denial of, the sensible realm.

But to end thus would be to neglect the second aspect of Platonism. It affirms that, to save oneself, one must flee the world, but adds that this must be done *without abandoning it*. This looks like an untenable paradox. Actually, it is intended to prove that Platonism is not merely a beautiful and unrealizable dream. Nothing, indeed, was easier than to mock the famous *ekei*, the "there above" so frequently invoked by Plotinus. So long as we have not found our way "there," he says again and again, we cannot possibly find "here" the serenity we seek. His "there," then, produces the effect of a convenient loophole. Are the Platonists not incurable charlatans? Is not Plotinus' mysticism a way of escaping at a tangent and answering every possible objection with a "he who has seen it knows whereof I speak" (VI, ix, 9)? And this would be so, if there were in Plotinus only that "loathing of the world" that has so often been imputed to him. But we must be careful not to attribute to the intelligible realm what in principle it cannot possess: the reality of the corporeal. What, in fact, is meant by the statement that ideas "really exist"? Obviously, it is not meant that they possess the kind of existence possessed by fire and stone and wood. Hence, *the reality of ideas does not absorb and dissolve the reality of bodies.* The two realities can coexist and even mutually support each other. Only when the claim is made that there is nothing but ideas does the danger arise of making these ideas—impossible to understand in any other way —into bodies. If we would understand it rightly, then, the Plotinian "there above" must be interpreted in some other way than by equating it with the world of dreams or transferring to the intelligible realm what belongs only to the sensible universe.

Hence when Plotinus admitted that the body of the sage "counts" in his life *and* that happiness does not consist solely in avoiding sickness and suffering (I, iv, 5), he was not saying anything self-contradictory. This statement was simply the result of a continuous oscillation between the obverse and the reverse of the same medal. In order not to become lost in a labyrinth of contradictions, there was nothing to do but employ the one instrument that constant use had not yet completely blunted: dialectics. To be sure, the "real universe" is not in space (VI, iv, 2) if we view space as an indefinite extension, as a multidimensional reality. But as soon as we *view it as* a continuity capable of being "concentrated," of reaching the same "place" from any starting point, its "unreality" vanishes. The "real universe" has no extension. But this only means that the "places" where it "is" are "indifferent" to it, and that hence it can be found *at any point* so long as it does not "feel itself" confined and "localized." Similar considerations can be applied to the body. They would all lead us to the same conclusion: What is "above" and what is "below" are such because we view them in a particular way. Therefore, despite his affirming that only "what is above" possessed genuine reality, the Platonist realized that, to reach it, he had no need to change his "place." Why, then, despise the world and the beautiful things that it contains (II, ix, 16)? In truth, the world—the sensible world—is admirable (V, i, 4), provided that we consider it in its greatness, beauty, and order. In the last analysis, *the "there above" is simply the sensible world viewed from the standpoint of the intelligible.* Hence, as Plotinus said, experience and suffering play an important role in human life. Hence the Platonic sage, at the same time that he allows his body to grow weak, that he rejects power, that he accepts infirmities, must learn the art of combat and prepare himself like a skilled athlete who fights against the blows of fortune (I, iv, 8). Good and evil do not battle each other as if they were separate and irreducible entities, but good permeates evil and finally justifies it. The sage must aid this process, whose final aim is the transfiguration of all reality. He must be ready to see "evils" as necessary aspects of universal Reason, which contains everything—evils as well as goods (III, ii, 18). To say that the world is evil is not false; it is illogical. Strictly speaking, in itself the world is nothing; only when it is illuminated by universal Reason does it acquire a definite reality. And then the sensible world becomes the best possible image of the intelligible realm (II, ix, 4). If at times we do not know it to be such, that happens because we are embroiled in action instead of devoting ourselves to contemplation. At such times we see the world as if it were autonomous, forgetting that it is part of a whole (III, ii, 3) and that the flute of Pan does not give but a single note. Moreover, daily experience confirms this lofty wisdom: unexpectedly, out of evil, good arises; adulteries produce natural sons who may become distinguished men; from prisoners of war arise cities more flourishing than those captured and sacked by the soldiers who took those very prisoners (III, ii, 18). But the fact that evils cannot be isolated from everything else means that, in themselves, they do not exist. Evil is a perturbation of good, as disorder is a perturbation of order (III, ii, 4). Evil is not a basic and subsistent reality: it is the tendency to dispersion, to diversity, to heterogeneity; something, in short, whose fate consists in being "changed." And what happens in the case of evil happens in the case of the soul. Wherein does its "badness" consist? Simply in its desire to be itself alone (V, i, 1), forgetting that its very authenticity depends on its participation in the One. The soul must endeavor to see itself as an element of *the* Universe (III, iii, 3). Only thus will the soul become free (III, iii, 4), and will recognize that, if it suffers evils, it must attribute them to its own faults and failings (I, iv, 7). These are summed up in one gigantic fault, in a single "mortal sin": failure to comprehend the universal order; not understanding that to be born into slavery is not a chance but a test; not perceiving that the incessant war of all against all will end as soon as a purely inner *idea*—the idea of order and peace—dominates the tumult of life.

Why, then, concern ourselves with the problem of the "existence" of the intelligible world if "even here" we can live the life of "there above"? Simply in order that we may fully understand what it means to lead a life similar to the life of the gods, a life of contemplation and of such "bliss" that it need not even be "conscious" (V, iv, 1; V, vi, 2). Strictly speaking, the "final enemy" of the soul is not death, but consciousness. Consciousness introduces disquiet, instability, dispersion. But the suppression of consciousness must be brought about by raising its powers to the utmost. Only then is it possible to attain to pure contemplation, the foundation for the famous "impassibility of incorporeals" to which the Stoics already had referred. But while the Stoics reached this impassibility through resistance, the Platonists sought to reach it by flight. A flight of a most peculiar nature, a flight that consisted in remaining in this world, and in seeing it *as if* one were in the other world. Obviously, this new demand made it still harder for the common man to become a Platonist. It was not enough to believe in ideas; one had to believe in them "from here below." The sage was no longer allowed even the subterfuge of escaping into a vague world of dreams. Hence the Platonist gave the term "impassibility" a peculiar meaning: "infinite production," which at the same time was the result of the absolute tension engendered by complete immobility (III, viii, 3). Only upon reaching this stage could man plunge into the current that flows from a single fountain (VI, vii, 12), take part in a dance in which souls, moving in a perfect circle, will contemplate the wellspring of life and intelligence (VI, ix, 9). When this end is attained, the body will no longer be an obstacle; it can even become an instrument. To be sure, Plotinus often said that the body was an impediment and that because of it contemplation could not be continuous. After all, the first fact we learn about him is the fact described by Porphyry at the beginning of his *Life of Plotinus:* "he seemed ashamed to possess a body." But let us not be misled. The "real obstacle" of the body is not its materiality: it is the inability of the soul to transfigure it entirely (III, viii, 7; IV, iii, 22). For even those who have been converted to the Platonic attitude continue to be beset by vestiges of that "mediocrity" which drags man downward and prevents him from fully realizing the only motion worthy of the name—approach to the One.

With this, the great cycle begun by Greek philosophy came to its close. Hence "Neoplatonism" is not only the name of a philosophic doctrine; it also designates the culmination of a long intellectual history. It is the history of a retreat. It was not an easy retreat. To accomplish it successfully, it required the courage to face many dangerous ambuscades: the ambush of thinking that everything consisted in knowledge; the ambush of supposing that one could always confidently cast oneself upon the irresistible suction of the One. . . . Fortunately, in the difficult combat, the Platonist possessed the best of all arms: a belief. It was the belief that one could live "here" *as if* one were living "there"; the belief that, once vain agitation and perpetual change were done away with, one could *even now* see the "there" *as if* it were wholly present. It was, in short, the belief that the world itself would change as soon as we contemplate it in its intelligible truth. The Platonist might very well say the opposite of what the Marxist says: so far, philosophers have done nothing but change the world, but what is needed is to contemplate it. Or, as Plotinus wrote: "Behold mankind, when contemplation weakens in them, they devote themselves to action, which is but a shadow of contemplation" (III, viii, 4).

Notes

The theme of "flight," although closely connected with belief in the immortality of the soul and especially in the possibility of its ascent to the "celestial kingdom," is to some extent distinct from it. If the two themes coincided completely, we should have to identify Plotinism with the Middle and New Stoicism, especially that of Posidonius and Seneca. But when Seneca, in various passages of his works, spoke of the ascent of the sage's soul to the celestial kingdom, of its dwelling in a luminous and ethereal world, he did not do so in the same spirit as Plotinus, still less did he have in mind the Plotinian idea of the imprisoned soul. The statements are similar, but what was meant by them was very different.

In his *Lux Perpetua*, Paris (1949), Franz Cumont recognizes the Plotinian duality between the conception of the soul as pure spirit and the old beliefs concerning astral immortality, as well as the duality between the "purity" of the soul and its "descent" into the body. On the one hand, "when Plotinus admits that the soul begins by lodging itself in the heavens in a spherical body like that of the stars, he is not dealing in pure metaphors, in mere verbal reminiscences, he is referring to common opinions which had spread with the doctrine of astral immortality and to which he did not hesitate to refer in his conversations with his pupils" (*op. cit.*, p. 355). On the other hand, the descent of the soul cannot be understood as a real journey (as Numenius of Apamea conceived it): "For an immaterial soul there can be no question of change of place. Its fall is a purely psychic transformation."

We shall not enter into the question whether it is the soul itself or its image which lives and is incarnated in matter, but we will call the reader's attention to the importance of this question from the historico-philosophical point of view. One's conception of Plotinus will inevitably depend upon the stress laid on the dual nature of the soul. The problem does not concern us further, since the *function* of the soul in Plotinus remains the same whether the soul be real or a simulacrum.

In his *L'Existence temporelle*, Paris (1949), Jean Guitton very justly observes that Plotinus' experiences betray "the solitude of consciousness in the midst of nature." This took place at a moment when "the spirit became conscious of its impotence to rule" (*op. cit.*, p. 12). But this impotence of spirit in nature is not only, as some philosophers hold, a moment in a dialectical process within philosophic thought, it also has concrete historical roots, some of which we have tried to illuminate in our chapter.

Our exposition of the "Platonic attitude" has been made almost entirely on the basis of Plotinus' *Enneads*. Beginning with page 40, we have indicated in parentheses the passages from the *Enneads* which corresponded to our description. In accordance with accepted practice, the first figure, in Roman capitals, gives the number of the corresponding *Ennead;* the second, in Roman lower case, the number of the treatise; the third, in Arabic figures, the paragraph. By this procedure we obviate a long note on our citations from Plotinus. We have purposely chosen them from a wide variety of treatises (omitting those of a purely "technical" nature), in order to give a sufficiently broad "sampling" of Plotinus' thought. The passages in our chapter which are immediately followed by references to the *Enneads* are those that most closely follow the philosopher's text.

Heraclitus' remark on the difference between the world of waking and the world of dreams, in fragment 89 (Diels-Kranz).– On the flight of the soul as the "principal theme" of Plotinus' Neoplatonism, see Émile Bréhier, Introduction to his edition of the *Enneads*, Vol. I, Paris (1924), xxxii.–A number of writers have stressed the constant tension in Plotinus' system between the conception of this world as a prison for the soul and the conception of it as a noble and necessary part of the universal order. Among them we will mention A. H. Armstrong, in his *The Architecture of the Intelligible Universe in the Philosophy of Plotinus*, Cambridge, Mass. (1940), in which he coins the expressions "world-accepting temper" and "world-rejecting temper," between which the tension is set up. However, in our view, it is not so much a question of "tension" as of a clear consciousness that each of these worlds acquires its meaning when viewed from the other.

4. The Futurists

Futurism as an attitude.–The desert Semite: his conception of reality.–An illuminating quotation.–The absorbing nature of "Him Who Is."–Prayer and its meaning.–The Covenant.

Images of the Promised Land.–The Greek city and the Hebrew tribe: nature and history.–Life as hope.

Hebrew history: traditionalism, futurism, and providentialism.–The fundamental facts.–From the Babylonian captivity to domination by Rome.–The birth of prophecy.–Prophecy and Messianism.

The life of Israel after the Captivity.–"Collaborationists" and "resistants."–The idea of the "New Jerusalem" or the "Return of Israel."–"Eternal interests" and "created interests": opposition and collusion between them.

Israel from within.–The fall of the politician and the triumph of the prophet.–Different attitudes toward the Awaited One.–The Sadducees.–The Pharisees.–The "extremists."–The Essenes.–The zealots.–The great problem: closing or opening.–Integration of futurism.

The attitudes so far described fed on the present or the past; the one that will now occupy us fed on the future. To understand this fact, we may recall the image of history as a gigantic, irresistible wave. Some men tried to remain *standing* under its impact; these were the philosophers. Others tried to *mount* it;

these were the powerful. Others took up their station *ahead* of it
—the Christians. Preceding these, there were some who believed
that they were *in the center* of the wave, guided by the hand of
Providence—the futurists. They were those who scorned the "is"
and the "has been" and concerned themselves only with what
"will be."

Among the various human types who adopted this last attitude,
one will serve perfectly as our example—the Hebrew, at a particular moment of his history. Assailed, like many other men of
his time, by disorientation and despair, he discovered a singular
way of filling the void thus produced in his life—the way of
hope.

Neither the problem nor the solution were wholly new to him.
For obvious reasons, we are concerned with the Hebrew people
only at that period of their history which can be connected with
the end of the ancient world. But what happened to them then
had millennial roots. The theme around which their history re-
volved, from the Babylonian Captivity to the Diaspora—the
theme of the future of the community—is comprehensible only
against the ultimate background of a most ancient and apparently changeless form of life—that of the desert Semites. Hence
a brief analysis of this form of life, and of Hebrew history before
the Babylonian Captivity, will be necessary if we would thoroughly understand what we shall call the "crisis of Israel"—
which, in the last analysis, is only an exacerbation of the ancient
Israel's permanent crisis.

If we ask what "reality" meant to these Semites, we shall get an
entirely different answer from that given by the classical Greek.
For the latter, "reality" meant "nature." For the Hebrew, "nature"
designated only the desolate setting in which the great dialogue
between the two only existing realities—God and the tribe—was
carried on. The desert Semite believed that he was led by the
hand of God, of one God, who was sometimes paternal, sometimes implacable, but always providential and absorbing. To illustrate this type of belief let us turn for a moment to the Arab
tribes who still live in a very similar "atmosphere." We shall cite
the testimony not of a historian or a philosopher, but of a soldier
and traveler. Here we have a long and fascinating book—*The*

Seven Pillars of Wisdom. Its author, Colonel T. E. Lawrence, was first of all a writer. This made him able to tell us far more in a few lines than others can in elaborate analysis or countless pages filled with historical details. Chapter III of Lawrence's book contains the following illuminating paragraphs:

> The common base of all the Semitic creeds, winners or losers, was the ever present idea of world-worthlessness. Their profound reaction from matter led them to preach bareness, renunciation, poverty; and the atmosphere of this invention stifled the minds of the desert pitilessly. A first knowledge of their sense of the purity of rarefaction was given me in early years, when we had ridden far out over the rolling plains of North Syria to a ruin of the Roman period which the Arabs believed was made by a prince of the border as a desert-palace for his queen. The clay of its building was said to have been kneaded for greater richness, not with water, but with the precious essential oils of flowers. My guides, sniffing the air like dogs, led me from crumbling room to room, saying, "This is jessamine, this violet, this rose!"
>
> But at last Dahoum drew me: "Come and smell the very sweetest scent of all", and we went into the main lodging, to the gaping window sockets of its eastern face, and there drank with open mouths of the effortless, empty, eddyless wind of the desert, throbbing past. That slow breath had been born somewhere beyond the distant Euphrates and had dragged its way across many days and nights of dead grass, to its first obstacle, the man-made walls of our broken palace. About them it seemed to fret and linger, murmuring in baby-speech. "This", they told me, "is the best: it has no taste."

This supreme reality, so pure that it is without qualities, always bears the same name—"God." God is defined as "That Which Is"; or, better, as "He Who Is." For He is a person, a "will," not a thing. In principle, there is only God. Everything else is an "attenuation" of "Him Who Is," the consequence of a divine "arbitrariness." Hence, when an important problem arises in the life of the desert Semite, he turns to God with the same impassioned certainty with which the Platonic philosopher turned to Ideas. Yet the difference between the two above attitudes is considerable. Ideas can be contemplated. But the act of contemplating them is the concern of men able to believe in them. Ideas themselves are indifferent to contemplation; the source of all movement, they are themselves immutable. But God is not indifferent; He is active, partial, "interested." Hence the tangle of any extreme situation can only be unraveled by prayer—with all the derivatives which prayer implies: imprecation, complaint, protest. Thus any solution is ineffectual if it is not based on the fundamental act of commending oneself to God.

There is a reason that accounts for the above attitude—the belief that human life is not self-sufficient. Why, then, is not human life torn with continual despair? For even if it is admitted that God created an environment in which man can live, that environment will always be on the verge of being taken from man. Now, to escape this permanent despair, the Hebrew possessed two methods. One is common to all men. It is action, by which the human being rebounds from those depths of the self to which an extreme situation had driven him. The other is specifically Hebraic. It consists in coming to terms with that supreme reality whose will is absolute law, by means of a curious artifice—the Covenant.

This solution was a stroke of genius. For as one cannot always be thinking, so one cannot always be praying. It is necessary to discover the divinity's "law of variations" and to be certain that one can rely on it. But since such a "law of variations" is not a natural law, but a personal law, its foundation cannot be a proposition or a formula but an agreement. It is the Covenant between man and God—between the tribe *of* Abraham and the God *of* Abraham. Because of it, man will do what it pleases God to have him do. But God, on his side, will fulfil what he has promised to man. The original state of despair will give way to a complicated structure, composed of prescriptions, rites—almost of reflexes. Thenceforth the Hebrew will live under its protection. The Law revealed by the Covenant is thus the Hebrew's unique way of repairing the breach that arose in his life when he did not know what to do in relation to this God without color, without taste, without form, this God who was all tension and will, fire and wrath. In exchange for certain observances, the Hebrew made God's will propitious to himself. Thenceforth God could become the protector of his seed, God of the Chosen People, God of victorious battles—the true Isra-El.

If from the conclusion of the Covenant the Hebrew continued to be led by the hand of God, he at least knew where he was being led. It was to the Promised Land. To be sure, his ideas of what the Promised Land might be were not always very clear. Was it a particular soil, in which all seed produced fruit? Was it dominion over the surrounding peoples? Was it something that lay beyond geography and history? The "classical" Hebrew lingered over each of these images. And when the last of them came to overshadow the others, it could be said of the Hebrew, as Xavier Zubiri has pointed out, that "in his radical solitude," he awaited the "consummation of time"; that, in this solitude, "the horizon of destiny from which the universe appears as history" took shape. In any case it was a single Law which governed his destiny. Beyond any particular interpretation of the Promise, there was something in which all things took on meaning. It was complete faith in the future—or complete lack of faith in it. Hence the perpetual oscillation between the height of illusion and the depth of despair which has been typical of Hebrew life for so many centuries.

The Hebrew tribe was, then, something quite different from the Greek City-State. Perhaps it was physically closer to nature than the latter. But spiritually it was far from nature. For in the last analysis, nature was only the setting in which the drama of history could be played. To the Hebrew, reality was not an eternal repetition, an endless succession of Great Years; it was a continuous episode. Only one thing remained immutable: the Law.

The whole of Hebrew history can be understood from this assumption. But there was a moment in that history when the virtues and faults of such an assumption were more strongly manifested than ever before; this was when Hebrew history moved not only parallel with that of Rome but also as a tangent of it. At a certain moment the particular crisis experienced by the Hebrew people could form part of the general crisis of the "Mediterranean world." We can thus add a fundamental attitude—that of futurism—to those already described. Our description applies to a definite period: the last two centuries B.C. But before coming to this point, we must briefly summarize the "classical" history of the Hebrew tribe, for this history established the conditions that make it possible to understand how far we are justified in writing the equation "Hebrew man = futurist."

We have written "the Hebrew tribe." For, through all its various forms of government—from the rule of the patriarch to that of the politician, passing through the judge, the king, the priest, and the prophet—Hebrew history was always tribal in character. The Hebrew community possessed a strong feeling of solidarity. It saw itself as a stream that had one source—tradition—and one direction—Providence. For the Hebrew, other peoples—the Egyptians, the Babylonians—were not real communities, but States, Empires—instruments of sin. At most they could—like the Babylonians—prove to be useful historical instruments. Contrary to what pan-Babylonian philology thinks on the subject, the legends of Ur, Babylonian cosmology were probably not the origin of the idea of the one great God, though they enabled the Hebrew to penetrate more deeply into His mysteries. Hence the surrounding peoples could explain the history of the Chosen People, but they did not make it. Through all his wanderings, the Hebrew preserved his inmost self untouched. The Exodus, the establishment of the Law and the Covenant, the settlement in Egypt, the organization under the Judges, the power of the Kings, the splendor of David and Solomon, the wars with Judaea, slavery under the whips of Tiglathpileser III, the Babylonian Captivity, the Liberation, and the return when the brilliant star of the Achaemenids blazed in the sky of the East—how many were not the historical experiences of this people, which had begun by being, according to some, the first inhabitants of the earth and, according to others, the people "on the other side" of the Euphrates? Yet this history, which sounds like a great symphony, had but a single note. It was this people's consciousness of possessing a truth that must be transmitted; its consciousness that it existed in order to bear witness to that "future" truth—among the great powers and, if need be, against them.

One moment of this history singles out for distinction. It was a "moment" that lasted for several centuries, continuing from the Babylonian Captivity to the Roman domination. It was the decisive period—the crisis by antonomasia.

It began with an event pregnant with consequences—primitive

innocence was lost. The Promise continued to breathe in the heart of the community. But it was no longer expressed by a thundering Voice, nor was it even living memory of the Covenant; only the Law was remembered. The entire life of the people was organized around the Law. To be sure, there seemed to be an increasing disparity between the more and more exact fulfillment of the Law and the more and more obvious unfulfillment of the Promise. But if the Promise is not fulfilled—the Hebrew thought—this cannot be because it is false, but because the Law is not observed with a pure conscience. What would happen *if* the Law were observed completely? Or *if* it remained completely unobserved? These questions formed the main theme of the prophets. The past was forever on their lips. But actually they were referring to the future. They could not fulfil their mission by merely knowing or consulting Destiny; they must curse, pray, and announce. And the last above all. Preaching against the practices of the East, against forsaking tradition, against magic, was only the preface to announcing the return of God. Around the prophets, audiences grew. For in addition to the disparity already mentioned between fulfillment of the Law and unfulfillment of the Promise, the Hebrew discovered a terrifying truth. And it was that at the moment of the "abomination of desolation" which followed the expedition of Antiochus the Syrian, some members of the community weakened—and not before worldly temptations, but before something worse: foreign power. Yet those who weakened were rewarded with earthly goods; while the faithful, those who resisted, were martyred. The old conceptions, then, were inadequate. New conceptions were needed to re-establish the lost equilibrium.

In fact, however, what was needed was not a new conception, but a Savior, a Messiah. From this moment began the most significant phase in the history of Israel—the phase of Messianism. With it commenced the proliferation of sects and groups. They had already begun to spread during the period of the Babylonian Captivity. It was then that the spirit by which Israel at once saved and condemned itself was formed: the spirit of resistance —of collective resistance—to any "contamination."

To explain this transformation, historians have found two causes. One is the influence exerted by the conquerors. The other is the will to resist this influence. They are two aspects of a single cause. From this point of view, the "collaboration" of the most compliant classes was no less responsible for the accentuation of Hebrew futurism than was the "resistance" of the classes who most zealously clung to tradition.

At the beginning only one group appeared to have a voice. It was the same group who, even before the Babylonian Captivity, had presented themselves as the genuine conservers of the essences of Hebraism—the disciples of Jeremiah, the *Anavim,* the *Hasidim,* the "pious." Out of them arose the new prophecy, and especially the consoling prophecies of Ezekiel. These prophecies were preceded by all manner of threats. If the son of man looked upon the mountains of Israel, it was so that he might "prophesy against them." Now, the "mountains of Israel" designated those who had fallen away from the faith. And there were many, indeed, who were in this case. Thus, if Jerusalem was guilty, she must be destroyed and scattered. Bread must be eaten "in fear and trembling," for only thus could the abominations that had been committed become known. The prophets turned their artillery against all kinds of targets—against the Ammonites, the Moabites, the Edomites, the Philistines; against Tyre, Sidon, Egypt. But through all these, a single target was discernible—the group who had not resisted the force of the New Empire. Only they were to be excluded from the "New Jerusalem," which was not only to be rebuilt but, as Ezekiel proposed, to be rebuilt in accordance with definite rites and exact measurements.

All prophecy was reduced to this announcement—"Israel will return." The voice of the prophets grew louder when, in fact, Israel returned after the New Babylonian Empire fell into the comparatively gentle clutches of the Achaemenids. But from the same moment "eternal interests" had to combine with "created interests." Reconstruction was carried on with *both.* And this coincided with the articulation of what was thenceforth the backbone of Hebraism—the Book, divided into a Law, a number of Prophets, and several hagiographers or "historians." In accordance with the Book, the conception of the Hebraic community as a people destined by God to become the axis of history consistently developed. This tendency appeared clearly as early as the so-called "Second Isaiah" (chapters 40-56 of the Book of Isaiah); the Hebrew community did not regard itself merely as a "people," but as the salt of mankind.

The "salt of mankind"—which at the same time means the hammer of God, the instrument of Providence. The idea was never lost. It even grew to be an obsession. And so, very soon, prophecy was identified with Messianism. The latter burst forth in its full power when the new historical constellation—the State of Alexander—rose like a meteor. Relations with the "West" now became constantly closer. This is not paradoxical. For it was precisely at the moment when the Hebrews conceived of their own community as the axis of history that a "relation" with other communities became acceptable. It was not even necessary to cling to Jerusalem as the only "seat." Many other "seats" were already envisaged; Alexandria, Rome, Athens. The history of the Hebrew people during this period proceeded at unbridled speed: revolt of the Maccabees, principate of Judas, Asmonaean "liberation," violent struggle, capitulation, and, finally, intervention by the other great world power, which for centuries was to be for the West *the* world power—Rome. With this we approach the moment when the great paradox arose in the heart of the Hebrew community: the very same forces that brought this community to exercise its greatest influence on the world made it an island of resistance.

To understand this fact, we must examine Israel "from within." For several decades, in Herod's time, the politician seemed to predominate over the patriarch, the judge, the king, the priest, the prophet, or the hero. Prophecy and Messianism seemed doomed to disappear. With all the arms at his disposal—with cleverness, with cruelty—Herod tried to persuade his people that neither nostalgia for the past nor apocalyptic vision of a future could save them from humiliation and slavery. To this end, he undertook to set up a semi-sceptical priestly class as a rigid politico-religious orthopaedia. But it soon became clear that this was not the age of the politician but of the reformer. All "political" efforts were bound to break down in the face of the problem raised by the disparity between what was promised and what actually happened. The great question was not the organization of society, but the meaning and future of the Alliance. The "politician" could turn the current from time to time, but he could not reduce its volume, still less do away with it. The moment had come when God would make known his Word—the moment of the Messiah, of the Envoy, of the Anointed. How was this event —hoped for by some, feared by others—faced by those who kept alive the sacred fire in the heart of Israel?

There were the Sadduccees. Their views have often been discussed. Dozens of books and articles have examined them from every possible angle. As a result, the image of the Sadducees has become very dim. We do not know who they were or what they professed. Some historians call them the *licim*, the "libertines," of the period. Some other historians regard them as the "reasonable," "realistic," "clear-sighted" group—as those who tried to understand "reality" instead of dreaming about some vague future. They were the organized priesthood and those who gathered about them. Their Hebraism was official, ritual, built on the Temple, with little sympathy for the Synogogue. Their motto was the motto of every well-organized Church—*quieta non movere*, "let sleeping dogs lie." They were astute; their solutions were not religious but "political." They did not deny the Messiah entirely—as some writers suppose—but they did not put much stress on him, nor wish that he would appear very soon; the appearance of the Messiah would certainly bring on upheavals, and everyone remembered the exile, the wars, the bloodshed. They did not *usually* accept among their doctrines either the resurrection or angelology (least of all in its accepted "new form"). Their conception of human existence accorded exactly with these presuppositions. Why should man be a plaything of God, be *entirely* in His hands? Man possessed a certain "freedom." The Sadducees, then, were the "moderates," those who wanted to commit themselves neither to God nor to the ruling power here on earth. They were, of course, severe and even extremely strict. But—so far as the term can be used of men who lived in an age so little propitious to the thing—they had a certain "irony." Or, in any case, a certain prudence. The Asmonaeans protected them. They suffered to some extent during the reign of Herod the Great, but in the end it proved unnecessary to be too much concerned over a choice between the opposed political constellations. The great Roman power burst into history like an irresistible gale. And that power had no intention of abandoning the only group who could guarantee "order" in Israel. Hence Sadducean thought even gave birth to a doctrine that could be termed "natural Jehovism," something not to be forced on other nations by fire and sword but which would allow the Jews to say to all nations: "You see, our religion is not intolerant, fanatical; it can come to an agreement with yours." Thus the Sadducees could become the "enlightened," though it would be going too far to call them—as some have done—"free-thinkers." Power for them had no lure because it was too great a burden, but resistance to power had no appeal for them either. When all is said and done, they conjectured, power will one day yield because, unlike spirit, it is something essentially pliant.

Their opponents, the Pharisees, are supposedly well known. It is not for us to discuss whether their name means "the separated." We incline to think not; yet there is no denying that the translation fits them like a glove. For the first thing we observe in them is the spirit of indifference. It was not an indifference to everything, but to whatever did not flow through a pre-established channel. This channel was the Law, so that the life of the faithful Hebrew could consist only in living *by* the Law and *for* the Law. The Pharisees were, then, the "unyielding," the "severe," those who proclaimed themselves heirs to the prophecy of "resistance." However, by this time, prophecy was no longer a glimpse into the future; it was a series of traditions, and quite often a series of formulas. The only solution for our ills, the Pharisees carped, is strict, almost infinitesimal observance of the Law. There is no other science. The Law must first be known; then, interpreted; finally, obeyed. The order here is not chronological but logical; to know, to interpret, and to obey are acts that must be performed simultaneously. All are equally fundamental. To us, however, the second is particularly important. For, unlike the Sadducees—for whom, roughly speaking, only the written Law counted and who consequently held few dogmas, leaving other matters "free"—the Pharisees tied up all loose ends, so that not a loophole should be left. Once all the strands were woven together, however, the individual was not trapped but "freed." The world had been delivered over to the powerful, the malignant. But those who knew and obeyed the Law

would be just, faithful. They need not be troubled. In words
often quoted, the prophet Habakkuk had said: "The just man
shall live by his faith." The Pharisees did not deny this truth.
But "Faith" for them did not mean what it meant later for St.
Paul—the substance of things hoped for—but only confidence
that knowledge and fulfillment of the Law were the salvation of
Israel. The Pharisees frequented the Synagogue. They hated the
"corruption" of the Temple; and though they often despised the
humble and ignorant, they felt obliged to teach them. They
met in brotherhoods, competed in obeying the Law and its infinite complications. These they discussed interminably. From
among them arose the great doctors: Hillel and Gamaliel, the
master of St. Paul. This shows that our description of the Pharisee spirit must be taken *cum grano salis*. For did not some
among them soften the strictness and harshness of the Law by
allegorical interpretations? Were there not some who everywhere
sought an "opening" which the "letter of the Law" forbade, but
which was not against its "spirit"? So we must not confuse the
"Pharisaic spirit" with the "Pharisee." Nevertheless, in the end the
former became predominant. Hence we may say that the general
run of the Pharisees in this period were not very different from
the description we have just given. Most of them were fanatics
of observance and purity, of a formalism always on the verge of
becoming formulism.

Besides the Pharisees there were the "extremists." "Besides"?
Were they not, rather, "among" the Pharisees, in order to provoke
them? For, rather than a "sect" or a "party," we find here an
"attitude." Some of the "extremists" were "pious"; their hatred
for the adherents of the Temple was almost indescribable. Even
more than the Pharisees the pious extremists lived "closed." Apocalyptic and Messianic above all things, they expected the
Anointed "from minute to minute." The Sadducees believed in
the Anointed, but they were in no hurry. The Pharisees announced him; but what was announced and what was hoped for
were not always one and the same. The pious extremists almost
saw him: "May the Lord come!" Naturally, they considered
themselves the true descendants of the prophets and of the ancient patriarchs. In addition, the way the world was going

seemed to confirm their outcries; the world—they thought—had gone mad. With the exception, of course, of Israel, which knew what had to be done—that is, what was bound to happen. The pious extremists—the Messianists—had no doubts about that; it was the coming of the Awaited. And he had a definite mission—to save his own people. For "the others" did not need anyone to save them, but rather someone to condemn them. With the pious extremists, futurism reached its furthest consequences. They did not, as is sometimes said, constitute the whole of Israel, but they were one of its most typical phases—the seed that dies not. Hence the extremists alternated between complete despair and insane hope. The Sadducees reacted to the crisis by intriguing, sometimes by smiling. The Pharisees reacted to it by isolating themselves. The Apocalyptics reacted to it by shouting.

From the period of the Asmonaeans, the strictest Messianists had gathered in special groups. One of these groups took a road that paradoxically ended by doing away with all traces of violent Apocalypticism. These were the Essenes. Their name has been given various meanings: the "silent," the "guardians," the "strangers," the "pious." It does not matter. They represented another way of reacting to the same crisis. The isolation of the Pharisees was obviously not enough. The isolation of the Law must be completed by that of life. Hence the monasticism of the Essenes, organized in closed communities, difficult of access. They were not, then, anarchists, but ascetics. Their life was training, a militant life. Their dwelling was not the town, but the country. Secluded in communities around the Dead Sea, they formed a girdle about Jerusalem, constantly reminding it that if there is anything eternal, it is not of "this world." For the world of the Essenes was not yet "the other," but neither was it "this world." It was an "intermediate" world, made up of strictness, hope, and mutual aid.

If we follow Josephus' classification—which, despite the many attacks on it by historians, still remains practically unshaken—there is still another group: the zealots. Strictly, they were neither a group nor a religious sect, still less a "school"; they were a "splinter faction." They had neither a doctrine nor even a settled and foreseeable attitude. Their appearance at certain moments of Israel's history is nevertheless more illuminating than the regular development of the "ordinary" sects. In their "normal" state, the Hebrews are neither fanatical nor desperate. But they have desperation in their innermost souls. The zealots were like the percussion-cap that could set off the overcharged weapon. Their fanaticism led them to the destruction of everything that was not the "purity" of the Hebrew tradition. In order not to introduce useless complications, we will identify this tradition with the Law. Now, for the zealots, the Law was the sword of God, and whoever did not obey it must perish by the sword. It was the fanaticism of the ignorant. The zealots played a decisive part in the rising of '66, and persecuted Sadducees and Christians with equal rage. We may say of them what Tacitus wrote of the inhabitants of Jerusalem in his account of the taking of the city by Titus: *vulgus, more humanae cupidinis, sibi tantum factorum magnitudinem interpretati, ne adversis quidem ad vera mutabantur*—"in accordance with the wishful thinking common to mankind, they interpreted these great events as a great destiny, so that not even misfortunes could make them look at reality face to face." They were the same people who *major vitae metus quam mortis*—who "feared life more than death." In short, they were the *violently closed*, a bare fact rather than a seed of history.

There were the "violently closed." There were also the "gently open." Every possible combination of violence and gentleness, of openness and closeness, made its appearance among the Hebrew groups at the moment of their greatest crisis. For this was precisely their problem—to determine whether to open or close themselves, how to do it, and in which direction to go. It was also one of the problems of the period. Now, none of the attitudes adopted appeared to be adequate. Those who were (comparatively) open lacked the drive to make their "opening" fruitful. Those who had drive, closed too soon and ended by writhing in their own flame, victims of their own fire. Those who were at once open and had enough drive, did not know where to direct it. They ended, then, at very different points—cautious adaptation, exaggerated subtlety, extreme severity, furious violence. But not in the one place that would have enabled the community to make the perilous leap that the necessity for radically changing position without ceasing to be itself represents for every human society. Hence this particular society was offered only a choice between three extreme solutions—annihilation, dispersal, or transformation. And this was what actually happened; some "committed suicide," others went into exile, others ceased to be what they had been and took refuge in a new type of community, in which futurism remained alive, but with order and measure.

Pure futurism, too, then proved to be no "solution," even for those who seemed to have found the meaning of their existence in its atmosphere. Like the other attitudes described, the one with which we have been concerned here could only survive by ceasing to be unique. The time did not care for exclusivisms, nor yet for eclecticisms. It called for something more difficult, perhaps impossible—a real integration.

Notes

For the foregoing interpretation of Hebrew life I have made use of Xavier Zubiri's valuable suggestions, pp. 93-99 of his "Sobre el problema de la filosofía," *Revista de Occidente*, XXXIX (1935). The phrases quoted on page 53 above are from page 96 of his essay. These ideas should be supplemented by those set forth by José Ortega y Gasset in his *Esquema de las crisis*, Madrid (1942), 92-93 and 97 (*OC.* V, 97-101), and in his "Notes on Thinking" cited in the note at the end of Chap. I (*OC.* V, 531-532). The thesis of truth as fulfillment of the promise, referred to by Zubiri and Ortega, is set forth in Hans Freiherr von Soden's *Was ist Wahrheit?* (1927). A number of suggestive clarifications, both philosophical and philological, on this point, in Zubiri, *Naturaleza, Historia, Dios*, Madrid (1944), 29, note. A clear comparison between the three different meanings of truth—the Hebrew, the Greek, and the Roman—will be found in Julián Marías, *Reason and Life: The Introduction to Philosophy*, New Haven (1956), 95-97 (an English translation of *Introducción a la Filosofía*, Madrid [1947], 104-107).

For Hebrew history in general, we have made use of various books—some longer (such as the works by H. Graetz and S. W. Baron), others shorter (such as the works by Giuseppe Ricciotti, Theodore H. Robinson, Max L. Margolis and Alexander Marx, Cecil Roth). Especially pertinent for our purpose were works treating in greater detail of the period studied in our chapter (such as those by Emil Schürer, E. Meyer, E. Bevan, M. Friedländer, J. W. Lightley, C. Guignebert, and Joseph Bonsirven). We have also made use of material contained in works that study the various sects separately. Among them are those by Geiger for the Sadducees and Pharisees; those by Caspari, A. T. Robertson, and R. T. Herford for the Pharisees; those by Hölscher and Lesynsky for the Sadducees; those by Ginsburg for the Essenes. Of particular value to us was J. W. Lightley's book on the Jewish sects in the time of Jesus Christ, a book that summarizes many earlier studies, including articles not reprinted in books, and articles appearing in the various biblical and Jewish encyclopaedias. We have also consulted the sources themselves. For our purpose, these were the works of Josephus (the *Jewish War*, the *Jewish Antiquities*, and the *Life*), the New Testament, and certain sections of the palaeotestamentary literature—partly apocalyptic in nature—not included in the Canon. For the passages on prophecy, we have taken into consideration the corresponding portions of the Old Testament. The quotation from Tacitus is from *Historiae*, V, xiii.

The reader may ask why it was necessary to consult so many books if, in the end, the facts adduced in the chapter are so few. But anyone who is acquainted with the problem will agree that extensive consultation of authorities was necessary simply to enable us to present a formulation of a plausible opinion. This is particularly true in the case of the Hebrew sects. Were the Sadducees really "libertines"? Were the Pharisees really "strict"? We thought it proper to refer to the doubts expressed on these questions by some historians and philologists. At the same time, we consider it our duty to give the opinion that best accords with the demands of the entire complex of facts. Hence we have left out the "contradictions" that have often been emphasized in descriptions of the Sadducees, Pharisees, Essenes, and zealots. Such "contradictions" are almost always due to forgetting the many occasions on which "extremes meet." To give an example: We do not see why it should be surprising that the strict conservatism of the Sadducees goes hand in hand with a comparative "liberalism." For the Pharisees, *the* tradition consisted in the Law, both written and oral. In some cases even, the oral tradition, fixed in all its details, was followed still more strictly than the written Law, which, being ambiguous, was therefore more susceptible of various interpretations. The Sadducees, on the other hand, held chiefly to the written Law, and though, as a number of writers have shown, they did not reject some of the oral Law, this oral Law did not have the importance for them that it acquired among the Pharisees. Hence the Sadducees, although more "conservative"—or alternatively, for that very reason —could be more "liberal" and "open" than the Pharisees. This passage from conservatism to "liberalism" is a consequence of a general historical (or sociological) law, and can easily be verified by anyone who studies the process by which dogmas become settled. The Marxist who holds to Marx's writings is usually more "open" than the one who "already" interprets them in the light of Lenin. A return to the "sources of Christianity" can be considered "suspect" if it is not accompanied by the commentary brought in by earlier "settlements." Thus, the more a text has been interpreted, the less possibility it affords for introducing different opinions.

What we have said on the subject of the Sadducees and Pharisees can also serve in regard to the Essenes. It has been possible to consider them as precursors of Christianity or as very different from Christianity, because in either case only one element—either prophecy, or ascetic ceremonialism, or some other— has been emphasized at the expense of the whole sociological complex. On the other hand, as soon as the general attitude of the Essenes is considered, we see that each of the above elements has its role in the whole. We do not hereby claim to solve the problem of different interpretations. That can be done only by a historical study *sensu stricto*, which, furthermore, would always be subject to empirical verification.

5. The Powerful

Power as office and power as benefice.–Principles and results, means and ends.–Power as reaction.

The figure of the "politician."–The "wave of the times" and attitudes toward it.–The impotence of power.–Once again, history and geology.

The psychological motivations for world conquest.–The powerful and the "frivolous."–Catonism and Caesarism.–The rationalization of power: ancient tyrannies and modern tyrannies.–Adaptation to power.–Power and intelligence.

Description of the "barbarian."–Politics and force.–Power and its means.–The appearance of power.–Power and society.–The example of Rome: monarchy and anarchy.–The quantitative factor.–"Inevitable periods."–Equalization and leveling.–The one problem: survival.

There are periods in which power is accepted as an office. There are others in which it is sought as a benefice. As the human mind is complex, neither of these attitudes is usually manifested in complete purity; every exercise of power is a mixture of the two. The distinction between exercising power responsibly and conscientiously, and exercising it unscrupulously is, then, by no means an easy one to make. We often think, for example, that "power for power's sake" always produces catastrophic results. Experience shows, however, that there are many exceptions here. Therefore, we cannot simply say: In "critical" or "abnormal" periods, power becomes a prize that certain men want to enjoy at all costs. Or, as the present situation would tend to make us think: In such periods, power loses its justification before morality, utility, or even history, and tends to become an autonomous reality. All evils, we could conclude, arise from this independence. Man no longer exercises power for the benefit of anything, not even of himself.

We cannot give our assent to this simple conclusion, because the principles that men follow and the actions that ensue from these principles are not always logically correlated. As the proverb has it, the road to Hell is paved with good intentions. Since Mandeville's day, it has been clearly acknowledged that private vices may become public benefits. According to Gide's well-known and wrongly interpreted phrase, bad literature can be made out of good sentiments. Conversely, out of dark passions, as Proust has shown, the conditions necessary for great spiritual creations *can* arise. Hence the first thing to be said on the subject is this: Our description of what happens in the exercise of power at certain moments of history is for the time being independent of any value judgment. The problem raised by the presence of the "power as reaction to a terrifying historical situation" should not be judged solely from the point of view of its ethical justification or lack of justification.

We have written: "power as reaction to a terrifying historical situation." For all its vagueness, the formula is not inadequate. This reaction has been described many times. There is even something monotonous about history. While resistance or flight or the projection of an ideal into the future are exceptional events, power is a normal phenomenon. But as long as there is no crisis, it is viewed as a delegation, a transmission—whether human or divine—and hence as an activity implying responsibility. He who exercises power is normally supposed to be responsible before some higher authority and also before himself. He believes that he possesses a margin of freedom sufficient to permit his intervention to bring a substantial change in human affairs. But as soon as the crisis becomes more serious, the ship of power is swept along by the current. To continue in metaphors, a void is produced, which draws toward itself a whirlpool of passions. Whereupon the intriguing figure of the "politician" makes its appearance in society. It emerges with such force that power seems to exist only by virtue of it, the organ appears to produce the function, and not vice versa. This impression is corroborated by the way in which the direction of affairs is often assumed; instead of transmission or delegation—more or less astutely handled—illegal seizure of power becomes increasingly frequent. Power is no longer a degrading or ennobling, a repugnant or desirable function; it is a singularly abrupt way of resolving a human situation. This situation is at once individual and collective. In both cases, it has one characteristic feature—it looks as if it were hopeless. Hence the decision to conquer power is comparable to resistance to it. Both are responses, or, better, reactions. What matters least is their particular content. Naturally, there continue to be great differences between the man in power and those whom he dominates. Indeed, the differences are greater than in "normal" times. But the ruler and the ruled have something fundamental in common —in either case they take a *decision through reaction*.

Perhaps the best way to express our thought in this connection is to quote a reflection that Balzac put into one of his novels: "The world is a quagmire; let us try to stay on its surface." This, the novelist goes on, means that at such moments "there are no principles, there are only events; no laws, only circumstances; the superior man seizes upon events and circumstances in order to direct them." Here we have one of the attitudes to which we referred when introducing the image of the irresistible "wave of the times." One of the ways of confronting this wave is precisely to mount it and try to stay on its ever unstable crest. Instead of planting one's feet firmly on the ground, shutting one's eyes, and summoning up one's courage (by meditation or by prayer); or instead of escaping from the wave by a transposition that is first intellectual and may then become mystical; or instead of following it as if it were the road of Providence or Destiny— man can try to *use* it. This is just what the man of power does —whether he is the head of the empire or the most insignificant of all bureaucrats. It is not even necessary for such a decision to be taken to become a tyrant or a despot. Tyranny or despotism are concrete ways of exercising rule and can exist in all periods. The ruler can hold many different functions. He can be a vicar of God, a guardian of the State in the Platonic fashion, an ignorant or enlightened despot. He can exercise power because he believes that it is a service to his fellow men, or he can throw all scruples to the winds and devote himself to rule for the sake of rule. In all these cases, power will possess a certain "independence," a certain "legality." Neither a "decision" nor a "reaction" will then make sense. They will make sense only when the consequences of the decisions taken by the ruler become increasingly unforeseeable, when power itself is driven away by the fearful whirlpool of the epoch.

Here we have an answer to our problem. Even absolute power looks as if it were a rudderless ship, as much at the mercy of the great gales of the times as the frailest skiff. At moments of crisis, no one, including the absolute ruler, can control the effects of power. In normal periods, "power" means not only a force, but the direction that the force takes, a direction that is assumed to be, if not consciously determined by men, at least freely accepted by them. There is then a sort of play between the force—physical or moral or intellectual—of power and the direction of power. It is a play that almost never goes beyond certain limits. In unstable periods, on the contrary, all limits are trespassed. The force has become independent of its direction; what is known in technical language as "heterogenesis of ends" has set in. Power can do everything except one thing—it cannot direct itself. Power—we must repeat—has become a geological process; its effects are comparable to the enormous pressure that some strata of society exert on the others (and vice versa), until it becomes impossible to know who is on top of whom—who rules. So that our "man of power" really has no power; our "ruler" rules nothing. It follows that the phrase "power for power's sake" is wholly inadequate to describe such a historical situation. In normal times the man who exercises power is able at least to keep his balance, to keep firm hold on the reins not only of society but also of his own person. None of this takes place in a "geological" upheaval. Some men, in view of a certain historical situation, "decide" for power. But from the first moment, they discover that it is a decision only in name. I said earlier that in such moments power is usurped. It will now be clear that this was only a first way of putting it. For power has lost its rudder, and the man who is embarked on it has only the appearance of command.

But why does he decide for power? The psychological root of the decision is always the same—it is a case of "getting on," of "establishing himself." These men seem to have everything—except scruples. If life asks—they seem to say—we will give it what it asks for. We choose to be carried by the current of the times instead of being drowned in it. Let us make use of all the means at hand while it is still possible. To be sure, power does not have this realm all to itself. There is also frivolity. If that be our choice, we shall surmount destiny by seeking out the areas which its sinister side has not yet darkened—the surfaces of life. Some even manage to combine frivolity and rule; there have been many examples since Alcibiades. But to devote oneself to frivolity is not as easy a task as it appears to be; it takes a prodigious degree of skill, intelligence, and art. It implies to accept many risks. Rule can be conquered more "easily," perhaps more "directly." Certainly, to conquer it, one must first pretend, then completely embrace, fanaticism. Power is also won through cynicism; but it is doubtful if it can be kept in the same way. The frivolous man seeks only to live well (with the accent on the adverb); the man of power wants to live (with the emphasis on the act). Scepticism and fanaticism, love of frivolity and appetite for power cannot, then, always be made to coincide. No more can the means that they employ—distant and apparently benevolent irony on the one side, enterprising astuteness on the other. But they are effects of the same causes, different ways of getting astride of the great wave, in full knowledge that it will carry us where *it* wants to go, not where *we* want to go. In periods when everything that happens seems to be inevitable, power is exercised neither as a means nor as an end. Even classic examples cannot instruct us here. If we believe the historians, Cato wielded power as a means, without an instant's slackening; Catonism was inflexible *precisely because* Cato's power was not absolute. Caesar, on the other hand, exercised power as an end; he had to shape his power as if it were a work of art, but a necessary work of art. Like an artist, he was inclined to think that his creation was self-sustaining; society, intrigue, friends, enemies, were merely means. There was no possibility of following a straight line. On the contrary, constant adaptation was required. But it was not adaptation to an ideal but to a "material"; as the material from which the statue is shaped conditions the artist's movements, so the men on whom he "works" oblige the seeker after power to adapt all his public acts, and the greater part of his private life, to them—to their passions, their vices, their virtues. Caesar exercised power as an end; Caesarism was not inflexible *precisely because* Caesar's power was absolute. Now, Catonism and Caesarism were still "normal" historical phenomena; in both, the exercise of power continued to have a *meaning*. This is not the case in the situation we are trying to describe. If we look for a historical example of what the phrase "power as reaction" means, we shall find it rather in imperial Roman power, once it was established not only with its personal rule, its increasing authoritarianism, but also, and above all, with its constantly growing bureaucracy. Some historians have pointed out that the characteristic feature of the Roman power was its increasing "bureaucratization." The conditions investigated by Max Weber or Karl Mannheim account for this process; the bureaucracy represented a rationalization of power —a functional rationalization, which did not necessarily affect the irrational nature of the rule. If the combination did not yet appear to be pure madness implacably directed by reason, this was because, as Tocqueville said, there is a great difference between the ancient tyranny of a central government and "our" tyranny. When the emperors were at the height of their power, Tocqueville observed, a great variety in customs and manners was still preserved. There were provinces that were separately administered, and much of public and private life escaped the control of a central hand and its functionaries. Even with unchecked power at their hands, even abusing power on frequent occasions, the emperors could oppress only a few— though those few, of course, became constantly more numerous. Like Ivan the Terrible in Russia, they battened principally on the dominant strata, which were within their reach; like the Muscovite monarch, they only occasionally destroyed some distant group, a city, even a whole district. All of them, however, lacked the technical means necessary to rationalize the ruling function completely. They began to discover a Siberia, but they could not yet exploit it. Nevertheless, the exercise of power was subject to the same conditions as in "our" epoch; it continued to be "at hand," ready to be seized by anyone with enough vigor, good luck, lack of scruples, or fanaticism. Or, better: ready to be seized by anyone who could adapt to it—the only way to secure it. In a moment of deep pessimism, Ortega y Gasset set up a distinction between "life as freedom" and "life as adaptation." There is no doubt that in the epoch described, adaptation predominates over freedom. Some men feel that they are free only in the measure in which they know how, or are able, to jettison scruples. But since the "politician"—as the man who expresses a certain human attitude—is the very one who does this to perfection, it is the politician, and not the legislator or even the plain tyrant, who becomes predominant in such periods. He will assure himself that at least he has made his freedom coincide with his adaptation. Hence his distrust of all "thought." For thought is interested in origins and principles, and instead of getting rid of scruples, likes to accumulate them. To be sure, the politician does not entirely dismiss intelligence. He needs it too much to allow himself such a luxury. But the intelligence that he tolerates is increasingly "functional"; *it is not an intelligence in search of principles but one that carries out decisions.* We must not, then, confuse the rule of the politician with the exercise of pure force. The "politician" is not the "barbarian," even when he commits, or allows others to commit, all sorts of "barbarities." The "barbarian" is like the naked arm that strikes it knows not where—without "adapting." In his historical novel *Ekkehard,* published in 1857, Josef Viktor von Scheffel undertook to describe the collision of two worlds —the one, a vital, strong, unprejudiced world; the other, an intellectual, weak, decadent world, burdened with scruples. One passage in his description is particularly suggestive. As the quotation from T. E. Lawrence did for the man in complete solitude with God, the passage we shall now give, slightly paraphrased, will illuminate the type of the barbarian better than any minute historical description or any abstract philosophical analysis.

The passage in question describes a scene in which the Huns

Ellak and Hornebog, leaders of one of the most redoubtable invasions suffered by the West, stand before a heap of corpses, the victims of the siege, capture, and burning of a monastery. Among the corpses lie some manuscripts from the destroyed library, scorched and almost indecipherable. Hornebog thrusts the point of his sword through one of them, raises it to the level of his comrade's eyes, and asks:

"What are these scratches and crow's-feet for, brother?"

Ellak takes the book, leafs through it carelessly; he knows a little Latin, and after a long time he says:

"Western wisdom, brother. A man named Boethius filled these sheets; I think there are fine things in them about consolation from philosophy."

Hornebog thinks for a time, and seems to understand. But then he says:

"Phil-os-o-phy? And what has that to do with consolation?"

"Well," says Ellak, "it's nothing about a beautiful woman—or about brandy either. It's hard to describe in the Hun language. Look . . . when a man doesn't know why he is in the world and takes it into his head to find out, that's what they call philosophy in the West. I've heard that the man who wrote this book was a weeping prisoner in a tower in Padua until they beat him to death."

"Served him right," says Hornebog. "A man who has a sword in his hand and a horse between his legs knows why he is in the world! And if *we* hadn't known it better than the fellow who made these scratches on this piece of a donkey's hide, we wouldn't be here, but fleeing along the Danube."

He is silent for a time, but an idea seems to be flitting through his brain. Again he turns to his companion and says steadily:

"You know, it's a luck all this stuff was ever thought of."

"Why?" Hornebog asks.

"Because the hand that has once held a pen will never know how to grasp a sword that cuts into flesh, and the nonsense that has got into that head, once it gets put in a book, will be able to inflame a hundred more heads. And a hundred milksops the more are a hundred knights the less."

No—the "politician" is not always the barbarian. For the latter feels that his vital, unconscious, activity can give a meaning to his own existence. The barbarian, then, is he who lives beyond the frontiers of established society, or he who, although inside these frontiers geographically, lives and acts as if he were outside them. He is the unadapted man; hence he can sometimes even become an "idealist"—with an "idealism" that, unlike the idealism of philosophy, is never rationalized. But the politician, if he uses force, will do it quite without the ingenuousness of the barbarian—fanatically, perhaps, but at the same time coldly. He has no use for brute force—it is too "pure." Pure force sometimes has its own greatness. And in any case it is too close to the spontaneity of life to be compared with the implacable operation performed by a machine. I do not say that the barbarian's brutality is fundamentally good, or lies beyond good and evil; I am not enough of a Rousseauist for that. The dewdrops of purity that, according to Simone Weil, shine at great intervals in the web of baseness and cruelty that constitutes human history are not engendered by the dubious greatness of brute force or of unprejudiced muscle. We have undergone too many recent experiences of brute force to have any illusions as to what it might have been in other periods of history. The "politician" is not the unadapted man; he is perfectly adapted, the only man who has really succeeded in "finding his place." To be sure, he runs the risk of being thrown out of it; but if that happens, it will be because he was not "political minded," because, consciously or unconsciously, he will have resisted the great wave that is constantly bearing him along, or he will have taken it into his head to think about it and find a meaning in it. In the periods we are describing, however, the meaning of events consists in the fact that they seem to be meaningless. If they do continue to have some meaning objectively, men do not know it or cannot find it; hence they act as if events had no meaning. And to act in history as if historical events had no meaning, is the nearest possible thing to history's being meaningless. The Antonines tried to justify power. Camus's Caligula tries to prove, by abusing power, that he is free—that he is the *only* free man. It might seem that we here have two completely different human types, and that the difference between them gives the lie to our conception that power in such periods cannot be properly controlled by men. But this is not so. In the first place, the exercise of power appeared as one of the "solutions." It was not the only solution, nor the most valid, nor even the most generally accepted. In the second place, the various ways in which the powerful men of the time exercised power are much less important than their consciousness that they all had something in common —their own *powerlessness*.

"What!" someone will ask, "powerlessness at a moment of history when the powerful are really powerful?" The inconsistency would be obvious, if power depended entirely upon the means at its disposal. The man of power—emperor, soldier, or bureaucrat—finds himself holding an office upon which the acts, the thoughts, and the lives of a vast multitude of human beings appear to depend. He has only to turn his will in one direction or another, and this vast multitude will feel that their lives have been radically changed. Here the objector will raise his voice again: "And could anyone ask for a more obvious manifestation of power? Or are you going to come at us with subtle metaphysical arguments and deny what is self-evident?" Yet, we must insist on denying it. For what use is power if the material on which the man of power exercises it is the same material that completely determines his "decisions"? Now, when historical inevitability prevails, this is what actually happens. Great landslides are caused by the land that slides; the cataclysm is the cause of the cataclysm. The strata of humanity are so arranged that the pressures exerted on them are unforeseeable. Events that appear to be the result of absolute personal power are nothing but the consequence of the force possessed by the apparently subject human masses. And since such human masses are unaware of this power of theirs, or are still unable to channel it, it follows that, in the last analysis, power belongs to nobody and to nothing; it is *dependent* on everybody, but nobody *exercises* it. In such a situation it is not surprising if some men say: "Since we cannot have power, let us at least have the *appearance* of it."

The appearance of power! Here we have the "secret" of these periods. If they are viewed superficially, it seems that in them policy becomes what it always is to some extent but never quite so shamelessly—that is, "realistic." It will have nothing to do with any "ideas," any "programs," any "Utopian chatter." Why, so much the better, it will be said, by doing so, political decisions become more flexible, more complex, more aware of the subtle structure of social reality. But this is not the case. A complex and sinuous policy, a truly realistic policy, exists only when reality is not completely ungovernable. Perhaps men cannot choose, as they frequently imagine that they do, between different realities or ideas. But at least they can choose between different shades of realities or ideas. When this last thing happens, we have the periods in which skilful, astute politicians actually rule society. These are the "happy" times of the "Machiavellians." Thus the prerequisite for such a policy is a reality that at times offers stubborn resistance but that can always be molded. But in periods in which the exercise of power is only an appearance, nothing can be molded; whoever holds the reins of society in his hands, he can do nothing but follow their insane tugs and pulls. He has quite enough to do just to remain in the saddle. Social reality has become so inert that it offers fewer and fewer openings for the "play" of politics. From Augustus down to the Antonines the illusion still survived that the rulers truly represented society—or the best elements of society. The emperor—the "king"—could be, or was supposed to be, the *primus inter pares*. This illusion very quickly vanished; he who would be emperor had to renounce being *princeps*. Society was undergoing an implacable process of leveling, and thereby lost all possibility of engendering a complex structure through whose chinks freedom could find an entrance. It will be said that this leveling was necessary, and that it was a step ahead toward a social ideal in which there would be neither oppressors nor oppressed. But the actual historical development quickly undertook to show that the above ideal was no more than a pious wish. For leveling is not always equivalent to equality and still less to fraternity; men do not become brothers *merely* by becoming equal; what happens is that *the center of power becomes progressively less localizable and hence less responsible.* All appeared to rule; actually, no one did. Well, it will be said, the most immediate organs of society ruled—the army, the bureaucracy. Both were formed on the basis of the most numerous, and previously dispossessed, classes. Quite true. But as soon as these organs functioned, they proceeded to pulverize the very classes from which they emerged. Society appeared to be a monarchy, perhaps without a monarch, but with only one authority; what it was however, was anarchy. Under the crust of organization to the utmost, under the universal militarization of all social functions, lurked a void. It was a perilous void; each time that readjustments became necessary, whole classes had to plunge into it, had to physically disappear—the slightest movement gave rise to countless upheavals and ills. Society appeared to have become simpler; but the result had been to make it less manageable.

The principal characteristic of a society such as we are attempting to describe was its almost complete lack of flexibility. One of the reasons for this was quantitative; a constantly increasing number of human beings found themselves compressed in the same political organization. This happened to the Roman Empire when the ideal of Romanism was losing more and more ground to the idea of the *Imperium*. Such a process was, of course, inevitable; any elegiac recalling of the past could only be helpless. But this is just what we want to emphasize; our digression concerns periods in which what happens cannot be said to be good or bad, repugnant or welcome, but only one thing: inevitable. These are the epochs in which the most frequent comment to be heard is: "There is nothing else we can do." From Commodus to Diocletian, and from Diocletian to Theodosius— two phases of a single period—we witness a historical process whose most general and permanent characteristic was political impotence. The senatorial class could not save the tradition, and was doomed to extinction. The emperor could not save the senatorial class; strictly speaking, he could not save any class and had to put them all at the orders of the bureaucracy and the army. But neither could these decide for themselves; not only were they without consciousness of authority, but they believed that authority was incarnated in the person who was merely their instrument—the emperor. In such moments, then, each social class depends on all the other classes, and each individual depends on all the other individuals, but no one knows if there is any structure—good or bad—which guarantees such a dependence. It could be argued that this fact contradicts the previous thesis, and that there is never so much flexibility as when rigidity vanishes. And this would be true, if the expression "flexible social reality" had the same meaning as the expression "formless social reality," if society became more complex as it became more uniform. But we must be on our guard not to confuse two different processes: equalization and leveling. "Equalization" means submitting men to a common standard. "Leveling" means that all men are submitted to the same absence of a standard. They will then all be equal, but it will not be equality in common justice, or in the common enjoyment of goods. They will all be equal in their anxiety, in their failure to foresee the future, in their slavery.

At certain periods, society has a single and urgent problem—to survive. Nothing else can be thought of; "politicians" and "men of power" alike are haunted by the same problem. All their efforts are bent to this one end. They cannot control society as the artist controls his material, with a peculiar mixture of love and domination. They have to confine themselves to keeping society from collapsing, although to attain this end they have to destroy—physically or morally—a large proportion of society's components. Hence they are almost as much slaves as the slaves themselves. Their advantage is that they are "on top," and hence that the psychological motivation referred to earlier—"getting on"—still exists for them. But as soon as they reflect on their lives and the lives of those around them, they realize that there is the same void in everyone, and that the great wave of the period carries all men with it, ceaselessly and mercilessly. The one hope is that the great crisis that all are experiencing together proves to be a crisis of growth and not of senescence; that everything that is happening may have a final justification in future history. Now, future history is hidden from the eyes of man, and the doubt will always remain whether, supposing that the case is one of rebirth, the pains are worth the result. The Stoic and the Neoplatonist would say that the above fears are unfounded, since there is no pain for him who has enough inward strength to resist, or whose soul is pure enough to contemplate the intelligible world. The Cynic would say that the problems raised in this connection are meaningless, because everything that happens is a symptom of an evil that will disappear as soon as we have removed its cause—the perversion of nature which social life causes. The Futurist, of course, would not say that the question is meaningless, but he would insist that it has no meaning in the present moment, and in this particular respect he would be in agreement with the Stoic, the Platonist, and even the Cynic. The man of power, on the other hand, can never say that the problem in question is a pseudo-problem. In whatever way he has managed to scale the unstable heights of authority, the problem of a great historical crisis will always be a living one for him. For the man whose existence consists in authority—small or great—there is no way of separating reality from appearance; what society appears to be, it is. He does not understand, nor will he ever understand, that to save the appearance it is not necessary either to deny it or to exalt it; it will suffice to discover that it can be renewed, transformed, transfigured. Thus, anxiety and philosophy have brought us to the threshold of renewal.

Notes

We recognize that there is a certain vagueness in our description of the period to which the present chapter refers. In the chapters on the Cynics, the Stoics, and the Platonists, the vagueness in respect to the period was somewhat diminished by our references to the various philosophers. In the chapter on the Futurists, the period in question was clearly delimited. But in connection with power, we are confronted by a problem similar to that raised in the first chapter. For what, once again, is meant by "end of the ancient world"? The expression is decidedly ambiguous. Shall we say that it refers to the "decline and fall of the Roman Empire"? But then when did that process begin and end? And what justification have we for using such markedly evaluative terms as "decline," "fall," "decadence," and the like? It does not solve our problem to say that the periods involved are "unstable." This only yields a verbal definition. There is nothing to do but to admit that we are in a sea of doubts.

In order not to drown in it, we must determine the dates that our analysis embraces. The chief difficulty lies in the fact that the historical events to which the present chapter refers appeared in the "ancient world" at various periods. For example, some of the problems described arose quite critically in Greece from the time when Alexander put the finishing touch to the breakup of the ancient City-State system. However, we thought it better to choose a particular phase of the Roman Empire as the example for analysis. Concretely, our digression is to be understood in the light of the events of Roman history from the death of Marcus Aurelius to the so-called "division of the Empire" by Theodosius the Great. The new attitude toward the Church represented by Constantine is one of the decisive events of this history. But the axis around which this history revolves lies probably in the period of Diocletian. After Constantine and Theodosius, a new epoch in the history of power began, which continued several important characteristics of the preceding period (the imaginary but possible scene from *Ekkehard* takes place in the tenth century, long after Boethius, when "our" history was already over and the cycle that we are trying to describe had ended, but it is applicable to the situation we have described). Hence it is ambiguous to talk of "fall" and "decadence." If we continue to use these words, we must give them a relative meaning—such as all general evaluative terms ought to have. There can be in the above period a "fall" from the viewpoint of the Principate, but not from that of the Middle Ages, which the period in question forestalls. The vacillations of which many historians are guilty validate our own vacillations. The usual practice is to distinguish between the Empire properly speaking and the Later Empire, of which works on the "decadence" of Rome usually treat. But such a distinction is vague. Some writers begin their descriptions of the Later Empire in the period of Diocletian—for example, Otto Seeck in his classic *Geschichte des Untergangs der antiken Welt*, 6 vols., with appendices, Berlin (1901-1920), or Ernst Stein in his *Geschichte des Spätrömischen Reiches. Vom römischen zum byzantinischen Staates 284-476*, Vienna (1928); Vol. II, in French, *Histoire du Bas Empire. De la disparition de l'Empire d'Occident à la mort de Justinien 476-565*, Paris-Brussels-Amsterdam (1949), published posthumously by Jean-Rémy Palanque, in which the equation "Post-Roman = Proto-Byzantine" is formally established. Others begin with the death of Theodosius the Great, as for example J. B. Bury in his *History of the Later Roman Empire*, 2 vols., London (1931). Yet others prefer to begin with the so-called "crisis of the third century," and the "restoration of the Roman world," as Ferdinand Lot does in his *La fin du monde antique et le début du moyen âge*, Paris (1927; English translation: *The End of the Ancient World and the Beginnings of the Middle Ages*, New York

[1931]). We shall not mention other historical treatises, since it has been enough for our purpose to give a few typical examples in which the comparative and comprehensible indecision of historians on the subject is patent (works that deal with the entire process of the Roman Empire from Augustus, or with the entire history of Rome, are of less concern to us here than those that specifically set out to describe the "fall"). Divisions of a political nature, on the other hand, are of little help; it is not too important to know whether the tradition of the Principate (or of the Diarchy) was broken with the Later Empire, whereupon the so-called "Pre-Byzantine" Empire began; or whether that tradition had already been interrupted by Diocletian's inauguration of the so-called "Dominatio." Political processes as such are less significant for our purpose than social, economic, and—if we may be forgiven for the vagueness of the term—"vital" phenomena. It must be made clear that the question of power arises in the form in which we have stated it, not when there is decadence in the strict sense but when power can accomplish no more than to keep society in a reasonable state of cohesion, and must sacrifice everything else to this end. In a period of real decadence, power, becoming more chaotic, becomes more plastic, and benefits by possibilities that do not exist in the epochs which we have described.

To sum up: before Commodus and Septimius Severus, power still flowed in "normal" channels. The upheavals of the civil wars before Augustus cannot be compared with the upheavals that took place between 200 and 300 A.D. It was only then that historical inevitability made its appearance. Thus though externally more "chaotic" and "confused," the times after Constantine, and especially after Theodosius the Great, were at least the ferment of a new community—the feudal-rural community—so that the sufferings of society already had more of birth-pangs than of dying agony. It will now be clearer why the period we have chosen is the one analyzed, under the names of "The Military Monarchy" and "The Military Anarchy," by M. Rostovtzeff in chapters IX and X of his *The Social and Economic History of the Roman Empire*, Cambridge (1926), and the one described by E. Altheim in *Die Krise der alten Welt*, I Berlin (1943). We would stress the fact that the situation in which, according to our analysis, power was then placed has also appeared in other periods—and is partially manifest in our own. But if our concepts are to be illustrated on a particular historical basis, we believe that the period proposed is the most fertile in examples and warnings.

Nevertheless, the problem of the causes that produced this situation remains unsolved. It is an important subject, but one with which we cannot be concerned here. With the reservations to be pointed out in a note at the end of our chapter on "The New Man," the examination of such causes is the business of the historian and not that of the writer who confines himself to seeking the meanings that a particular historical situation holds for various groups of human beings. In addition, the opinions maintained as to the nature of the above causes are so various that it would take much time to mention even the most important doctrines formulated in this respect. Some writers look primarily for political causes (this was the dominant view in the nineteenth century, and gave rise to Renouvier's curious and ingenious theory, set forth in his *Uchronie*, according to which the change in the political situation upon the accession of Marcus Aurelius completely altered the course of history). Others allege various other "causes"—economic, geographical, biological, technical, historico-cultural, religious, or even "metaphysical." Others, finally, maintain that all these so-called "causes" are merely symptoms, or favor an eclectic view that sees the process of history as determined by a combination of all the factors mentioned. If such a combination is meant to name a historical complex whose structure is constantly changing (in which case, for example, economic causes will be more influential at one period than at another), the resulting theory seems to us to have considerable plausibility. But then it would remain to explain why at one or another moment there is a greater or less predominance of particular causal factors—so the problem would be raised again.

A review of the various theories concerning the "decadence" of ancient civilization will be found in the last chapter of the book by Rostovtzeff mentioned above. How the problem of the decadence of Rome has been reflected in the thought of the West, from Polybius and Saint Augustine to Gibbon and Nietzsche, is studied in Walter Rehm's *Der Untergang Roms in abendländischen Denken. Ein Beitrag zur Geschichtsschreibung und zum Dekadenzproblem*, Leipzig (1930). The most recent sociological, philosophical, or historico-philosophical theories (Spengler, Toynbee, *et al.*) are too well known to require particular description. As a model of a historical treatment that is neither "philosophical" nor strictly "causal" in approach, but which is not limited to mere description, we will mention Max Weber's still illuminating essay, "Die sozialen Gründe des Untergangs der antiken Kultur," *Die Wahrheit*, Stuttgart, VI, 3 (1896), 59-77.

On the bureaucratization of the Roman Empire, Ernst Meyer, *Römischer Staat und Staatsgedanke*, Zürich (1948), 98 ff. Max Weber's observations on the role of bureaucracy and its various types will be found in Volume IV, Chapter VI of his *Wirtschaft und Gesellschaft* (1922).–For Karl Mannheim's distinction, his *Mensch und Gesellschaft im Zeitalter des Umbaus*, Leyden (1935), is fundamental. This book is a rehandling and enlargement of two earlier works of his, published in English: "Rational and Irrational Elements in Contemporary Society," Hobhouse Lecture (O.U.P., Cambridge) and "The Crisis of Culture in the Era of Mass-democracies and Autarchies," *The Sociological Review*, XXVI, 2 (1934).–The quotation from Tocqueville is from Vol. II, Book IV, Chapter VI of his *De la démocratie en Amérique*, 2 vols. (1835); English translation, *Democracy in America*, 4 vols. (1835-40), revised translation, New York, 2 vols. (1945).–The novel of Balzac's is *Le Père Goriot*.–The reference to Ortega is from his "Del Imperio romano," first published in a series of articles in *La Nación*, of Buenos Aires, and then in his *Historia como sistema*, Madrid (1941), reprinted in *OC*. VI (1947), 51-107. There is an English translation of Ortega's articles, *Concord and Liberty*, New York (1946), 9-47.–Simone Weil's book is *L'enracinement*, Paris (1950).–On the problem of the view of power held in the ancient world, see Joseph Vogt, "Dämonie der Macht und Weisheit der Antike," *Die Welt als Geschichte*, X, 1 (1950), with citations on the "demoniac" and "degrading" nature of power from many writers of classical Antiquity. For the Greek "classic" period, which furnished many of the ideas later developed by Roman writers, see Hertwig Frisch, *Might and Right in Antiquity. From Homer to the Persian Wars*, Copenhagen (1949), English translation of *Magt og Ret in Ildtiden*. A careful historical description and comparison of "Catonism" and "Caesarism" will be found in Chapter VIII of Lily Ross Taylor's *Party Politics in the Age of Caesar*, Berkeley and Los Angeles (1949).

Thornton Wilder's *The Ides of March* depicts a Julius Caesar who is acutely conscious of the "fatality of power": "Rome as I have shaped it," Caesar is supposed to write, "*as I have had to shape it* [our italics], is not a comfortable place for a man whose genius is the genius for ruling at the top: if I were not Caesar now, I would be Caesar's assassin."

6. The New Man

Christianity as a "solution."–Truth and efficacy of
Christianity.–Natural religions and human religion.–The
philosopher and the religious man.

The figure of Jesus.–Messianism and Christianity.–
Pharisaism and anti-Pharisaism.–The "Gospel paradoxes."

The unique character of Jesus.–The opening of the
new man.–Love of God, love of one's neighbor, and love
of the world.–The Law and preaching.–The relation between God and man.–The role of the "Mediator."–
Death and resurrection.–Christianity and history.–Purifi-
cation of the soul and transformation of life.

The "causes" for the triumph of Christianity.–Its unity
and variety.–The ambivalence of faith: renewal and
stagnation.–The necessity for a "Church."

Solving the three disequilibriums: (1) the disequilibrium between this world and another; (2) the disequilibrium between man and society; (3) the disequilibrium
between action and thought.–Truths for the initiated and
salvation for all.

It is a commonplace to say that Christianity alone represented
a complete "solution" for the troubles of the period. The "collapse" of the philosophical systems—or of the philosophical

"ways of life"—is pointed out. The "invasion" of the Empire by Oriental religions is then emphasized. It is added that *if* circumstances had been different, Mithraism for example, and not Christianity, *would have* been victorious. In short, the common man of the period is depicted as a hopelessly astray, desperate being, deprived of any firm belief. A vacuum thus having been produced—which, as in our period, some call thirst for the absolute, others stupidity—nothing more natural than that Christianity should proceed to "fill it." Thus Christianity is interpreted as a consummately adequate "expedient" for a particular historical moment. In this case, Christianity would be a "reaction," which, thanks to favorable circumstances, could find its place both in the heart of society and in the souls of men.

The point of view adopted in this book does not allow us to dismiss such assumptions. As a matter of fact, it obliges us to take them very seriously. After all, similar considerations were raised in regard to Cynicism, to Stoicism, to Neoplatonism. We never believed that these philosophical doctrines could be exhaustively defined as human reactions to certain historical situations, but we emphasized the fact that to study them as human reactions was a very illuminating approach for our purpose. It does not seem preposterous, then, to begin by considering Christianity as an "expedient," without prejudice to whatever affirmations it may contain that "transcend" the human condition.

From this viewpoint, we do not need to inquire into the truth of Christianity, in much the same way as we did not need to inquire into the truth of Stoicism or of Platonism. To declare them "true," it was sufficient for us to accept them as real—that is, as undeniable facts in the history of mankind. Now, to the Christian nothing is so real as the figure of Jesus, his life and death. To become a Platonist, it is not necessary to believe that Plato once existed. To become a Christian, there is nothing for it but to believe in the existence of Christ. We even suspect that one of the reasons for the historical victory of Christianity depends on the fact that, instead of being a "natural religion" or an "intellectual religion" or a "mythical religion," it is—with the reservations to be made forthwith—a "human religion." We are not using "natural" or "intellectual" or "human" as philosophical terms here; for the moment we are not concerned with philosophical theses, but with a very simple fact, which consists in recognizing the difference between following and worshiping a man—whether he is thought of as "natural" or as divine—and worshiping a myth, a principle, or a phenomenon of nature. The famous Oriental gods who "invaded" the Empire were not human gods in this sense. Almost all the humanity that they had was borrowed. It did not arise spontaneously and inexhaustibly; there was nothing "dramatic" about it. Hence the figure of Christ has always been a central theme in understanding the Christian attitude and distinguishing it from others. We can even conceive the possibility of a "religion" founded by a philosopher—a Zeno of Citium or a Socrates. But the philosopher will always be over-shadowed by his doctrine—or by the doctrine attributed to him. His life may have been entirely devoted, even sacrificed, to the doctrine; yet his doctrine will always be taken as something apart from his life. He was a philosopher, not a "religious man." Therein lies all the difference. It is immense. It is the frontier between two worlds, even if we end by admitting that they both lie within the universe of man.

For us, then, the figure of Jesus will be the center and the starting point. As Messiah, the figure of Jesus does not seem to raise any great problems; it even appears to be a "natural" culmination of the crisis of the Hebrew people. Otherwise it would be impossible to find so much "Christianity" among that people before Christ. A few decades before the birth of Jesus, Christianity was, so to speak, "in the air." Everywhere the Hebrew was looking for some crevice through which he could put his head into the world outside, could escape from the constantly more rarefied atmosphere that had been produced by his bewildering mixture of despair and mad hope. Closed upon itself, his society could scarcely function. The reason for this fact was not metaphysical but historical. Being a community that was called on to live among others, and refusing to be "penetrated," it could do nothing but disperse. The prophets had opened it, but only to itself. Christ opened it to all. He opened it so much that it fell to pieces; it should not surprise us that, from a purely historical point of view, the message of Jesus, although bathed in a Hebrew atmosphere, appeared to many of his people to be a dissolvent. Like the condemnation of Socrates, the condemnation of Jesus was "nationally-historically" justified. What the majority of the Hebrew people hoped for was *their* Messiah, not *the* Messiah. To call oneself the Son of God, and at the same time be the Son of Man, was a scandal for a community accustomed to expecting the Son of David and thinking that the words of the prophets had meaning only for their own people. A single point marked the touching of two lines which soon turned out to diverge—one was the seed of Christianity, the other was the culmination of Messianism.

The conflicting arguments over the figure of Jesus are chiefly due to the fact that, out of the rich tapestry in which he is depicted, only a few threads have been taken in each case. One could even amuse oneself by showing that many of the threads could never cross. Let us take one of the Gospels, St. Matthew's. In one place (10:5), we are told: "Go not into the way of the Gentiles, and into any city of the Samaritans enter ye not." In another (28:19) we read: "Go ye therefore and teach all nations, baptizing them in the name of the Father, and of the Son, and of the Holy Ghost." Philologists and historians can spend their lives attempting to demonstrate that the composition of the New Testament—not to mention the rest of primitive Christian literature—is the result of a complicated process involving any number of unknown sources, successive versions, and interpolations. With it all, they will only end by showing that the tapestry has a great many threads; they will hardly succeed in convincing us that the tapestry does not exist. Are we, then, to be importunately "logical" and ignore the fact that, despite everything, such "contradictions" were accepted and acted upon? This means that they form part, at least historically, of Christianity, and that in consequence they cannot be left out of what concerns us here—the appearance of the "new man" through what we shall call "the Christian fact."

The figure of Jesus, the source and center of this renewal, is infinitely complex. Was he a founder? Was he a prophet? Was he "violent," "sweet," "severe," "ironic"? To begin with, we do not know what we should accept as his image of the world. Eduard Meyer has said that "the religious image of the world possessed by Jesus was, point for point, the Pharisaic image of it." In proof of his view, he has emphasized characteristics that seem to be incontrovertible: There is a "Kingdom of God," with the hierarchy of the angels, and a kingdom of demons under the rule of Satan. After death there will be a judgment that will raise some to eternal life and cast others into ignominy, Hell, *Gehenna.* Resurrection and Last Judgment are presupposed (Mark 12:26). In addition, the Law is to be strictly obeyed (Luke 14:17; Matthew 5:18). If with all this we think of the verses already quoted from Matthew (10:5 ff.), we shall easily round out the Pharisaic image. Are we to say, then, that Jesus was "the good Pharisee," so much the more angered by the "bad Pharisees" because the latter in their hearts betrayed the principles that they claimed to defend? As soon as we admit all this, we realize that we have sacrificed life to doctrine, and the Kingdom of God to a dogma about this Kingdom. With the same abundance of evidence that allows us to assert the "Pharisaism" of Jesus, we could maintain his "anti-Pharisaism." Ferdinand Prat has observed that "the Christian spirit could be defined as the direct antithesis of the Pharisaic spirit." The proofs for his view are also convincing: "fear of God instead of fear of men, simplicity and self-forgetfulness in place of ostentation and self-love, genuine virtue in place of sham, substance in place of shadow." These are not mere metaphors, for Ferdinand Prat's view is supported by Jesus' own words: Pharisaism is lack of genuineness and hypocrisy (Luke 12:1; 12:4-7; Matthew 5:20). We have cited these two views; we could add many others. The result would always be the same. Not "*either* this *or* that," nor yet "this *and* that," but "this *and nevertheless* that." For the mentioned incongruity is not the consequence of an opposition, nor yet of an easy eclecticism; it is, to use Unamuno's profound phrase, the consequence of the interpenetration of contraries that "embrace fighting." Obviously it is not here where for the first time the paradoxical nature of the Gospel maxims is emphasized. Nor is it the first attempt made in order to explain it. Bergson had already pointed out that the paradox of the Gospels disappears and the contradictions vanish if due consideration is paid to the "intent" of these maxims—the production of a "disposition of soul." For this reason the maxims are never formulas, petrifications of a movement, but the very expression of that movement. Without accepting Bergson's metaphysics, we may make use of this Bergsonian intuition. But, unlike Bergson—and indeed reversing his approach—we shall not regard the formulas as a descending movement, as a reduction to the motionless, the static. The formula is only *one* of the extremes between which the true movement of spirit occurs, between which—but never fixed at any one point—the Christian attitude dwells. We shall not, then, be surprised to find how infinitely mobile the image of Jesus proves to be, and to what an extent it is only understood when it is "imitated." The Christian attitude arises as an endeavor—forever failing—to practice the *imitatio Christi*. Hence nothing whatever is explained by the fact that Gamaliel or Hillel *could have* delivered the Sermon on the Mount. Similarly the vigor with which Christianity took root is not solely explained by the fact that in the Hebrew community before the Savior there were figures strangely like his. For one of the most remarkable paradoxes in the figure of Jesus is that it is at once universal and unique. Without that figure, *as it was*, we should not have the source from which the type of the "new man" arose.

We have already mentioned the fact that this new man was "open." Above all, he was open to God. Seventeen centuries later, Quevedo put this condition into one splendid line: "A soul whose prison has been—a whole God." It is a fundamental condition. For it is only *because* he is open to God that the Christian can open himself to his neighbor and to the world. This is what the life—and the death—of Jesus say more clearly than if Jesus had handed down a decalogue graven on stone. For the decalogue need only be obeyed, while the life of Jesus must be followed too. The one commands and ordains, while the other merely "recommends" and "suggests." Now, this recommendation is not a simple "do it, if you feel so inclined." Jesus did not always speak *suaviter in modo;* few threats have been so terrible as those he made to men whose minds and hearts were closed, or tortuous, or indifferent. Rather, it is a warning: The Kingdom of God will come; no one is obliged to do this and to avoid that; but he who will hear, let him hear. What he can hear are various warnings, which appear to be mutually contradictory: To him who has much, much will be given, and from him who has little will be taken even the little that he has; be as innocent as doves and as subtle as serpents, and so on and so on. What remains of all these warnings? Is it only the constant movement that follows the pattern of a "this, and nevertheless that"? Is there not, together with the warnings, a "doctrine"? There is one, indeed. It too sets forth many norms. One of them is superlatively important: Man is master of the Sabbath, but the master of man is God.

What changed with the coming of Jesus was not so much the idea of God as the relation between God and man, and, in consequence, the relation between man and the world. But this required that God himself should be seen under a quite uncommon aspect. Christianity as a new religion, mother of a new man, really arose only from the moment when it was admitted that Jesus was not a mere preacher, a prophet, a bringer of the good tidings of God's forgiveness—but the *Lord*. Hence it is impossible to talk of Christianity if Christ is taken to have had only a human nature. But the contrary is also true—it is impossible to talk of Christianity if one imagines that Christ had only a divine nature. The great innovation of Christianity was, then, the idea of God become man. There was no lack of "mediators" between God and man in the various ancient religions— and not only in the conservative religions, which had "triumphed," but also in the countless lost religions, which had "failed." It is almost a question whether a religion is possible without "mediation." But what is essential in Christianity is that mediation coincides with the Incarnation, that the raising of man to God coincides with the actual, not merely "mythical," descent of God to man. This explains why the image of Jesus constitutes the source and center of Christian renewal. We are not trying to reduce Christianity to evangelism; we only wish to emphasize the degree to which, without the radical openness and sacrifice that Jesus exemplified, the later openness of his followers would be inconceivable. Of course, Christian theology is something more than an *imitatio Christi*. But no one would have tried to renew himself if there had not been someone—and precisely a God—whose life and teaching could be the inexhaustible fountain of all renewal.

Hence the central role played by the death of Jesus, and therefore by the mystery of the resurrection. It has been said that the most surprising thing about Christianity is the way in which it kindled the enthusiasm of Jesus' followers despite the ignominy of his death. How can fervor be aroused by a religion that begins with dire "failure"? But to ask this question is to forget that there is the fact of the resurrection—that is, together with the human factor, there is always in Christianity the sacramental element. Christ did not come to continue, or slightly change, an old world, but to begin a new. It is not surprising, then, that when the preaching of Christianity began to be widely received, it was above all received in the souls of the Gentiles. For the majority of Hebrews, Messianic preaching was stubbornly connected with "the new Jerusalem," with "Jerusalem delivered." Now, for such Hebrews the "deliverance" of Jerusalem was equivalent to the conquest of freedom in the face of power— of external power, which appeared to be overwhelming. It was not equivalent to the freedom that can arise even under power, amidst the greatest affliction and the harshest slavery. But the freedom promised by the death and resurrection of Jesus was of this latter kind; no historical "failure" could affect it. For him who regards the coming of Christ as containing history and not as contained in it, everything merely historical in his coming will appear insignificant. Which does not mean that history is foreign to Christ; it means that, for the Christian, Christ is the sum of history, if not its source.

Thus the new man appeared. He was not the only one at the time. On the contrary, this moment of history swarmed with men seeking salvation in a complete transformation of life. Not even the philosophers held aloof. In one of Seneca's *Epistles,* we read: "I think, Lucilius, that I am becoming not only better, but transfigured." Could the situation have been perceived more clearly than in this sentence? Nevertheless, the distance between the philosopher in search of salvation and the Christian was fundamental. True, Socrates accepted death in order to commit his life to his own philosophy, in order that no one should have the slightest doubt that his philosophy had not been a mere dialectical exercise, a Sophistic game. And if this was not enough, Socrates (the Platonic Socrates) transmitted an eschatology at the moment of his death: the doctrine of the immortality of the soul. But none of all this accomplished what was most important for the time: to place man in a world that should

be at once sacramental and fraternal. In the *soteria* of the philosophers, the relations between souls were too much like the
relations between ideas. Then, too, the philosophers did not go
much beyond fraternity among the inhabitants of the City-State,
and when the City-State spread to all the shores of the Mediterranean, they continued to think of it as a cosmos whose inhabitants were primarily "citizens," "enlightened souls," or perhaps "members of nature." Overflowing and "arbitrary" love was
debilitated by the thinker's final goal—transformation, but
without surrender. In the philosophers' world the soul was
purified, as in the futurists' world it was shaken, but it did not
succeed in being "converted." It continued, at bottom, to be the
same soul, with all its old memories and all its old scars. It had
not been driven by the impulse that would make it feel a new
lightness, make it forget the burden of ideas, of history, of nature.
The distance between the philosopher and the new man was,
then, still great. Nevertheless, the new man did not remain for
ever the enemy of philosophy. After the first exaltation of his
difference from other men, he understood that he had been repeatedly forerun by them. There had been, in fact, many who
had sought salvation not in a reform of the City nor in individual
withdrawal, but in a complete transformation of life. This should
not surprise us. The triumphs in history are made up of countless failures; willingly or unwillingly, the victor takes his seat on
ruins. Around Christianity lie the corpses of many religions that
have failed, including those that constantly arose from within
it. Like the healthy tree, the new man needed not only space in
which to grow undisturbed, but also a periodical, and perhaps
violent, pruning of his own aspirations.

We have not to explain here why Christianity won such an extraordinary victory. The causes of its expansion—its appeal to
the minds of the humble people; its prompt and definite establishment of an ecclesiastical community; its propagation through
a world previously unified by Rome—are of no more interest to
us than it would be to know why a stone thrown blind lands in a
particular place. The fact is that the anxiety that tortured vast
multitudes in the ancient world finally ceased only under the type
of life exemplified by the Christian. Many types of men aimed at

the same goal. But only one succeeded sufficiently to write the equation, "Christian = new man."

One fundamental condition was, however, required—to be "open." Many religions had attempted to fulfil this condition, but none of them had completely succeeded. To be sure, certain religions of Near Eastern or Hellenistic origin had emphasized the necessity of freeing man from his close ties to his City or his people. But they very soon "closed." Some—like the mysteries—finally became "official"; others ended in myth; most of them succumbed to the most unbridled fantasy. Yet Christianity cannot be reduced to openness, as it cannot be reduced to faith—which many other men possessed for different reasons. Its significance is more complex.

It is superlatively complex. First of all, it presents different historical aspects. Do we not see it oscillate between moralism and prophecy, between the Jerusalemite type and the Roman type, between a pure tendency to brotherhood and the most rigid hierarchy? Do we not see it pass from an attitude of loyal submission to the Empire to declaring that Rome must be destroyed? Let us take but one of its representatives—St. Paul. What was his doctrine? A Pharisaism supplemented by a sacramental Christology? A Hellenism that adopted the Stoic-Cynic form of the diatribe? One more manifestation of the abundant syncretism of the times? Or let us raise the question of the relations between philosophic systems and Christian dogmas. The opinions held on these relations will be no less abundant—for some, Hellenic thought was a paganism to be avoided at all costs; for others, it was a forerunner of Christianity; some emphasized intellectual content, others spiritual life. We seem, then, to be in a sea of confusion. To escape from it, a first—and wrong—answer comes to mind. Christianity, we may say, is an attitude so open that to be a Christian means *not* to be attached to a particular formula or a strict system of propositions. But we very soon realize that the unity in Christianity is no less patent than the diversity. If this were not the case, it would be difficult to understand the violence with which Christianity rejected the tendencies that endangered its existence—not only external tendencies, but some internal tendencies as well. Christianity must, then, have possessed an inner, self-stabilizing force, which allowed it to accept some elements and reject others. This force was the Church. But then the problem arises again in reverse. If Christianity was so soon obliged to "shut itself up" in a dogmatic shell and reduce the Churches to *one* Church, why do we insist that it was an open attitude? Have we not here another manifestation of the famous "brotherhood or death" which, some say, was proclaimed by the French revolutionaries? Have we not here, in short, a mirage, of which we can only be cured by trying to understand—even if we do not accept—Augustine's or Bossuet's "Force them to come in"?

Perhaps the mirage can be dispelled when we recognize that the dynamism that brought the new man into being had an ambivalent character. Let us take faith. There is no doubt that without some amount of faith, human life—that of the majority of men—would be unlivable. Hence the course of conduct to be adopted seems obvious—loneliness, anxiety, rootlessness can be cured by faith. Nevertheless, it is a cure that sometimes breeds new evils; faith *can* lead to salvation *or* to destruction, to renewal *or* to stagnation. This ambivalence of faith has a cause that was revealed by the genius of Dostoevski. Man, said the great novelist, does not only want to save himself by faith, he wants to save himself *with* others. To achieve this, he does not hesitate over the means; thus he can end either in the charity and abnegation of the missionary, or in the fanaticism and terrorism of the inquisitor. No less evident is the ambivalence to be seen in the community that claims to incorporate the new desires, ideas, and norms. To begin, it appears to segregate itself from other communities and even to become an "enemy of the human race." Men gather into a community to renew themselves, but the community soon becomes stagnant. Hence the common objection: "The Christian, like every new man, tends to constitute a separate community, a church of the faithful, but this is a betrayal of his own original idea, and, above all, of his own original impulse." How is this objection to be answered? Simply by showing that the existence of an organized community is essential to the believer, just as a higher organism requires a skeleton to articulate its movements and a skin to give it a supple covering. The most that can be demanded is that the skeleton does not ossify too much, and that the skin remains always firm. Otherwise there will be no genuine "adjustment," either for the individual man or for society. We said "genuine," because the adjustment in question is not equivalent to the withdrawal of the philosopher nor to the adaptation of the man of power; it is the possibility that the freedom of society will coincide with the freedom of the person and vice versa. Hence a "Church" is historically unavoidable whenever an impulse for total salvation appears. For the salvation we are discussing here is not a matter of solitary individuals or of small minorities; it is something that affects all men and that cannot be solved by the simple, but unavailing expedient of direct communication between persons.

But all this would not yet be justification enough for talking of a new man. What made Christianity a complete solution for the time was its extraordinary ability to maintain a threefold equilibrium. In times of deep crisis, various types of disequilibrium appear in human life. At the end of the ancient world they could be reduced to three types. First, the growing disequilibrium between this world and the other world (however that world might be conceived). Second, the disequilibrium between man and society, manifested not only in vague uneasinesses, but in concrete political, social, and economic disturbances. Lastly, the disequilibrium between action and thought. Now, Christianity undertook to remedy these three kinds of disequilibrium. It will perhaps be said that the concrete life of man in this period—and in any other—cannot be embraced in such vague formulas, and that if there are problems, they concern the organization of society and not undefined states of disequilibrium. We have stated our opinion on this subject in a note at the end of this chapter. Let us merely say now that a society is really organized and men within it are (or feel themselves to be) something more than members or slaves, only when these disequilibriums have been resolved. To attain this end a "spiritual doctrine" must be set forth. It does not suffice to exert an adequate amount of physical pressure or to create a perfect organization; men themselves have to be firmly convinced that the above disequilibriums have ceased to exist. In short, men must be given a new consciousness. The genuine—and, of course, always relative—solution for great human conflicts requires that the majority of men in the society that is undergoing them succeed in acting and thinking *as if* the conflicts did not exist, or, what comes to the same thing, *as if* the conflicts could always be resolved by a sovereign arbiter whose laws or whose decisions command universal respect.

Once again, then, it is a problem of belief. But the word "belief" does not designate here a mere willingness to accept a dogma or a truth. Nor is belief a state of mind engendered by pure compulsion. The belief that, at certain historical periods, makes possible the appearance of the type that we have called "the new man" presupposes the simultaneous presence of personal experience and of universal truth. Thus such a belief must resolve all the disequilibriums between the individual and society. The three above mentioned types of disequilibrium are, however, particularly important from our point of view.

Let us take the first of them—the one that raises the problem of the relation between "this world" and "the other world." From the beginning, Christianity felt capable of rendering to each of these worlds what belonged to it. Christianity succeeded in doing so not only through the famous Gospel maxim about God and Caesar, but also by virtue of the constitution of the Christian community, which had to evolve against the State, but at the same time after the pattern of the State. Much was said about this earth as a vale of tears. But as a point of fact the Christian never showed any great inclination to detach himself from this world. In this the temporal and the spiritual directors of the community were at one. St. Paul, to be sure, said that "the time is short" (I Cor. 7:29), that "the fashion of this world passeth away" (I Cor. 7:31), that the faithful must not be "conformed to this world" (Rom. 12:2). But he also wrote, "that which may be known of God is manifest . . . God hath shewed it," so that the invisible perfections of God, "even his eternal power and Godhead, from the creation of the world are clearly seen, being understood by the things that are made" (Rom. 1:19-21). Hence although the Christian renewal was accomplished in a supernatural atmosphere, according to which only God is *fons veri, lumen mentis,* the idea of a complete elimination of "this world" was never formulated. Actually, the new man tried to mediate between supernaturalism and naturalism, continually oscillating between the two. To be sure, the Platonist had arrived at a sim-

ilar "solution" in interpreting the Principle of Unity in two ways—
first, as a culmination of the movement of nature; second, as a
reality transcending all nature. But while the Platonic solution
was built on an intellectual foundation, the Christian solution
was founded on a new experience. Hence the Christian mediation between this world and the other, between the immanent
and the transcendent, the natural and the supernatural was not a
rational eclecticism. It was the mediation imposed by one who
believes that he can save this world without destroying it. This
was why there could be such frequent agreement between "God"
and "Caesar," from the moment when the latter found himself
obliged to recognize the power of the community in which the
new doctrine was deposited.

The second disequilibrium appeared in the type of the relation
between man and society. By enlarging itself to the limit attain-
able by the primitive technique of the period, society imposed itself on men as an ineluctible destiny. In consequence, it produced an increasing mechanization of the relations between man
and society. To alleviate this situation, many devices were conceived. But there seemed to be only two solutions, both extreme
—either to adapt to society, or to flee from it. The dilemma became more acute when a constantly increasing number of men
did not merely suffer the brutal uncertainty of the age in their
flesh, but became conscious that the age itself was uncertain and
brutal. But a moment arrived when a truly radical solution made
its appearance—the solution that consisted in changing society
and the men who were members of it. From this moment the
earlier problem vanished. But a new "problem"—the same "problem" that torments so many minds today—seemed to demand
solution: "Shall man reform himself in order that society may
change, or is society to be changed so that man will be renewed?"
It took great effort to understand that this was a pseudo-problem. For man and society mutually imply each other; the one
cannot be changed without a substantial change being produced
in the other. This takes place, furthermore, in such a way that
the more society succeeds in renewing itself, the more will man
be renewed, and vice versa.

At this decisive point, Christianity intervened and proposed a
way of finding a dynamic equilibrium between opposing tensions.
The individual and society were united through an "element"

that constituted at once their intermediary and their foundation—God. The society of men was presented as a possible—and never attained—image of the community of the saints; the *civitas ter-rena,* if it was to cease being a *civitas diaboli,* must follow the plan of the *civitas divina.* This plan, at one stroke, solved the greater part of the problems that had accumulated before the "ancient man." The solution consisted in showing that each man's station in the world, even the wretchedest, offered him the pos-sibility of freeing himself from all fear except the fear of God. And this liberation was held possible not through such a ration-alization as we have seen in the Platonists, or such a resignation as we have observed in the Stoics, or through any of the many means that had previously been tried, but through a living faith that allowed the individual to be integrated into society without violence. Hence it would be wrong to suppose that all this was merely a device to keep man in subjection. How can such a thesis be defended, when we know that Christianity offered man, *every man,* what no *"ancien régime"* would have permitted him—a personal, independent, "separate" life? For some, perhaps, preaching the doctrine that all men were sons of God was a way of preventing particular groups from rebelling against the estab-lished power. Even so, Christianity affirmed something new and revolutionary concerning man. Christianity did not address itself to some men, or even to the majority of them, but to all. Now, the word "revolutionary" meant something different from what it means today; it meant "power of renewal," not only for society but also for the individual. In any case, Christianity was not a revolution of classes, but of men. Hence it was able to realize one of the greatest paradoxes in history—changing the type of rela-tion between man and society without touching the foundations of society.

The third kind of disequilibrium—the one that had arisen be-tween action and thought—is the most important. To a certain extent, this disequilibrium is essential to man. Without it, there would be no progress in history. But at moments of crisis it be-comes so extreme that it follows the pattern of some poisons; in certain quantities, they are beneficial, but an overdose is fatal. The overdose stage was reached in the period we are considering.

Increasingly numerous groups felt an uneasiness for which there seemed to be no cure, because, instead of being probed to the bottom, it was treated with purely external remedies, some of them decidedly ingenious, but all of them inadequate. The commonest of these remedies consisted in eliminating either action or thought. Since it was so difficult to accord them, why not act without thinking, or why not abandon action and give oneself up to the delights of a purely "disinterested" thought? It was upon these one-sided premises that the majority of the attitudes described in the foregoing chapter were based. In any case, it seemed increasingly difficult to square action with thought. Many men seemed even to believe that such an operation could never be performed. Since this operation, however, was performed with consummate energy by the Christians, we may use the same expression that they preferred to any other when they tried to emphasize the necessity of squaring thought with action: "To live by the truth."

"To live by the truth": no formula better expresses the *desideratum* of the epochs we have been describing. In the Christian human type we can see with utmost clarity what was probably the reason for the conversion of so many—we can see a man who acted in accordance with his beliefs, who was entirely committed to them, but not unconsciously or foolishly, like the man who says, "It is so because I want it to be so." Perhaps some Christians tended to stress the dependence of events on desire, perhaps some other Christians, in their eagerness to differentiate their beliefs from all others, were inclined to think that what was believed was true because it was unbelievable, irrational, or absurd. But from the beginning the predominant attitude among Christians was the typical attitude of every sincere believer—the attitude that consists in looking anywhere and everywhere for arguments to provide rational support for belief. Anyone who has ever thoroughly believed in something knows that true belief is no mere matter of words; in addition to leading his life in accordance with his belief, the believer tries to justify his belief by thought. His perspicacity in discovering all sorts of arguments in support of his belief is a sufficient proof of this deeply rooted tendency in him. For the genuine believer is not one who only believes or who only acts, but one who consolidates belief and action into one compact, unbreakable block. His missionary and dynamic spirit can be explained in no other way. And his "open-ness" consists primarily in seeking out the respective arguments that will convince every man that what he believes is true. Hence we have not truths for initiates, but arguments for all. Without this condition, the expression "to live by the truth" could not designate an operation which seems to be its opposite but is rather its complement: to make life true.

As soon as the above way of living was set in motion, theory and practice, that for so many years had been separate, reunited. Our own epoch, which has repeatedly experienced the discord between thought and action, will understand what their reunion meant for society. Perhaps, once again, a certain disequilibrium between theory and practice is befitting for the human being; if they were too closely identified, they would become paralyzed. What is needed, then, is neither a separation nor an identification —it is a correlation. For, if practice is blind without theory, theory is powerless without practice. Not only in human life, but even in science, rules or principles are ineffectual without the corresponding operations. Particularly in human life, theory must not be merely a series of statements that are declared to be true, but that at the same time are "put in parentheses." Theory has no meaning in human life unless it is thought of as something that can fill all of life's contents. Theory is unavailing if it is merely conceived as a "Sunday truth" in which we believe condescend-ingly and which is forgotten whenever any temptation to aban-don it arises. Theory must therefore provide truth for every day, and permeate the whole of human existence. Now, whatever idea of Christianity one may hold, there is no denying that *it appeared in the world under this aspect.* For a long time the pagans thought of Christians as "obstinate," "ignorant," "mad," "rustic." The dynamism with which they lived and increased their num-bers seemed "vulgar." At times even, it did not merely seem so, but was so. But at the bottom of this "obstinacy" and "boorish-ness" was the fact that thought tended not to detach itself from life, that even subtleties themselves were the result of an effort to adapt thinking to the contradictions between belief and life— the fundamental fact of the intimate relation between theory and practice. When an item of this magnitude stands in the credit column, it does not take much more to balance the accounts of history.

Notes

By calling Christianity a "human religion" we have probably laid ourselves open to the accusation that we have forgotten the most essential thing about it—its divine dimension. But we have not forgotten it. Christianity preaches not only the "kingdom of man" but also and above all the "Kingdom of God." It is curious that in this conception Christians are at one with anti-Christians and the indifferent. Only those Christians who have "lost their faith" and wish to save the "moral" and "admonitory" aspect of Christianity consider the problem of the divine aspect of the Christian beliefs as a meaningless problem. For believers and for "anti-believers" the divine has a connotation; the only distinction between them—an extremely important distinction, of course, but one which has no place here—is that for the former it also has a denotation. For the moralizers, on the other hand, even the connotation has disappeared. In our text, we have left the denotation of the term *in suspenso*, but have maintained its connotation. We have been concerned with the actual way in which some men adopted the Christian attitude, and with the historical consequences of this attitude. Hence, to say provisionally that Christianity is a human religion is not to affirm that only the human factor—in contrast to the natural, the intelligible, or the divine factors—plays a role in it; it is to stress an aspect of Christianity that is generally absent from the ancient religions.

Among the "anticipations" of the Christian attitude which were mentioned in the present chapter, one has produced something of a sensation. I refer to the "anticipation" disclosed by the partial publication of scrolls discovered, beginning in 1947, in various caves in the vicinity of the Dead Sea. A manuscript of *Isaiah*, a *Commentary on Habakkuk*, a *Manual of Discipline*, *The War of the Sons of Light with the Sons of Darkness*, *The Thanksgiving Psalms*, the *Lamech Apocalypse*—these are some of the texts that have created the greatest stir. The bibliography on the subject is already impressive; a considerable number of Hebraists and biblical scholars have produced editions of texts, or analyses, or commentaries. The reader interested in obtaining full details may consult the publications of S. A. Birnbaum, W. H. Brownlee,

Millar Burrows, M. Delcor, R. de Vaux, G. R. Driver, A. Dupont-
Sommer, O. Eissfeldt, R. Goossens, P. Kahle, G. Lambert, J. T.
Milik, S. Moscati, Isaac Rabinowitz, L. Rost, H. H. Rowley, M. H.
Segal, E. L. Sukenik, J. L. Teicher, J. C. Trever, G. Vermès, S.
Zeitlin (many of these are cited in the bibliography included in
the book by Millar Burrows referred to below). Of particular
value for the subject are the publications of S. A. Birnbaum, Millar Burrows, R. de Vaux, G. R. Driver, A. Dupont-Sommer, Isaac
Rabinowitz, H. H. Rowley, E. L. Sukenik, and G. Vermès. A
general description of the documents, discussion of their dates
of composition, and of the origin, history, and organization of
the community with which they are connected, an analysis of the
importance of the texts, and selections from them in English
translation will be found in Millar Burrows' *The Dead Sea Scrolls,*
New York (1955). A vivid account of the circumstances that led
to the discovery of the scrolls and of the problems which they
raise is given in Edmund Wilson's *The Scrolls from the Dead Sea,*
New York (1955).

The documents in question appear to reveal the existence of a
community or sect, the "New Alliance," which some consider
very similar to, others identical with, the sect of the Essenes.
Originally military, this sect became a community devoted to
peaceful preaching under the aegis of a "Teacher of Righteousness," whom the *Damascus Document* (discovered in 1896), calls
the "One Master," the "Founder of Justice," the "Anointed," the
"Lawgiver"—a martyr-prophet and Messiah who died between
67 and 63 B.C. and who preached an eschatology similar to that of
Jesus. Some of the most violent controversies have arisen around
the problem whether or not the contents of the scrolls affect
what is known about the origins of Christianity. As usual, much
of the controversy has centered on chronological problems. Do
the documents (or some of them) date from the beginning of the
first century B.C.? Is the *Habbakuk Commentary* from the middle
of the same century? Must the *Isaiah* scroll be dated not earlier
than from 200 to 500 A.D., in view of its careless language? Our
total lack of competence in such matters makes it impossible for
us to pronounce on any of these points. But we will venture to
say that some of the texts—for example, the fragment translated
from the *Manual*—appear to contain much more "Hebraism"
than our analysis of the "Christian attitude" would allow of. In
addition, we will go so far as to maintain that, even were this not

so, none of these discoveries would invalidate our idea of the *unique* character of the life and death of Jesus. In any case, it was this unique character that did in fact provide the desired "solution." Similarities between different doctrines, though historically illuminating, cannot solve certain questions. Not everything lies in the "doctrine" or the "rule"; there is, in addition and above all, the movement begun by the concrete life of the person. We cannot, then, turn history into a series of "counter-factual conditionals": "If *A* had not occurred, *B* would have happened," and so on. For us, it is meaningless to say, "If Jesus had not existed, the 'Teacher of Righteousness' would have been the founder of 'Christianity,'" or "If the 'Teacher of Righteousness' had not existed, Jesus would not have been the Christ." These counter-factual conditionals can help understanding history, but actual writing of history can easily dispense with them.

Among the religions that attempted to transcend the circle of the City even in the classic Greek period, that is, among the movements toward "segregation" of the individual in respect to *his* community for religious reasons, were the mysteries (especially those of Eleusis, and, in a more "intellectual" way, Orphism). However, the small communities of the initiated did never completely disregard the City-State to which they belonged; on the contrary, they often tried to reform it. But "reform" did not coincide with the "fame of the City," the only ultimate with which the official cults were concerned. To be sure, in these mysteries there was the idea of salvation—of a salvation at once individual and collective, since the corresponding community usually believed that it could extend itself through various City-States. And it was this idea that linked the mysteries to some of the philosophical schools. But it was not long before the mysteries were "officialized," and became an essential part and even the cornerstone of the City-State. Throughout the course of Western history, this process of "officialization" has always distinguished the ancient religions from Christianity or even Eastern from Western Christianity. Western Christian society, although it has frequently tended toward theocracy, has never been actually theocratic (the sixteenth-century dictum, *cuius regio eius religio* meant something quite different). The powers of church and state were several times on the verge of coalescing, but they never did fuse together. Hence we cannot say that Western Christianity became "official" in the sense of constituting a part—or the foundation—of the structure

of the State. This fact has had the most far-reaching consequences. Many of the peculiarities of Western civilization derive
from a continual interplay between the religious and the profane.
Therefore, the formation of a "Church" must not be confused
with the "officialization"—or, better, the "statification"—of the
religious impulse.

The distinctions set up by some writers—for example, Yves
M.-J. Congar in his *Vraie et fausse Reforme dans l'Église*, Paris
(1950)—between the "life" and the "structure" of the church
(distinctions that, in principle, are applicable to any human
community organized in accordance with certain beliefs) is
highly illuminating for our purpose. We do not need to defend
such a distinction as if it dealt with two realities, nor to adhere
to one of them as representing the sole truth. It is a matter of a
method that we consider fertile for understanding the history of
such a community as the Christian Church. The Church has
possessed life and structure in equal measure, and has never been
able to do without either; its existence has consisted precisely in
maintaining an unstable equilibrium between them. It has, in
short, had constantly to face the eternal question of the relation
between feeling—or experiences—and principles—or dogmas.
With feeling alone, principles disappear; with principles alone,
feeling withers. Both, then, are subject to the same rule that,
according to Kant, holds for intuitions and for concepts—they
mutually imply each other. An organism that is at once strong
and flexible cannot be a pure skeleton, still less a carapace, but
neither can it be a flabby entity. Hence we are not to consider
whether the life of a Church must prevail over its structure or
whether its structure must predominate over its vitality; it is a
matter of an endosmosis that is all the more delicate and hazard-
ous because, while each term struggles to impose itself completely on the other, it divines that it is certain to perish as soon
as the other is eliminated. In the period that we are considering,
the "community of the faithful" had both a missionary spirit
and an organizing spirit. It could not have an equal quantity
of both, because this would have produced a static equilibrium
—which would be as fatal as the complete absorption of one
of the two terms by the other. Its having accepted an unstable
and dynamic equilibrium was in fact one of the reasons for its
historical triumph.

It was not our intention to discuss in detail the structure of the society in which the type of the new man arose. To do so would involve describing, even though but briefly, the immense political, social, and economic changes of the period. In our analysis, such changes are taken for granted. After all, the history of man can be written in various languages. To choose one of them is not to forget that the others exist; it merely implies recognizing the limitations of the mind in the face of that most complex phenomenon, human history. By neglecting this fact, philosophers and historians have constantly involved themselves in problems of causal relations without taking into account that epistemological investigation in this respect is still in its infancy. Such problems are usually put in questions of the following type: "Was Christianity a product of the social and economic milieu, or could the Christian, by virtue of being such, give social and economic relations a new direction?" To answer this question either in the affirmative or the negative is equally a reductionist fallacy. The fallacy appears clearly as soon as it is realized that different answers can be given with the same historical material. Before we can formulate questions in which historical causality is implied, our epistemological foundations need to be somewhat broadened.

The quotation from Eduard Meyer is from his collection of studies, *Ursprung und Anfänge des Christentums*, 3 vols., Stuttgart and Berlin (1921-1923), Vol. II, 425.–The quotation from Ferdinand Prat, S.J., is from his *Jésus Christ*, Book III, chap. VII; English translation: *Jesus Christ. His Life, His Teaching, and His Work*, Milwaukee, 2 vols. (1950).–The reference to Bergson is taken from *Les deux sources de la morale et de la religion*, Paris (1932), 56-58; English translation: *The two Sources of Morality and Religion*, New York (1935).–The line of Quevedo's is in his sonnet "Amor constante más allá de la muerte," and will be found on p. 43 of Luis Astrana Marín's edition of Quevedo's *Obras completas*, volume entitled *Obras en verso*, Madrid (1943).–The quotation from Seneca is from *Ep.* VI, 13.–The reference to Dostoevski is from the chapter "The Grand Inquisitor" in *The Brothers Karamazov* (Part II, Book V, chap. V).–We have, of course, used other books, most of them read long ago and assimilated to the point where we can no longer distinguish between "our own" thought and "another's." The biliography on Jesus and the origins of Christianity is practically inexhaustible; since it was not the task of this book to supply bibliographies except to the extent of giving specific sources for references in the text, we consider it preferable not to mention even the best-known works in this field. The reader will easily discover that in describing Christian doctrines or attitudes we have constantly had in mind the literature of primitive Christianity and particularly the New Testament canon.

PART II. *Crisis and Reconstruction*

7. The Problem of the Modern Age

Ancient world and modern world: similarities and differences.–The modern age: the West and its geographical expansion.–Traditional divisions of the West: their
faults and virtues.–Comte's thesis: the modern age as
"crisis."–Difficulties of Comte's thesis: the existence of
"stable moments."–The "stable" and the "unstable" in
the modern age.–The westernization of the world and
de-westernization of the West.

The process of stabilization: the conditions for it.–The
function of socially prominent groups in times of crisis.–
The function of "lower" groups.–The accommodating
and the revolutionary souls.–The question of the relation between real factors and ideal motives: their interpenetration.

The three stages of the modern crisis: the crisis of the
"few"; the crisis of the "many"; the crisis of "all."–The
periods corresponding to the three stages: fourteenth
to sevententh centuries; eighteenth century; nineteenth
and twentieth centuries.–Their characteristics.–The two
doctrines concerning the modern age: "progressivism"
and "traditionalism."–Their falsity and their truth.–"Progressive" and "regressive" aspects in the same period.–
The fundamental problem of the modern age: the assimilation of crises.

The problems that arise for contemporary man are in important respects the same as those that arose at the end of the ancient world. We too have the feeling that the direction of history has slipped from our hands and that the world—the entire planet, no longer only a part of it—is being borne on by a great wave. We do not mean to say that this is what is actually happening. The motive force of history is one thing; its particular reflection in men's minds is another. The latter is all that concerns us here. Whatever man's real possibilities in respect to his history may have been, there are times in which he thinks of himself as master and others in which he thinks of himself as slave. This is not meant to imply that all men always find themselves in the same situation or have always the same consciousness of it. As at the end of the ancient world, historical consciousness began to be incarnated in a few human groups. They were the same human groups that, in later times, were said to have faithfully reflected their period, even though in the period itself they had been regarded as extravagantly astray.

An adequate understanding of the problems that arise for contemporary man is not possible without a previous examination of the problems that have arisen for modern men in the course of modern history. We have to presuppose, then, that there has been a modern history. Moreover, we have to presuppose that there has been a modern age, which has developed in a series of phases, and that the so-called "contemporary period" is one of these phases. These seem to be obvious and commonplace ideas. But when we examine them a little, we find that they bristle with difficulties.

To begin with, what is the modern age? If we could confine ourselves to the West—to Europe (with a frequent inclusion of the Near East and Russia), to America, and to the zones of expansion of European man—the above question would not be too difficult to answer. After all, it is no mere chance that the division proposed in the eighteenth century between an ancient period, a medieval period, and a modern period has been so persistently accepted by, and so widely useful to, historians. To be sure, historians during the last hundred years have subjected these concepts to minute analysis, and have demonstrated *ad nauseam* that they are without meaning. Yet when the same historians have had to treat of the West, they have not hesitated to employ the above division. To be sure, they have employed it in a cautious way. They have shown, for example, that in the so-called Renaissance there was a considerable amount of medieval elements, or that the Middle Ages already anticipated in many respects the Renaissance. They have pointed out that if we continue to talk of periods we must not understand them merely as sections of a single line. But they have often presupposed the same division that they have tried to eliminate. This means that such a division is still useful—provided, of course, that it be not interpreted too literally. It is the way we shall follow in our investigation. We will consider the proposition, "There is a modern age," as an "open statement" whose variables are constantly changing. The range of these variables is very broad. As a matter of fact, a description of the modern crisis extends from the anxieties experienced many centuries ago by a certain number of Western men to the upheavals that affect the whole of contemporary society over the entire surface of the planet.

We said, "the modern crisis." For we shall have to describe a long phase of instability, which is the more difficult to perceive because, on some occasions—as in the period of absolute monarchies—certain definite stabilities cannot be ruled out entirely. Now, the terms "stable periods" and "unstable periods" which we shall often use are not respectively equivalent to the terms "peaceful periods" and "turbulent periods." A period can display the utmost calm externally, and at the same time be torn by strong internal tensions. In the modern age the turmoil has often been external and internal. From his earliest writings, which reflected what Saint-Simon and others had often surmised, Comte declared that what took place through the sixteenth, seventeenth, and eighteenth centuries was the disorganization of an earlier system; that in the course of this long period there was "an inevitable time of anarchy," and that during the latter all imaginable efforts were made to "destroy the theological power." These various factors caused the predominance, during three centuries, of a "critical doctrine," which, however, must not be considered as a necessarily destructive ideology. This doctrine erected into dogmas various principles which would overthrow the old order: first, unlimited freedom of conscience; second, the sovereignty of the people; third, equality. Something more than a play of internal tensions was then set up; externally, the modern age was characterized by a continuous breaking down of the different social orders, a tireless replacing of some principles by other principles, without ever reaching an enduring system of principles, capable of producing a permanent stabilization of human society. As Comte emphasized, all "earlier revolutions were no more than mere modifications." Hence this long period could be called "the Great Revolution."

We need not subscribe to Comte's philosophical system in order to recognize that his ideas on the above subject contain some important truths. Comte perceived with unusual clarity not only that there was a modern age, but also some of its chief characteristics. Henceforth the word "modern" did not mean simply "new"; it did not refer to a way of life that had become the fashion among those who least clung to tradition; it designated a historical period that was not yet concluded but whose complete intellectual and political structure was already clearly discernible. To be just, we should recognize that this sort of consciousness had already dawned in the eighteenth century and that its major intellectual figures felt that they were living—some like Voltaire, comfortably; others, like Rousseau, uncomfortably —in a period different from all preceding periods, and whose structure they were beginning to explore. In justice, too, we should mention another philosopher who, though in many respects the complete opposite of Comte, perceived the nature of the problem we raise no less clearly than Comte himself; we refer to Hegel. As a matter of fact, the meaning of "modern age" here proposed could not have been worked out without the previous contributions of all these philosophers. But we differ from the eighteenth-century philosophers, from Comte or from Hegel in two respects: first, in our ideas about the internal structure of the modern age; second, in our ideas about the function that the modern age performs in the total economy of human history.

Let us disregard the latter point. It alone would force us to develop a whole material philosophy of history. For our purpose, only the first point is pertinent. Now, once admitted that there has been a modern age, we deny that it has been as homogeneous as Comte and most philosophers have assumed. If it has been a critical period, it has not always been an unstable period. There have been in it a certain number of "crises" that *could* have dissolved society but which in fact helped to reorganize it. Society's powers of cohesion during the modern period have been as evident as society's powers of dissolution. To be sure, periods of crises and efforts to overcome them can also be perceived in the Middle Ages. For the Middle Ages were not the stable, well-ordered, "organic" period that Comte had so hastily described. It has even been possible to speak of "Renaissances" during the Middle Ages—to the point where it has even been doubted whether the Middle Ages have existed at all. However, the succession of critical periods is far more evident in the modern age than perhaps in any other period of Western history. Therefore, we can define the modern age as a period that has had *its* own problems, *its* own solutions, and *its* own models for life. Like all historical periods, it has been open to other epochs, and hence it is difficult to assign definite limits to it; rather than like a segment of a line, it is like a fragment of a melody that began before the previous phrase was quite finished and that ends when new phrases make their harmonies heard. It is not, then, like a compact, solid mass, but like a complex edifice supported on an unstable equilibrium, by virtue of which there are evolution and progress. Thus we shall not understand the modern age as a period of anarchy, any more that we have considered the Middle Ages to be a perfectly stable epoch. But while the Middle Ages maintained a comparative stability, the modern age has accentuated instability, to the point of appearing to be an essentially unstable, insecure age, incessantly producing "crises," "explosions," "breaks." By using these terms, we are not trying to escape the difficulties implicit in a concrete examination of the period. Any one of the said terms designates an intricate combination of vital, social, political, economic, and spiritual phenomena by virtue of which what a certain group of men had once thought to be a "solution" proved later to be no solution at all.

What, then, do the terms "critical" and "unstable" designate in such expressions as "the critical modern age," "the unstable modern age"? They designate the fact that from a limited geographical area modern man steadily spread out through constantly wider zones—first, through the Americas; next, through the peripheral colonies; finally, through the whole planet, including the interior of the immense Euro-Asiatic zone. The "ferments" now manifesting in regions that until quite recently were completely immersed in their own secular traditions—in India, in China, in the Arabic world, in various places in the Pacific—are one manifestation of this spread of modern man. This seems to foreshadow the westernization of the world. The statement cannot be accepted as a plausible one if we interpret its meaning literally. But it can be accepted as a highly probable statement if we take it *cum grano salis* as the expression of a certain tendency to the (comparative) unification of human groups hitherto confined to separate areas. We shall not, however, be able to explain what the expression "westernization" signifies until we have reached our last two chapters. For there we shall see that the process of westernization runs parallel with another that is no less evident: the de-westernization of the West. In the second place, the term "critical" in the expression "critical modern age" designates the peculiar character of the process referred to earlier—the successive and increasing production of disequilibriums in the course of which Western civilization has assimilated ever more numerous groups of men with new ways of life and thought. The first fact and the second process are closely related. And in our own period we seem to have in them two manifestations of the same historical phenomenon. In our day, then, it would be wrong to regard as merely a Western crisis what is already a "planetary" question. Hence our analysis can be divided into two sections. In the first section, dealt with in chapters 7, 8, and 9, we shall refer to the crises of the modern age in so far as they can still be limited to the European and in part to the Euro-American West. In the second section, the subject of chapters 10 and 11, we shall consider what is taking place today throughout the world. The world of today cannot, of course, be measured solely by the standard of what has previously happened in the West. But without the history of the West contemporary society could not be properly understood.

1. If, then, we continue to use the name "crisis" for the modern age, we do not do so exactly in Comte's sense. The modern age is not solely a transition to another age. Nor is it a "deviation" or a "mistake." It has its own nature. As this nature reveals itself by means of a considerable "freedom" in respect to new forms of life and thought, the impression produced by it is one of perpetual instability. But soon we perceive that such an instability is interrupted by several important "stabilities." These we call "the stages of the crisis." In each of them arise new social, political, and economic phenomena, accompanied by spiritual and ideological changes. These new phenomena and these changes do not entirely dissolve society. But they produce a breach, through which all sorts of novelties rush in. And then something happens, which follows a certain typical pattern: after apparently submerging everything, the new tendencies solidify, the waters draw back, and society becomes again stable. The change, then, has been quickly and skillfully "assimilated." This process has occurred three times in European history. Each time the solution given to a crisis has coincided with the consciousness that a new crisis had arisen. There is no logical contradiction in this statement, for what we mean is the fact that the historical situation had become stable for some human groups while a disequilibrium had already arisen for other human groups.

2. The "crisis," then, does not affect all the members or all the groups of Western society in the same degree. It appears first in certain groups—those that occupy a prominent social position or those that are intellectually alert. If it seems perplexing that instability should set up first of all in groups that, because they are at the top of society, have situations that are supposed to be intellectually and socially stable, the perplexity is only due to the fact that the peculiar character of historical crises is not sufficiently understood. In short, *the instability does not always "manifest" itself in the same groups in which it is "produced."* The group that is socially underneath, and that, because of some political or economic changes, feels uneasy and agitated, dreaming about "rising" or about improving its social status, commonly experiences such a status within the traditional modes of living and

thinking; it obscurely feels that something is in process of changing, but it has the tendency to interpret the change according to traditional ideas. The mind of this group is an accommodating, not a truly revolutionary mind. On the contrary, some individuals belonging to a group comparatively unaffected by the above changes succeed in describing clearly the nature of the changing process. In fact, they do more than merely describe such a nature; they describe, besides, the historical goal in sight. They become the spark that sets the social powder magazine afire. Here we have a key to making our way through the intricate labyrinth of the relations between real factors and ideal motives. The former are the potential forces, held back, ready to explode, but unable by themselves to begin moving toward a particular target. In order to reach the target, a directing impulse is required—the "idea." Toward the end of the last century the Spanish statesman Emilio Castelar began one of his essays with the emphatic statement: "Human society is a condensation of ideas, as the terraqueous globe is a condensation of gases." At the same period, many European thinkers subscribed to a view that is the opposite of Castelar's and that proves to be no less implausible than it—the view according to which only real factors (economics, race, or geography) set society in motion. In point of fact, society does not move unless ideas and real factors enter into close relation, or, more accurately, into fusion. Max Scheler has contended that real factors contain the power and that ideas furnish the guidance. This view, though suggestive, is too dualistic for our taste. The relation between ideas and reality is not comparable to an occasional contact between two different entities. Strictly speaking, there are neither pure ideas nor pure real factors. Both are names of limiting concepts, of mental instruments that make it possible for us to understand the actual processes of history. The only distinction to be made rests on the predominance of one over the other. When a real factor predominates too exclusively, the ideas do not possess sufficient force to set society in motion, still less to blow up the powder magazine of society in a revolutionary upheaval. And when ideas predominate excessively, they waste themselves in a pure, ineffectual speculation.

3. It would be wrong, then, to hold that the series of crises in

the West has depended solely on real upheavals affecting the majority of the population. But it would be equally wrong to suppose that the crises in question have been merely of an ideological nature, experienced and discussed only by minorities. It is necessary to state this once and for all, because our vocabulary will at times lack the necessary precision. We have chosen three principal moments of crisis and have called them *the crisis of the "few," the crisis of the "many,"* and *the crisis of "all."* This would appear to indicate that in the beginning there were a few men who felt that the traditional system of ideas and beliefs was tottering and who tried to repair or to replace it by a new system; that there came a moment when increasingly numerous groups had a similar feeling about the new system and reacted to this feeling in a similar although more comprehensive way; and that, finally, the crisis was the concern of everyone so that the system proposed must be valid for everyone. But if things had simply happened in this way, it would be difficult to understand the type of relation existing between minorities and majorities. (By "minorities" and "majorities" we do not here mean respectively the "elect" and the "vulgar," the "aristocracy" and the "masses." Sometimes, in fact, the minorities are the elect and the majorities the vulgar, but such a coincidence is not always necessary.) Now, the above type of relation is a peculiar one. In the course of the modern age an almost invariable pattern was followed in this respect. A crisis appeared, and it entered the consciousness of certain men particularly gifted to perceive its nature and its implications. These men proposed a system of life and thought that was meant to be universal and, therefore, acceptable to majorities. In fact, however, the system proved to be valid only for those who had proposed it. In view of this, an attempt was made to amplify the system. But to amplify such a system implied falsifying it. This falsification was predominantly the work of the majorities. They took over the distorted, caricatured, and hence false, aspect of the very same ideas that the minorities had painfully elaborated. The minorities then cried out: "No, it's not that." But they were wrong—from the beginning, their ideas were "that" *too.* Hence we can formulate a proposition that has a semblance of paradox: the ideas proposed by minorities to solve a crisis remain viable only to the extent to which they are distorted. At this point a comparative stabilization of society ensued. It was not to last long. Several cracks appeared in the structures of life and thought, and grew until other men formulated an entirely new system in order to meet the new crisis. The previous process was repeated. But not in exactly the same way —not only because the new crisis had a different content, but also because neither the minorities nor the majorities remained in the same numerical proportion. At any rate, the crisis of the "few," even though it was not merely the manifestation of the intellectual anxieties of a handful of idle intellectuals, affected a comparatively small number of men. The crisis of the "many" spread rather widely through majority and minority. And the crisis of "all" is of such a nature that a most extraordinary phenomenon occurs in it: there appear to be neither minorities nor majorities, because every member of human society all over the world—or very nearly—at once feels the impact of the universal crisis and the need to overcome it.

4. A description of each of these crises will permit us to clarify the foregoing ideas. We thus hope to obviate the confusion that might result in the reader's mind from our division of the modern age into a series of crises or phases. As a matter of fact, all these phases intersect and overlap. For when a new critical phase appears, society is still in a state of agitation resulting from the upheavals occurred during the preceding phase. Only with these precautions can we accept the proposed "division." In accordance with it, we consider that there was (1) a long period whose origins some authorities put in the thirteenth century though others carry them back as far as the so-called "twelfth-century Renaissance," but which we see as commencing at the end of the fourteenth or the beginning of the fifteenth. This period— which culminated in the seventeenth century—consisted in a series of social and intellectual readjustments. Socially, it was characterized by the first birth-cries of the so-called "bourgeois spirit." But this term does not have the same meaning here as the expression "the bourgeois spirit of the eighteenth century." It simply designates the resurgence of the city—after a period of economic retrocession—and in particular the breakdown of the "organismic system" that had prevailed during the Middle Ages. Intellectually, the period in question was characterized by a series

of attempts to outline a system of the world that, without reject-
ing the "Inherited Conglomerate," should modify it at points
where it was considered antiquated. If we call this earlier "Inherited Conglomerate" the "medieval conception," we can say
that the first stage of the crisis consisted not so much in relegating
it to the dustbin as in amplifying it. Historians have frequently
stressed the chaotic nature of the Renaissance period—which is
included in this first phase. From our point of view, the chaos
vanishes. For the complex tissue of negations and affirmations
was not at that time applied to the whole conception of the world
and to the whole of the structure of society hitherto in force, but
only to various parts of them. What, at bottom, was sought was
another way of being the same. Too much stress has been laid
on the power of renewal in the Renaissance, at the expense of its
immensely strong conservatism. For, strictly speaking, it was
only through the coexistence of renewal and conservatism that
the fourteenth-seventeenth-century phase could remain what it
chiefly was—a series of opposing tensions, held in a precarious
equilibrium. Like all formulas of the kind, the one just propounded will seem highly inadequate to historians. The inexhaustible richness of human life cannot be reduced to a single
formula. But we do not claim that our formula gives an ex-
haustive description of the structure of human life in a particular
period; it is meant only to furnish a thread that will guide us
through its labyrinthine complexity. The above phase was followed (2) by a shorter one, which began in the seventeenth century and reached its culmination after the middle of the eighteenth; as we shall see in the proper place, the solution at which,
after so many groping efforts, certain men—the "few"—had arrived, proved to be inadequate for the "many." Hence the stabilization was only provisional. And thus began another phase
(3), the crisis of "all," *our* crisis, which, as it is part and parcel of
contemporary society, will receive more attention than any of
the others.

The reader will excuse the scantiness of these indications; their
only purpose was to point out the road upon which we are about
to enter. But what has been said already suggests the idea that
the modern crisis can be regarded as an accelerating series of
"openings" of society—"openings" which certain men tried to
close permanently, but which they succeeded only in closing

temporarily. These temporal closings we call "stabilizations." The modern crisis, then, was not, as was claimed by Comte and all those who have joined him in clamoring against the "deviations" of modernity, a single period, whose continuity consisted in its progressive deterioration. It was one stage in a larger cycle, first of Western and then of universal history. But this stage was decidedly broken up, for it was composed of "regressions" and provisional "accommodations," of "collapses" and "restorations," all of them affecting not only ideas and beliefs but also the organization of social strata, the consumption and production of economic goods, and the function of government. From a causal point of view, perhaps all these elements should be separated. But from the descriptive angle, they appear to be inextricably intertwined.

5. Our analysis of this period, then, differs in many ways from that commonly given by philosophers of the last few decades. In general, as soon as they have admitted that there has been a modern age, thinkers have set themselves to attack the problem of its nature. Two doctrines, based on two different conceptions of the world and on two different value judgments, have alternately held the field. According to the *first*, the modern age has been a movement toward total "liberation." Gathering up the crumbs from the Age of Enlightenment, the proponents of this doctrine proclaim that in the course of the period two objectives have been attained: "diminishing the authority of the Church and increasing the authority of science." For some, this process of liberation has been of a predominantly intellectual nature. Others have seen it from a social point of view: what has counted, they say, is not the fact that the new ideas have shed light on society but the fact that they have transformed it. This transformation has in its turn been understood in various ways: as a conquest of freedom, as a better distribution of wealth, as a subjugation of nature. According to the *second* doctrine, on the contrary, the modern age has been a complete "deviation," a "mistake," a gigantic "infamy." This idea came to the fore at the same time as the contrary one, and, strictly speaking, we should have to go back to the debates between those who followed the *via antiqua* and those who preferred the *via moderna* to find

precedents for them both. However, in explicit form it gained strength only from the time when the anti-Enlightenment school, nostalgic Romanticism, and traditionalism laid a finger on certain modern sores. As history has no lack of facts, both doctrines have succeeded in adducing many in support of their respective arguments. In the case of novelty-hating traditionalism, the facts are the "vacillations," the "confusions," the "instabilities" of the modern age. Thus a series of characteristics has been established, which, in the view of these philosophers, demonstrates the "perverse" character of the period. Chief among these characteristics are: secularism, anthropocentrism, individualism, immanentism. It has been declared, in every variety of tone, that modern man has been uprooted, led astray, emptied of substance, despiritualized. To these characteristics, others have sometimes been added, admittedly less permanent, but still vitiating: rationalism and materialism. In view of all which, the solution seems obvious: modern man must be recast, must be made an "eternal man" once again, and this can only be done if we inaugurate a new age— "a new Middle Ages." On the one hand, then, we are told that if there have been and still are evils, this is because tradition has burdened modern man too heavily. Hence, nothing will function as it should until the revolutionary process has been completed. On the other hand, we are told that all the evils of the modern age arise from the fact that man has turned away from tradition, which offered him security and confidence. Hence nothing will go as it should unless the revolutionary process is slowed down and stopped.

6. The reader will think that we have simplified the above views to an inadmissible degree, and that it is unfair to reduce the controversies over modern history to a perpetual battle between "leftists" and "rightists." But this has not been our intention. Even supposing that modern history is marked by a continuous tension between impulses toward renewal and impulses toward conservation, between philomodernism and misomodernism, we recognize that neither attitude has the comparative simplicity that they exhibit in the usual political struggles. But in addition, we acknowledge that the above doctrines have almost never manifested themselves in the extreme form in which we have described them. The "liberation" thesis has not always been characterized by an exalted utopian futurism, nor has the "devia-

tion" thesis always been guided by a stubborn regressionism. The majority of modern ideologies have moved, dynamically yet without loss of balance, between the two aforementioned extremes. Here too, then, we must regard them as limiting concepts and insist that only as such are they illuminating. Terms like "rationalism," "immanentism," and others put into circulation by extreme or moderate traditionalists, are not useless. Nor are the terms "freedom," "individualism," and so on, proclaimed by the progressivists. But the valorizations underlying them often make them ambiguous. Hence we prefer to include all of these over-static notions within a dynamic conception according to which the modern age has been a series of processes, each of which has included progressive and regressive elements, which in their course have exhibited with unusual vigor the ambivalent character of human history—its being at one and the same time a combination of possibilities that are being created and of possibilities that are being destroyed. The great question concerning the modern age—and an especially acute question at the present moment—is not, then, whether the total result is a good or an evil; it is to find out whether the number of possibilities created can make up for the number of possibilities that have had their day. The great problem consists also in knowing if the constantly more frequent and far-reaching crises, manifested first in the West and then all over the planet during the past five or six centuries, *can be assimilated by constantly increasing masses of human beings.* Terrified by the events of his time, man has often asked himself if all the evils do not originate in an illusion—the illusion that certain forms of life, well suited to a few, can spread without being corrupted. The answer that the West has given *up to the present* is: Yes, they can and they have. And this is so true that our description of the modern age will, in the last analysis, be the history of a growing assimilation, in which the evils themselves have, down to today, created new possibilities. It is this conviction, be it said in passing, which provides the basis for the optimism that is discernible in our portrayal. We cannot be sure that this optimism can always be maintained. But if, to the language of description and analysis, we may add a few drops of exhortation and persuasion, we will say: It is our mission to apply all our forces to maintaining it. In the face of the fanatical mind and the disillusioned mind, we preach the need for a mind serene and hopeful.

Notes

This chapter may give the impression that, despite the reservations that we have expressed, we continue to accept the strict division of the West into an Ancient, a Medieval, and a Modern period. We do not. By "Western history" we mean the history that embraces the Middle Ages *and* the modern age. What we said on the subject of the dividing line between the ancient and the Western worlds (in notes to chapters 1 and 5 of Part I) was based on this idea, it being a matter of indifference whether the extreme limit of the former was taken to be the sixth century or the partition of the Mediterranean world by the Islamic invasion. In any case, historians recognize that a number of centuries saw the development of a society (in Toynbee's vocabulary, an "affiliated society") which departed further and further from ancient patterns and for that very reason could on various occasions take them as models. We fully accept all the difficulties caused by our reduction of the crisis to the Western-modern world. Now, within the Christian-Western unit (we can find no better term to designate it) there came a moment when what had appeared to be a definitive stage—the feudal-organismic society—proved to be only one of the many unstable equilibriums of which history is composed.

For an understanding of the difference between the two phases, we think it relevant to make use of a fruitful notion— that expressed by the term "function." By "function" we mean the different roles played in history by certain elements—facts or ideas—at different times. In his *Razón del mundo,* Buenos Aires (1944), Francisco Ayala called attention to the fact that "obscurantism" and "illuminism" (two terms that are respectively equivalent to "regressivism" and "progressivism" or to "misomodernism" and "philomodernism") are not only two ways of thinking: "the difference between them lies not so much in their thought-content as in their style" (*op. cit.,* p. 26). This is why it is so difficult to discover the difference between periods in their several *contents.* Beliefs themselves, important as they are, are not sufficient. What counts is the use that men make of them. As Américo Castro has said, "the touchstone is not in the oldness or newness of ideas but in the intention and the meaning that are injected into them" (*Aspectos del vivir hispánico,* Santiago de Chile [1949], 37). Two communities can hold the same beliefs. But how different the meaning of those beliefs may be in the two can easily be seen if we compare what the term "Christian" meant to a man of the thirteenth century and what it means to a man of the twentieth; what the word "humanist" meant in the fifteenth century and what it meant in the nineteenth. Ortega y Gasset was right when he inveighed against the fallacies implicit in using these and similar terms as if they had only one meaning, and when he pointed out how preposterous it is to give the same meaning to "poet" when we are speaking of Homer as when we are speaking of Lamartine. Without the concept of function we consider it very difficult, therefore, to understand adequately any historical period. The historians or the sociologists who say, "Basically everything is the same," or "Everything repeats itself," are unaware that they are using the expression "is the same" or "repeats itself" in a most controversial sense. We can admit that, according to the classic dictum *eadem sed aliter,* everything is the same, but in a different way. Now, the "in a different way" is no trifle. It is what makes it possible for a twentieth-century capitalist to understand and be understood by—that is, to "speak the same language as"—a workman of the same century; while it is far more difficult—though as we shall see presently, not entirely impossible—for a capitalist of our century and another from the Rome of the first century A.D. to "understand each other." To emphasize this, we have frequently used the word "attitude" in the course of this book. By it we mean the fact that man *can* make different uses of the contents of his life. We recognize that this assertion in turn raises serious problems: "What are the 'contents' of man's life?" "Shall we, like some existentialists, attribute to man complete freedom to 'make himself' without taking into any account the tremendous pressure of circumstances—of facts of all sorts, of ideologies, and so on?" For our purpose, the importance of attitude consists in emphasizing the fact that identical or similar contents *can* function in very different ways. We do not go so far as to say that everything depends on attitude. In the last analysis, we introduce the term to indicate that, together with ideas, real factors, etc., it is one of the elements of history.

On the other hand, it must be borne in the mind that attitudes are not based only upon contemporaneousness. It is certain that men living in the same period have, by that very fact, common assumptions that enable them to "understand one another" on many points, independently of their opinions, or their social class. But there are other assumptions common to them. For example, there is a "common language" between a Spaniard of the sixteenth century and a Spaniard of the twentieth, which will not be found between a Spaniard and a Frenchman of either period. There are also common assumptions corresponding to "social classes" and to "psychological types." For this reason we now make the reservation announced earlier: A European or American capitalist of our period and a capitalist of the first century A.D. in Rome *also* have a "common language" and, *in certain respects,* can "understand each other." The most plausible approach is to apply here the thesis formulated by Georg Simmel in his *Soziologie* (Chap. VI) under the name of "the intersection of social circles." Like social circles, attitudes too intersect in all sorts of ways, their intersections producing zones of understanding and zones of incomprehension. Nevertheless, we continue to believe that the "largest circle" within a relatively unified community such as that of the West is constituted by "community of period." This is what allows us to give a meaning to the expression "modern age" without necessarily adopting a radically historicistic point of view.

One of the factors of which we have scarcely spoken in this book, but which must be given a great place in history, is "character." We understand this term in a sense similar to that given it by Kretschmer, Jung, and other psychologists in presenting classifications of psychological types. Hence psychology, characterology, and what Kant called "anthropology in the pragmatic sense" are very useful disciplines in understanding history. This is shown in two ways. One is the "psychological (or psychosomatic) type" to which each man belongs as an individual; the other is the "national (or communal) type" —a type that, like the individual, can never be defined by a single trait. We will not here enter into the thorny problem of the relation between psychological or national types and history. As in the question of the relation between ideas and real factors, here again two opposing doctrines have been held. One maintains that psychological types depend upon differences of "constitution" (in Kretschmer's sense) and hence are comparatively invariable. The other asserts that they are modified in the course of history and are even determined by its major changes. Our view is that psychological types—individual or collective—are functional in nature. They are not invariable, but invariant. Hence they persist throughout history, but history can modify them in two ways—first, in so far as, in advanced stages of human society, the behavioral can frequently prevail over the psychosomatic; secondly, because the historical situation favors the development of some possibilities of a type and exercises a restraining influence on others. Our lack of competence in the field makes it necessary, of course, that all these assertions should be taken as merely plausible opinions. But we think it almost certain that a careful description of human history must not overlook the existence of these factors. This seems obvious to many people when national types are concerned. But no less important is the influence of the individual psychological type in certain decisions which apparently affect only ideas or real factors. To give an example of the latter case: Between an anarchist and a Marxist there is not only a difference in ideology or in class-consciousness; there is—as the history of the split in the First International shows—a difference in temperament.

Our use of the formula "a new Middle Ages" is in allusion to the title of a book by Nīkolaī A. Berdiaev, published in part in Russian in 1923; in German in 1924. But the Russian thinker's ideological orbit was very large, and cannot be reduced to such a formula. The same is true of many of the manifestations of traditional thought during the nineteenth and twentieth centuries. Rather than any definite doctrine, they have represented a style of thinking that has assumed very different forms, has employed very different arguments, and has subscribed to many different orthodoxies. Particularly illuminating in this respect are certain extremist forms, such as those presented in the works of Joseph de Maistre and Louis de Bonald. A happy phrase expresses the attitude of these writers—they are "more Papist than the Pope." This is so true that the Catholic Church itself has always carefully avoided being carried away by tendencies of the integrationist or Maurrasian type. For various reasons, the Catholic Church has looked with misgiving on the rising wave of extreme traditionalism. Among these reasons, a leading place falls to the Church's psychological and sociological perspicacity. But in addition, even when the high ecclesiastical hierarchy has given its assent to the thesis of the modern age as a "mistake," it has nevertheless not ceased to pay attention to the conditions imposed by the modern age. Extremist traditionalism, on the other hand, has taken its stand on a pure regressionism. In some cases, it has not even made the reservation, manifested rather in action than in thought, according to which modern principles are to be rejected, but modern results—for example, techniques—may be accepted and even encouraged. Extremist traditionalism has, in short, declared modernity *in toto* a gigantic "error." This very opinion was held, among Spaniards of the past century, by Juan Donoso Cortés (the Donoso Cortés of the *Essay*). Prominent in this respect among Spaniards of the present century, was Ramiro de Maeztu, whose *Authority, Liberty, and Function in the Light of the War* (London, 1916; written in English) not only ably summarized several of the leading theses of traditionalism, but also anticipated the two-edged criticism (later plentifully expressed by Maritain and others) which sees "modernism" as leading equally to despotism and to anarchy. But in Maeztu's work there is also an interesting postulate; salvation would lie, he held, in recognition of the importance of objective reality, and principally of objective values. This, of course, can be considered "medieval" (and Maeztu's emphasis on the "estates" as a means of stabilizing society supports such an interpretation). But at the same time it expresses an idea of the highest importance for our period, and on which many could agree—the idea that the subjective arbitrariness and the despotism which are combined in a suprapersonal State can only be cured by a recognition that the "center of gravity" of society "lies in the object." What the "object" is, is the burning question of the times.

As to the representatives of progressivistic thought during the last hundred and fifty years, they are so well known that they do not need to be named. We shall confine ourselves to mentioning one of them, from whom we borrowed the phrase on page 120 about the inverse relation between the authority of the Church and the authority of science. He is Bertrand Russell. The phrase quoted is from Book III, Part I, Chap. I of his *A History of Western Philosophy*, New York (1945). Russell himself ironically recognizes his "neo-Enlightenment" position by reprinting in his *Unpopular Essays*, London (1950), a false obituary that appeared in 1937, which called his doctrine an "antiquated rationalism" and added that his entire life exhibited "a certain anachronistic consistency reminiscent of that of the aristocratic rebels of the early nineteenth century." We could term this position a "philosophical radicalism," opposed to all romanticism (which served as ideological pabulum to many traditionalists) but at the same time having a certain romantic spirit. It put forth two branches: on the one hand, utopian optimism; on the other, the optimism of disillusionment.

Obviously, European social reality is richer than the schemas offered in this chapter would suggest. To mention only the problem of the origins of the bourgeoisie, careful attention must be paid to the fundamental role played by a class that cannot be exactly placed either with the nobility or with the medieval artisanate—the so-called patricianiate (on which see J. Lestocquoy, *Les Villes de Flandre et d'Italie sous le Gouvernement des Patriciens, XIᵉ-XVᵉ siècles,* Paris [1952]). The fact that, at least in the beginning, this class was not industrial and commercial does not mean that it did not foreshadow many of the activities of the "bourgeoisie."

Comte's assertions concerning the character of the modern age are found in several of his earliest essays: "Sommaire appréciation de l'ensemble du passé moderne" (1820), "Plan des travaux scientifiques nécessaires pour réorganiser la société" (1822), "Considerations sur le pouvoir spirituel" (1826), etc. These essays have been translated into English and published in the volume, *Early Essays on Social Philosophy,* London and New York (n.d.); the three essays mentioned bear in English the following titles: "A Brief Estimate of Modern History," "Plan of the Scientific Operations necessary for reorganizing Society," "Considerations on the Spiritual Power." Most of Comte's ideas on the subject were collected and systematized in his *Système de politique positive ou Traité de Sociologie instituant la Religion de l'Humanité,* published in 1851 in four volumes, the early essays being included as an Appendix. English translation of the *Système: System of positive polity,* London, 4 vols. (1875-77), containing also the above essays. Similar assertions are found in Saint-Simon, in Ballanche, in Proudhon, and in other writers of the period, to confine ourselves to France.—For the theses concerning the modern age as "liberation" or "error" see the previous note.–Castelar's sentence is from the preface that he wrote for the Spanish translation of Thiers's *Histoire de la Révolution Française*.–There have been many writers who elaborated theories based on the assumption that history depended on real factors; Ratzel, Marx, and Gobineau were some of the most important.–The idea of Scheler's to which the text refers occurs in several of his works, especially in his *Die Wissensformen und die Gesellschaft*, Leipzig (1926), a revised edition of his *Versuche zu einer Soziologie des Wissens*, Köln (1924). All the writers who have worked in the field of the sociology of knowledge (Max Weber, Karl Mannheim, Ernst Grünwald, Pitirim A. Sorokin, Hans Barth, J. J. Maquet, etc.) offer suggestive ideas on the subject.–Books and essays on the problem of the "origins of the modern age" are innumerable and it would take a long time to cite even the most outstanding.. During the last few years there has been much work on such questions as "Renaissances" in various centuries (twelfth, thirteenth, fourteenth); "crises" of various centuries (thirteenth, fourteenth, fifteenth); relations between the crisis (both material and moral) in the late Middle Ages and the birth of the "bourgeois spirit"; economic and economico-social history of the transition from the Middle Ages to the modern period (with special regard to the communal movements in various European countries and to the differences between cities, to the antecedents of the *devotio moderna*, to the resurgence of autobiographical literature, to the role played by luxury and asceticism, by humor, etc.). Many of these studies have not only provided valuable data, they have also succeeded in evoking a "historical atmosphere" based on a detailed study of the sources, but at the same time on a conviction that all human life—individual or collective—must of necessity live within a certain "structure."–For the ideas of the "stabilization," "opening," and "closing" of societies and other related notions, we have found much to our purpose in Bergson, *The two Sources of Morality and Religion* (cited in a note at the end of Part I, Chapter 6); the basic concept itself is probably of ancient lineage and Toynbee has cited many of its antecedents in various places in his *A Study of History*.–The book of Juan Donoso Cortés referred to in an earlier note is *Ensayo sobre el catolicismo, el liberalismo y el socialismo considerados en sus principios fundamentales*, first edition, Madrid (1851); English translation, *Essay on Catholicism, Liberalism, and Socialism, considered in Their Fundamental Principles*, Philadelphia (1862) and Dublin (1874).

8. The Crisis of the "Few"

Ambiguity of the title.–Changes between the fourteenth and seventeenth centuries.–Middle Ages and modern age: differences between them.–The medieval idea of order.–Being and becoming.

Attempts toward a solution: disequilibrium and stability.–The premodern "ferment."–Ideas on modernity. –Traditional notions.–Phases of the first stage: Renaissance and Counter-Renaissance.–Religion and humanism.–The meaning of "experience."–Requisites for historiographical constructions.–Ideological and chronological phases.–Unity and variety of modern Europe.

Partial and total solutions.–The role of seventeenth-century philosophy.–Significance of Cartesianism.–The problem of reason: human and divine reason.–Traditional and modern reason.–St. Thomas and Descartes. –Rationalism and voluntarism.

Radical spirit and mediating spirit.–The *pax fidei* and the new conception of man and the universe.–Applications of the spirit of mediation.–The problem of God. –Monarchy.–Stability: cosmic and human.–The idea of perfection.–Reason as mediator between will and love.

The title of this chapter is ambiguous. The crisis that developed between the fourteenth and the seventeenth centuries did not affect only a few men. All manner of changes were constantly produced in society: new types of communities were established, among them the type that gave birth to the modern conception of the State. But all these changes took place without any great transformation being introduced in men's traditional image of the world. Naturally, there were some who did not confine themselves to trying to alleviate society's gaping wounds with soothing plasters; they wanted a permanent cure. But it would be wrong to suppose that whenever radical solutions are presented a new historical period is born. Extremisms have always existed. What counts is the function that they perform; what matters is whether they are influential or irrelevant. There have always been orthodoxies and heterodoxies, repressions and rebellions. But they have not always been able to change the face of history. We must, then, be very much on our guard in our description of the "crisis of the 'few.'" We are dealing with a historical phase in which all kinds of changes took place in increasing measure. But these were adequately reflected only in some men's minds. Hence the best expression to describe this phase would be: "the crisis of the 'many' manifesting itself in a 'few.'" Considerations of brevity alone have led us to adopt the formula given in the chapter title.

In what did this stage of the crisis consist? We do not intend to describe it. This is not a history book; it neither enumerates facts nor portrays an atmosphere. But we need to have in mind the type of events to which we are referring. They are the following: the rise of the bourgeoisie in the late medieval period—with the growth of city life and of trade; the fervor of religious reformation—of which the so-called Reformation was but one aspect; the search for new forms of expression—of which the Renaissance and the *ritorno all' antico* were corollaries; the dissociation of the various factors that had remained in equilibrium during the Middle Ages—one of the consequences of this being an alternation between pessimism and extreme confidence in life; the change in the historical "constellation"—from the "replacement" of the Byzantine menace by the threat from the Turks, down to the period of voyages and explorations and the discovery of America; the abandonment of the symbolico-static concept of the world; the first tentative voicings of a pure *raison d'État*. There were, of course, many other types of events. It will suffice here to have given a sampling of them, and to show that what took place, especially during the sixteenth and seventeenth centuries, was only the acceleration of a process that had already begun two hundred years earlier. The chronological "limits" of our stage are, therefore, the beginnings of the fifteenth century and the end of the seventeenth century. The terms used to describe this period—"Renaissance," "Reformation," "Counter-Reformation," etc.—are merely convenient abbreviations intended to group a certain number of facts whose most general characteristic appears to be a growing "dislocation." For, in the last analysis, this is the most striking difference between the Middle Ages and the modern age. The dislocations in the former were analogous to the type of dislocations manifested by the functions within an organism. Extreme poverty and extreme wealth; radical asceticism and full enjoyment of life; scepticism and faith, with a thousand other facets, were in comparative harmony. All this began to break up as early as the beginning of the fourteenth century. The old order persisted, but it assumed new forms. Huizinga has pointed out that the importance accorded by historical research to the rise of the communal bourgeoisie in the fifteenth century must not make us forget that in the same period the bourgeoisie were very far below the nobility. This confirms a historical law: that rising social strata long remain under the spell of the old strata, which they try to imitate instead of doing what finally happens—succeeding to them. The medieval world was supported by the notion of order and the orders. *In principle,* every person and every thing had its place in society and in the universe. The displacements that occurred did no more than to confirm what everyone knew already—that, though built after the pattern of the heavenly city, the human city was a mere copy, and sometimes a caricature, of it. Disorder only emphasized order the more; leaving one's place confirmed the existence of a "place." Already in the fifteenth century, however, the nobility sought to become rich differently and more quickly than the method of inheritance allowed, but at the same time the communal bourgeoisie felt the itch to become noble. This is only one example. But it shows us one of the principal characteristics of the modern period—acceleration. For medieval man, what one did depended on what one was. The Scholastics expressed this idea in a neat general formula: *operari sequitur esse.* For the modern man, what one is has increasingly depended on what one has done. The modern formula may read thus: *esse sequitur operari,* the foundation of being is operation—or action.

For two centuries, certain minorities sought formulas that would define any being on the basis of its "activity." This implied attaining a clear knowledge of several essential things: who should finally rule in a society; what things could and should be fundamentally believed; what solid reasons there were for believing them. To solve the problem, not everyone proposed ideas; some considered that the solution consisted in adopting new forms of life. And in fact the great abundance of these forms, the rapidity with which they were modified, the increasing ease with which they were transmitted to other strata of the population, clearly shows that something unusual was happening and that all sorts of postures were being tried out in order to find those most suitable for the new situations. The history of these "try-outs" coincides with the history of life in the fifteenth and sixteenth centuries. Not everything in them, of course, can be explained from this angle. In the first place, history is governed by many and various motives, which make a facile reductionism implausible. In the second place, the aforementioned search implied all sorts of "advances" and "retreats," of stabilities promptly thrown out of balance, and of disequilibriums presented as definitive formulas. In addition, the history of these centuries must include not only their different forms of life but also intellectual and spiritual movements of all kinds: "humanisms" of every shade; attempts at religious reformation, from those that remained faithfully within Catholic orthodoxy to those that violently cast it off; the new political thought that was being shaped along with the growth of national States and which usually revolves around Machiavellianism. But a "real" sedimentation of all such new ideas occurred only on the appearance of a philosophical system capable of organizing them in an imposing architecture.

When did this system arise? Certainly not before the seventeenth century. From the end of the fourteenth to the beginning of the seventeenth century, all Europe was in a constant state of agitation, both in regard to real facts and to intellectual attitudes.

The agitation was so intense that it has been very difficult to discern a reasonably clear pattern for this period. It has been customary to distinguish between two different movements: on the one hand, the "waning of the Middle Ages" (a longer period than the one so ably described by Huizinga); on the other, the ceaseless emergence of new forms of life and of new ideas, in conjunction with the phenomenon pointed out by Adolf Weber —the fact that for the first time in Europe the masses rose, "forming a wave of immense volume." But although there have been, in fact, such movements, their description does not provide all the clarification that is needed. The pattern introduced by Burckhardt in one of his famous books was also inadequate. Aside from the fact that the great historian was dealing exclusively with the Italian Renaissance, and even only with certain forms of it (the more "esthetic"; Cassirer pointed out that he "forgot" nothing less than philosophy), his attempt failed because of his insistence on emphasizing "aspects" rather than well organized systems of beliefs, ways of life, or ideas. Later attempts by other historians were no more successful. They failed in particular when applied to the field of philosophical ideas. One of the results of all these investigations seemed to be that nothing worth mentioning happened in philosophy during the fifteenth and sixteenth centuries. But if this were true, the great seventeenth-century attempt to find in reason—individual reason, finally supported and justified by divine reason—the sovereign arbiter before which all doubts should vanish, would appear as a complete novelty, prepared at most by vague suggestions lost in a farrago of nonsense. Since this view did not correspond to reality, it proved necessary to replace the "theory of aspects" by what we shall call the "theory of articulations." The latter is now being developed by some able scholars. They are convinced that terms such as "Reformation," "Renaissance," "Counter-Reformation," etc., are too general and ambiguous. But they realize at the same time that some general notions are indispensable to historians in order not to become lost in a chaos of facts. In view of this, the above scholars have tried to discern a certain number of "movements" which, without being strictly chronological, prove capable of imposing an order over the variety of facts and ideas. One of these scholars, Hiram Haydn, has proposed a quite plausible theory. As a point of fact, it applies only to intellectual movements. But since it is these which chiefly interest us here, we shall proceed to outline it.

Haydn would divide the period from the fifteenth to the seventeenth century into three movements: the Classic Renaissance, the Counter-Renaissance, and the Scientific Reformation. The *first* includes the entire humanistic Renaissance, which to a great extent prolonged the medieval conception and undertook to complement it. The motive force of this movement was the desire to attain an "intellectual peace" not based on purely orthodox restrictions and admitting even certain tolerations. The term "Classical Renaissance" is, certainly, a misnomer. It can hardly be claimed that the immense variety of ideas, desires, emotions of the period can be embraced in such an innocuous expression as "Classical Renaissance." It might, then, be better to call this movement "Humanism," were it not that this term has been used for very different purposes, and were it not that those who "joined" the movement were humanists in addition to bearing many other labels. The *second* movement was not humanistic; it included the aspirations to a "reformation," emphasized the importance of faith, stressed the living springs of tradition, and sought the final justification of all thought not only in humane letters but also in "experience." Now, Hiram Haydn's originality consists in his not having included in this movement only the *homines religiosi;* although it sounds paradoxical, he also includes all those who stressed immediate, and directly experienced reality. "Experience" is, of course, a highly ambiguous word. For it designates not only the "inward experience" through which it was expected that new sap would be injected into the old faith, but also "outward experience," which confronted men with something that both humane letters and abstract reasoning had disdained—nature. Hence a singular amalgam: scepticism combined with the most fervid faith; a radical naturalism united with extreme supernaturalism. As if this were not enough, the same movement has to include political realism of the Machiavellian type, not so much in respect to the maxims it propounded for the acquisition of power, but in its conception of the nature of man. In short, the Counter-Renaissance was characterized by an attempt to throw off every kind of rigid bond, by a search for "release"—not, however, in the sense of modern individualism, but as an expression of the desire to attain to a more genuine contact with "reality." What predominated in the thought of the Counter-Renaissance was not humane letters. But neither was it theology, and still less "logic." It was *devotio*, the "heart's reasons," experiences of all kinds, observation, facts, and pragmatic rules. The *third* movement, the so-called "Scientific Reformation," did already reach ahead to the specifically modern spirit, not so much through the importance it accorded to science, as through its unshakable faith in the power of human reason. Hence we should prefer to call this movement "Reformation of the mind" or of the "understanding." Hence too it can be regarded as the real prelude to the solution for the first crisis.

Probably these notions are also inadequate. It will be for future historians to propose others that more closely fit the historical facts. But it seems quite probable that some historiographical construction of this type is unavoidable. Any such construction, however, must not be made too rigid; it must be remembered that the movements in question are not only aspects, any more than they are mere chronological phases. They continually intersect, and it is difficult to find pure representatives of any of them in actual history. Not even a Montaigne was completely "experimental" and "sceptical." Nor was even a Luther completely antirational. Sometimes the confusion of boundaries is obvious; it is enough to cite the example of Erasmus. Dilthey called him a "Voltaire of the sixteenth century," a corrosive mind. True, but at the same time he was a passionate seeker for the *philosophia Christi*. From other points of view, finally, we must take into account the particular ways in which different European communities reacted in the face of a similar historical situation; this explains why the function performed by these movements was, for example, very different in Italy from what it was in France or Spain. Hence, without a certain preliminary "ideological ordering" of the critical phase, it is impossible to understand the solution that some men now proposed: to outline a great philosophical system.

What was this system? It has been usual to consider Cartesianism the leading expression of "the modern idea." The view is quite plausible. Though they were strong and influential, the spiritual and intellectual movements previously mentioned touched only one aspect—religion, morality, the conception of nature or of the structure of society—but not the whole of reality. If, occasionally, they did attempt to embrace all reality—as in the case of the Counter-Reformation—they did so by a strange mixture of inclusions and exclusions. They were not, then, a sufficient proof that the process of crisis had at last been met with a complete and stable solution. This is not merely an impression of ours. The majority of the men who contributed to the formation of these movements felt that they were contributing something essential to the stabilization of society and introducing an order in the growing chaos of ideas. But no one thought that he had attained the desired end. Or, more precisely, they thought that they had attained it for themselves (like Montaigne), for an enlightened minority (like Erasmus), for a society with which they shared common customs and a common language (like Luther). These limitations were not due to personal incapacity, but to a very simple fact—that the right historical moment had not yet arrived. The philosophers of the seventeenth century, on the contrary, and particularly Descartes, not only tried to find a complete solution for the crisis, they were also conscious of having scaled heights from which they could look out confidently over the previous historical panorama. Above all, they were conscious that from those heights they could draw dividing lines between jurisdictions that, as Lucien Fèbvre has observed, were still confused in sixteenth-century minds—the realms of the natural and of the supernatural, of the certain and of the uncertain, of the possible and of the impossible. We need not, then, be surprised by the tone of assurance with which they formulated their leading arguments. Taking on the previous conflict of ideas and interests, they set themselves to resolve it in its entirety, without exceptions but at the same time without compromises. In this sense their thought was far more "radical" than the thought of the Counter-Renaissance philosophers. For "radical" does not here mean "extreme," but as the dictionary defines it, "of, pertaining to, or proceeding from the root." The hope, then, was to find the roots

in accordance with which it was believed that life should be con-
ducted, and according to which it was thought that belief was
possible.

In consideration of this totality, we forgive Descartes'
thought its inadequacies. We are not even concerned that
many parts of it were notoriously false, even for his own time,
and that, so far as science—one of the outstanding ingredients
of the period—is concerned, the real axis around which
modern thought has turned has been not Descartes but New-
ton. All this loses importance when we consider Descartes'
purpose and especially the *clarity* with which it was expressed.
Instead of clinging to the old tradition, without deviating a
hair's-breadth; or instead of seeking the living source of faith
in the soul within; or instead of remaining content with some
modus vivendi based on sarcastic jibing or benign scepticism, Descartes searched for solid and unquestionable truths,
truths not dependent on individual whim, which could be
accepted, "believed," by all. In principle, the only prerequisite
for finding them was common sense. But how difficult to obey
it! That required a singular courage: one must get rid of all
soothing confidence, of all preconceived ideas, of all traditional
beliefs. One must be utterly alone—without advisers, without
guides, without witnesses. Such an attempt had never been
made earlier, for the existence of similar formulas does not
justify the assumption that they refer to the same intention, or
are based on the same experience. Descartes did not only
pretend to draw truth from the depths of his own self, but
also to show that this truth, and the truths directly derived from
it, constituted the law of the universe. If anyone wants to call
this "idealism," we accept the label. But we do not lay too
much stress on it. One tendency in modern philosophical
thought holds that thinking activity is creative in nature. Paradoxically, among the adherents of this tendency are not only
the rationalists but also many empiricists. When Vico asserted,
against Descartes, that only what is done is properly understood, he did not misprize reason; he was emphasizing its opera-
tive side. But it would be a mistake to forget the strong
dose of objectivism that is present in modern subjectivism. This

"subjectivism" has confidence—manifested in the form of an apodeictic proposition—that the reason of the individual, *when rightly guided and guarded from being led astray by demands foreign to it,* coincides with the reason of the world and hence with the divine reason. The first real and radical solution offered to men who did not know exactly to what they should adhere was expressed by that ambiguous term—"reason."

"What!" the reader will perhaps protest. "Is not that just what philosophers have always done? When you were talking about Socrates, did you not speak of reason, of 'his reason,' as being his last 'refuge,' the ultimate foundation of his life? Then why suppose that Descartes was the first to reach a conclusion so commonplace?" And it is true that, in a way, Descartes' contentions were one of the many reiterations of what the West has called the "philosophic attitude." Without a reason that should be at once individual and intersubjective, that should explain both the behavior of the human individual and the structure of the universe, it would be difficult to talk meaningfully of "philosophy." St. Thomas maintained precisely the same thing. His idea of *ratio* was quite complex; as with all philosophers, the terms he employed embraced many meanings. But if we do not let ourselves be led astray by details, we shall recognize in his conception of "reason" something that has always been at the basis of philosophical activity. Without it, how can one even become a philosopher? Like everyone else, the philosopher has to admit some sovereign arbiter that "decides," when a conflict arises. But unlike other people, he makes reason the sovereign arbiter. To be sure, the term "reason" by itself does not explain much. It is the logical consistency of propositions with one another? Is it a "faculty" that "reveals" reality to us by freeing it from the mists of prejudices, of momentary and contradictory sensations, of the obscure movements of the will and the affections? We cannot say. But at least we can say that when it is necessary to "decide," the philosopher, *as philosopher,* does not decide in accordance with what he knows by hearsay, or with what he wants. The philosopher can also be a believer. In that case, he will not confine himself to believing, he will look for reasons to support his belief. He will not say: "This is so, *because* reason contra-

dicts it." And if he happens to maintain such a view, he will
have his philosophical arguments in support of it: individual
reason, he will say for example, does not suffice; there is a
higher reason, to which it is difficult for man to attain, deposited
in an institution or revealed through some exceptional experience. Or if he subjects reason to severe criticism in the
name of experience, his critique will continue to be rational.
He will have shifted from *reason* to *reasons*. But he will continue to move in the rational realm. St. Thomas did not believe
that reason could know everything. In addition, he very carefully delimited its possibilities. Not being pure spirit, man can
not apprehend intelligibles by a single intuition; he must laboriously derive them from things. But all this is not expressed in the form of mere opinions; the limitations of human
reason are shown through rational arguments. Hence it seemed
nothing new that reason was a solution for the perplexities of
certain men. Is there not, then, in the Cartesian philosophy,
some other element, as important or more important than reason
in the above sense, and without which it would merely be the
repetition of an attitude frequent in history, at least among
philosophers?

Yes, there is. It is the *use* that is made of reason. Or, better
—the conception held of its use. Maritain has written that
Descartes' "sin" consisted in "angelism," in having conceived of
human thought in accordance with the type of angelic thought.
Let us dismiss the "sin." The fact will remain that Descartes
conceived of the use of reason differently from other philosophers. Reason, and reason alone, was the sovereign arbiter.
For even at the moment when the philosopher decides what is
the first thing that can be known—that he who doubts, thinks
—such a "decision" is not the result of a fundamental experience, of a "primitive fact." Descartes' philosophy was not the
philosophy of sufficient fact; it was the philosophy of sufficient
reason. To be sure, the will played a leading role in it; not only
was judgment an assent of the will, but—as in Duns Scotus—
the creation and its structure was supposed to depend on divine
arbitrariness. We can, then, add to Descartes' rationalism an
element that appears to contradict it—voluntarism. In this

respect, Descartes was one of those who continued to stress the separation between reason and faith established in the fourteenth century by Occam and other philosophers. But Descartes represented more than a link in a long chain. If he had been only this, he would have become an outstanding example of the great modern "deviation," but not one of those who proposed a total solution for the crisis of the period. So let us admit, with Xavier Zubiri, that "the supposed Cartesian rationalism" is "rather a vast and paradoxical voluntarism— the voluntarism of reason." It was, then, his *conception* of the use of reason—and not simply the idea of reason or the mere use of it—which constituted Descartes' originality. In one way or another, all the great philosophers of the seventeenth century shared this conception. Spinoza was far less "subjectivistic" than Descartes. But in the conception we have been discussing, he was not far behind him. Locke was much more of an empiricist; but we can hardly think that he was very far from the "Cartesian spirit" when he wrote (and italicized): *"Reason must be our last judge and guide in everything."* Nor is this all. When we look at the entire panorama of philosophical activity in the seventeenth century, we see that Scholasticism itself— especially the most advanced and aggressive Scholasticism, that of the Spanish Jesuits—arrived at conceptions very similar to those of Descartes—or, better, of Leibniz. Hence the current practice of calling the seventeenth century "the Cartesian Age" seems to us not very wide of the mark. For "the Cartesian Age" did not need to coincide exactly with the particular philosophy of Descartes, but with a spirit which Descartes represented better than anyone else and which could seem to some the only spirit capable of providing a defense against the age's uncertainties.

It was, as we have seen, a radical spirit. But it was also a mediating spirit. The two were not incompatible. When a "conflictive age" reaches its culminating point, mediation and radicalism go hand in hand. For "mediation" does not mean a vague eclecticism—it means the discovery of a new crossroads, at which the roads that had seemed so greatly to diverge prove to have been convergent. Hence it would not be right to regard Cartesianism simply as one—or the first—manifestation of modern rationalism, as the formulation of the metaphysics correspond-

ing to the new conception of man and nature. In addition, it was
an attempt to attain the so greatly desired *pax fidei*. Hence, the
"repose of the heart," the "banishment of disquiet," the "end of
anxiety," were primary in it. We must not forget the role played
in the great systems of the period by anything that might lead to
some firm conception of the relation between man and God, to
some clear idea of man's place in nature. Of course, nature had
to be known. But such a knowledge was conceived as a means,
not as an end. To quote Xavier Zubiri again, what was sought
was to bring man back into himself. Which, however, did not
mean to segregate him from things or from God. To have interpreted Cartesianism as an attempt at "segregation"—as Maritain
has done—is to have forgotten that in the Cartesian Age method
is not *yet* entirely its own justification.

In what did the above mediation consist? In very different
things, some of them extremely concrete. For example: it consisted in proposing a rational organization of society in accordance with monarchical principle. This organization did away
with the turbulence of the feudal lords, but at the same time
raised a bulwark against the factional politico-religious struggles,
the communal revolts, in which the previous three centuries had
abounded. Here, however, we shall briefly discuss only one type
of mediation—that represented by reason when it built a bridge
between supreme love and omniscient will.

At first sight, this seems a shining example of vague metaphysics. What have the urgent tasks of the moment—stabilizing
society, allaying individual and social anxiety—to do with such
sublime speculations? As urgent and immediate measures, almost
nothing. As signs of a vast intellectual construction in which the
solution proposed by the "few" was marvelously reflected, they
have much. This is seen above all in a problem that was central
for the period—the problem of God. What was man's position in
respect to Him? Much depended on the answer given to this
question. And it was not a matter of two easy and extreme answers: either God is continually in us and in this world; or He
exists in an uncertain "beyond," outside of the world, in lofty indifference to the toilsome strivings of men (one further step, and
it could be said that He exists nowhere). In this period there was

no simple alternative between religious men on the one side and free-thinkers on the other. In the social strata where such problems were debated, each man, like Faust, had two souls within him. This, be it said in passing, can explain to us the so-called "mystery" of scholarly literary production during the seventeenth century. Some writers published pious books immediately after they had—often anonymously—published works of scepticism. Others took refuge in the adoption of "cautious" literary styles; reading these authors three centuries later, we get the impression that they do not mean what they say, that they mean something different, but we cannot be sure quite what. Roughly from 1870 to 1930, the majority of European countries, and almost all the American countries, lost the idea that this kind of "double talk" was possible. Today we not only know that it is possible, but how to do it: it consists in not giving oneself completely, in shrewdly discovering what expressions are sufficiently ambiguous, in cleverly setting up all sorts of intellectual alibis. Hence today we can understand many seventeenth-century writers who until quite recently were almost unintelligible. To be sure, such devices were also practiced in the fifteenth and sixteenth centuries (and *to a certain extent,* in all periods). But in the seventeenth century this type of literature—and the controversy that it aroused—had its heyday. It was the "literature of indecision." Almost all of it centered on the same problem, as if the cornerstone of society and of nature rested upon it. This is why the mediation we have mentioned was so fundamental. It makes little difference, therefore, that Descartes and the other great seventeenth-century thinkers were also, as the former has been called, "philosophers in masks." At certain periods wearing a mask is universal. It is not always an evidence of insincerity and hypocrisy; *the mask that a man wears is at the same time part of his face.* But even within this "double talk" an equilibrium was possible—and the great philosophers found it.

It was the equilibrium between a God powerful enough to create any world that he chose to create, and a God loving enough to make his creation "reasonable." For three centuries, there had been a constant widening not only of the split between God and the world but of the "split" in God himself. St. Thomas had not run into difficulties in affirming divine reason; he could maintain the thesis without thereby becoming a "rationalist." But from the time of Duns Scotus and William of Occam, the cleavage between the several divine attributes increased. If this had affected only philosophical speculation, it would have created no serious problem. But conceptions of God had repercussions in ideas concerning man. Hence cleavage appeared, and quite markedly, for man too. Should reason rule in man? Or should he give himself to devotion, to spiritual effusion, to a humble life of action and love? These were all questions of the first importance. Cartesian conception of reason helped to put them in their proper place. The omnipotent divine will can make any world, even one in which the principles of logic do not hold. But God, who is supreme will, is at the same time supreme love. He introduces reason to correct the "excesses" of omnipotent will. Thus reason originates in the *clash* and *tension* between will and love. Reason acts as the great mediator, as the great moderator. The God of Descartes—like the God of Leibniz—has been called the Great Mathematician, the Great Architect. It would be better to say (and Leibniz did say): the Great Monarch. God is the true "Sovereign," not only of human societies but of the whole of nature. He is the keystone that supports the highest arch of the cosmic edifice. Without Him, there can be neither honor nor order nor knowledge. God is, in short, the pattern of nature, man, and history. With this there would seem to be a return to the medieval idea that the government of this earth is a copy, though an imperfect copy, of the divine government. But there is an essential difference between the medieval and the modern idea. In the Middle Ages, though the effective power belonged to the nobles, and the power of political unification to the Emperor, it was still believed—both Guelfs and Ghibellines believed it—that complete legitimacy of earthly power was possible only through the Pope. The Pope could be denied concrete power, but the final justification for the exercise of power as deriving from the Grace of God was bestowed through the Vicar of Christ. But in the modern age, the secularization of power became far more radical than we can suppose it to have been in view of the sovereigns' respect for the Churches. From the moment when it was recognized that the religion of the king determined the religion of the subject, it was admitted that only the king could finally prescribe the latter. Society was now completely "on its own," and with it, nature and history.

It was a perfect world—in its way. It was—intellectually—a moment of high noon. It suggests some lines of the Spanish poet Jorge Guillén:

> All is dome. Rests,
> Central without desire, the rose.

A perfect world—but at what sacrifices! Perfect for the "few," incomprehensible or suspect for the "many," foreign to the mass, to the "all." Like all great intellectual constructions that have claimed to give a complete image of the world, it represented a moment of delicate and unstable equilibrium between many opposing tensions. A few decades earlier, it would have seemed unattainable; a few decades later, it already seemed indefensible. Yet within its instability it carried certain seeds that, cultivated later, came to flower in the modern age. Their development was not foreseen by their authors. Indeed, had they been able to witness it, some of them would have considered it a sheer caricature. The view that "reason" was the sovereign arbiter could be accepted only by some. By whom? Precisely by those who could believe in it—or, better, by those who could live by it. They were not many—a few gentlemen who were at the same time "intellectuals"—or vice versa. For the rest, "reason" did not suffice. Or, rather, they needed another kind of "reason." In the Western world, constantly more numerous classes of men were rising to power, to wealth, to influence. For them, reason as a principle was not enough; they preferred it as an instrument. No sooner had the crisis of the "few" ended than the crisis of the "many" began. With it, a new problem arose: Could these new classes be "assimilated" without definite injury to the forms of life and culture established by the "first" modern men? The answer to this question was given in the course of the next hundred years. It began with what Paul Hazard has called "the crisis of the European mind," and ended approximately with the French Revolution. Its center was the eighteenth century; its chief expression, the Enlightenment. All the countries of Europe, and many of those in the Americas, entered into this immense movement. One of them—France, as it has often done—expressed what was universal in the new ideas. Another—England—always a little distrustful of ideas, sought the solution in discreet, and effective, social norms. Each acted in accordance with its respective "national spirit." But all, responding to the same historical situation, scaling the same steep heights, sought a new solution able to fire more minds than the idea of a Reason mediating between Will and Love.

Notes

We may still be accused of persistent vagueness in regard to a term of which we make constant use—the "West." We have said something to define it, but the reader will rightly think that our remarks in that direction have been decidedly scanty. Unfortunately, the term does not lend itself to precise definitions. For it is not a mere geographical notion—it is a historical notion, which, furthermore, concerns a history that is constantly in movement. Without any pretention to clear up the problem entirely, we will venture a few additional remarks.

By the "West," we mean, first of all, Europe, which we take as the *nucleus* of the West. Yet even in this apparently simple conception, difficult problems already appear. The Mediterranean world—especially as it was gradually "liberated" from the Islamic invasion—was "recovered" for Europe. But at the same time characteristics that had belonged to classical Antiquity reappeared in it. On the other hand, Russia—even Russia west of the Urals—is, as has repeatedly been said, an ambiguous historico-geographical entity. From Peter the Great, it appears to have been incorporated into Europe. But the incorporation has been intermittent, as was shown in the nineteenth century by the struggles between the Westernizers and the Slavophiles (who, be it said in passing, were less "Asianists" than "Byzantinists"). Are we to say, then, that the West, as equivalent to Europe, is only those modern European nations which, even though divided internally—as two of them were down to the nineteenth century—sooner or latter attained to economic, religious, or political influence: France, Spain, Italy, England, Germany, Holland, Sweden, etc.? This restriction would have several disadvantages. For example, it would exclude Poland or Southwestern Europe—an important intermediate fringe. The question of the meaning of the "West" seems, then, insoluble. Yet it is so only when we attempt to give strict definitions, without taking into account the continual flux and reflux of European civilization.

A more "dynamic" definition is tempting: The West is a civilization whose nucleus arose in Europe, which has gradually spread all over the planet, and which, finally, has been "choked" and "repressed" by the great forces which it was in large part itself responsible for loosing. The spread of the West has taken place in several stages. In the sixteenth and seventeenth centuries it consisted in two movements—the containing of the Ottomans, and the expansion to America (together with the voyages of exploration and circumnavigation). In the eighteenth century European civilization already included a substantial part of the Americas and incorporated the dynamism of Russia. It next spread through many areas of the planet—coastal and island zones (coast of China, Pacific islands), subcontinents (India), etc. In some cases there was a process of colonization, which still persists (part of Southwestern Asia, Central Africa). In others, there was a process of assimilation of techniques (Japan). The point of maximum expansion was reached at the moment of the maximum penetration of techniques. And at the same moment, the reflux of what it had itself let loose began for Europe.

The problem of the place occupied by Europe and the West in the world has often been treated, especially during the last few decades, and still more after the end of the Second World War. It has been observed that one of Europe's chances for maintaining, if not its hegemony, at least its independence, was lost with the fall of Germany; hence, largely through Germany's fault. Germany had not indeed succeeded in having a clear idea of Europe. Whether because of the comparative youth of Germany as a nation, or because of the frenzied ideology with which the Nazis sought to protect and extend that power, the European idea was almost completely foreign to most Germans; the famous *Festung Europas* was never anything more than a military term designating only the outer circles of defense for *Germany*.

Our opinion that the philosophical ideas produced in a given period are particularly valuable toward an understanding of that period is largely derived from Hegel. But we disagree in several respects with the Hegelian idea of the "spirit of the age." Above all, we do not think that philosophical thought is completely "representative." We take it only as a particularly clear example of certain human attitudes. We do not exclude other historical factors. In our description of the ancient world, for example, we took into account problems concerning power or the projection of a community's ideals into the future. In our analysis of the modern world, we have often stressed the real factors, and in our final chapters we dwell to some extent on the impact of science and technique on society. But in addition we disagree with Hegel in that we deny the direct and unequivocal relation between *each* philosophical thought and "its" historical reality. To be sure, Hegel did not speak of strict contemporaneity; if "philosophy takes its flight, like the owl, at the coming of twilight," this is because the form of life that it seeks to reflect is already passing away. But this view is still too "correlative" for our taste. The reflection of forms of life by philosophy takes place in various ways: simultaneously, in anticipation, posthumously. There can even fail to be any such reflection. It is, then, necessary to see in each case whether one can talk of the "spirit of the age" reflected by philosophy and to what extent philosophy reflects it.

The objection which may at once occur to the reader—that Leibniz did not share in the Cartesian conception of the "arbitrary God" and hence could hardly be regarded as a representative of "mediating reason"—is lessened as soon as it is remembered that the Leibnizian God did not need to introduce reason to mediate, because He appeared as the supreme "mediator," supreme equilibrium and precise point of balance of the universe. Hence Leibniz saw many similarities between his conceptions and those of the Schoolmen; neither had any need for introducing a cleavage only to repair it.

The reference to Huizinga is to his *Herfsttij der middeleeuwen,* Haarlem (1919), 2nd edition (1921). English translation with many corrections and additions: *The Waning of the Middle Ages,* New York (1924), reprinted in a cheaper edition in 1954.—The quotation from A. Weber is from his *Kulturgeschichte als Kultursoziologie,* Leyden (1935), p. 284. There is a second edition (München, 1950), with some additions; especially important is the new closing chapter on the present situation of man.—

The reference from Cassirer is from his *Individuum und Kosmos in der Philosophie der Renaissance*, Leipzig and Berlin (1927), 3.–Burckhardt's book is *Die Kultur der Renaissance in Italien*. The first edition appeared in 1860, a revised edition in 1890. This work has often been reprinted. English translation from the second German edition, *The Civilization of the Renaissance in Italy*, London (1878), several times reprinted in Great Britain and in the United States. The "aspects" brought out by Burckhardt are: the State as a work of art, the development of the individual, the revival of Antiquity, the discovery of the world and of man, society and festivals, morality and religion. Burckhardt's method of exposition by "aspects" is very fruitful only when—as the great historian also tried to do—there is an effort to discover an "atmosphere," a procedure which has today become an essential part of historiography.–Hiram Haydn's book is *The Counter-Renaissance*, New York (1950); see especially the Introduction. P. O. Kristeller's judicious reflections on the proposed divisions (in his review of Haydn's book in the *Journal of the History of Ideas*, XII [1951], 468-472) should be taken into consideration. Our insistence on the need for finding certain major "articulations" in order to understand the pre-modern period does not mean that we overlook other ways of approaching historical reality. Among them the method by generations deserves particular attention.–The quotation from Dilthey is from his "Die Auffassung und Analyse des Menschen im 15. und 16. Jahrhundert," I, *Archiv für Geschichte der Philosophie*, IV (1891), 604-651; II, *id.*, V (1892), 377-400, reprinted in Vol. II of his *Gesammelte Schriften*, p. 42. Dilthey's studies of the period contain most valuable suggestions.–Lucien Fèbvre's idea will be found in his *Le problème de l'incroyance au XVIᵉ siècle. La religion de Rabelais*, Paris, 1942 (1947), 473 ff.–The quotation from Maritain is from *Trois Réformateurs: Luther—Descartes—Rousseau*, Paris (1925), 78 ff. (English translation: *Three Reformers. Luther—Descartes—Rousseau*, New York [1929].–The two quotations from Xavier Zubiri are from his Prologue to a volume of selections of Descartes' works translated into Spanish: *Descartes*, Madrid (1944); the Prologue was later included in Zubiri's *Naturaleza, Historia, Dios*, Madrid (1944), 106-7.–The quotation from Locke is from his *Essay concerning Human Understanding* (Book IV, Ch. XIX). The possible objection to our comparing the Cartesian and the Lockeian reason—that for Locke, reason would be man's *total* intelligence, including sensation—does not hold. Once man is "constituted," according to Locke, reason is his highest faculty. The only difference lies in how reason is acquired: according to Descartes it is innate; according to Locke, empirical.–For the "modern" character of seventeenth century Jesuit Scholasticism, especially in Suárez and the Spanish Jesuits, see our article "Suarez and Modern Philosophy," *Journal of the History of Ideas,* XIV (1953), 528-543.–For the thesis of Descartes as a "masked philosopher," see Maxime Leroy's *Descartes, le philosophe au masque,* Paris, 2 vols. (1929). Bertrand Russell makes similar statements about Leibniz in his *A Critical Exposition of the Philosophy of Leibniz,* Cambridge (1900), new edition (1937). This thesis has often been attacked. If it seeks to show that Descartes was basically "insincere," it should be rejected. But if it is interpreted cautiously, it can render useful service. In this connection there is much of interest in René Pintard's *Le libertinage érudit dans la première moitié du XVIIᵉ siècle,* Paris, 2 fascs. (1943), which refers in detail to numerous "double-talk" phenomena of the period and which does not leave the impression that they represented pure "hypocrisy." Furthermore, there can be a difference between the "subjective aim" of a writer and the "objective result" of his thought. Lucien Goldmann (See *Le Dieu caché,* Paris [1955], 17) has even said: "Descartes is a believer, but Cartesian rationalism is atheistic." On the general problem of "philosophic double-talk" see Leo Strauss, *Persecution and the Art of Writing,* Glencoe, Illinois (1952).–Jorge Guillén's lines are from his poem "Perfección" (p. 240 in the *editio ne varietur* of *Cántico,* Buenos Aires [1951]).–The book by Paul Hazard referred to will be cited in the notes to the next chapter.

9. The Crisis of the "Many"

Quantity and intensity.–The "unhappy consciousness."
–Notional assent and real assent.–The beginning of the
new crisis: love of discipline and criticism of authority.
–The ruling human groups.–Differences between "national mentalities": England and the Continent.–The
new rationalists.

Orthodoxies and heterodoxies: their common assumptions.–Ideals and forms of life.–Transcendent reason and
earthly reason: the meaning of the new rationalism.–The
new idea of nature.–The world as permanent residence.
–Possession and realization of ideas.–The worldliness of
the lax and of the austere: where they coincide.

The representative type: the "philosopher."–The society of God and the society of men.–The inhabitants of
the earthly city.–Goodness and imbecility of man: history as tragicomedy.–The function of the "best": enlightened despotism and classic liberalism.–The spirit
of society and the spirit of the laws.

Victory and rout of enlightened reason.–Inadequacy
of the reason of the "many" for "all."–The birth of a
new spirit: criticism, revolutionary aspiration, and nostalgia.

Around 1700 many people entered into the great European debate.

It was not solely a matter of quantity. How numerous, in the twelfth century, were not those who, their minds fired by the words of Abelard, disputed interminably on the slopes of Mont Ste.-Geneviève? Nor was it merely a question of intensity. Could any arguments be more intense than those that went on during the sixteenth and seventeenth centuries over dogma, experience, religious philosophy? Of what, then, is it a question? Of something fundamental—of the fact that in the midst of all the ideological struggles that will now occupy our attention the minds of every one of the participants were divided. One of the few metaphysical concepts which is still useful for understanding history is the one that has been current since Hegel: the concept of the "unhappy consciousness," manifested in the "divided" or "split" consciousness. This type of consciousness is one of man's typical characteristics. But here we must find out to what a point it is sometimes accentuated.

Then why call this crisis the "crisis of the many"? Because the phenomenon of "double consciousness" *already* appeared in the minds of many people. Those who, rising above their own "doubleness," had found a total solution for the modern crisis, could not adequately communicate this solution to others. Was this because they were lacking in skill, unclear in their language, incapable of systematizing their thoughts? On the contrary. They were almost too clear, too "logical." They confused notional assent to the fundamental propositions of their philosophies with a real assent. Or better, they believed that real assent to such propositions could be expected of all men. The distinction between the two types of assent is taken from Newman. By notional assent, we understand merely an assent to notions— to "intellectual" notions, thus, contrary to Newman, excluding "beliefs." By real assent we understand, with Newman, a stronger type of assent than the former, but though in Newman it usually refers to "things," for us this is not necessarily so; on the contrary, we contend that some men have been able to live—or to believe that they lived—by certain notions. The distinction, then, serves two purposes: first, to show how different it is to assent to "things" and to assent to notions: second, to indicate that some individuals are able, and others are unable, to transfer to notions the "assertiveness" that commonly relates to "things." The former were the philosophers of the seventeenth century; the latter, the men—whether philosophers or not—of the same century, and more especially of the eighteenth.

When did the new crisis begin? As to concrete events, considerably earlier than it came to be reflected in intellectual productions. We have already said that the constant dynamism of the West never halts for very long. The seventeenth century seemed to have attained a *modus vivendi* that was not simply intellectual but also social: the great European monarchies were the model to which it was assumed that all forms of society could be adapted. Yet even by the end of the same century the beautiful historical edifice we have described began to totter. "An hierarchical system ensured by authority; life firmly based on dogmatic principle—such were the things held dear by the people of the seventeenth century; but these—controls, authority, dogmas and the like—were the very things that their immediate successors of the eighteenth held in cordial detestation." So Paul Hazard began his book on the crisis of the European mind. The crisis embraced the years 1680 to 1715; strictly speaking, it was a transition within a transition. Hazard's description is accurate. But the term "men" is equivocal. What men? Not all men in the seventeenth century loved the order that authority undertakes to assure. But those who did not, exercised no influence on society; they were a handful of Utopians without clear ideas about reality, or they were stragglers, left-overs from the ferment of the preceding centuries. The majority did what it always does— adapted. But, once the 1700 line was passed, there was an increase in those who, instead of adapting their lives and their ideas to the changes that society was undergoing, attempted to adapt society to their own ideas—or, more precisely, to their own attitudes. They were principally the rising classes—the "bourgeoisie." This name designates here not only the middle classes, but also the aristocratic classes which succeeded in readjusting to the demands of the time, which were not content to do no more than proudly display their nobility. These "rising classes," then, included very different elements: the aristocracy who were clever enough to preserve their old prerogatives; the economically

powerful bourgeoisie who tried to become enlightened; the steadily increasing number of the gentry and minor aristocracy who
were on the borderline between bourgeoisie and nobility; the
"intellectuals." From the sociological and economic point of
view, it looked as if it were a social chaos. But from the human
point of view, it was a society that took more definite shape every
day. For these were the groups which agreed on ultimate assumptions regarding man, society, and the world; which lived
by comparatively common norms; which had, all in all, similar
"interests." To be sure, struggles between different representatives of these groups gave the impression that a violent battle
was taking place between old and new conceptions. On the one
side there were the "rationalists," on the other, the "apologists"
(although, as the century progressed the vociferations of the
former silenced the clamor of the latter). But seen from today,
their quarrels look like a war between brothers, a civil war. Let
us take the country in which ideological warfare was most
violent: France. According to Groethuysen's description, there
were in France at least three well-defined conceptions disputing
the possession of men's souls (and their worldly goods)—*bour-
geoiserie,* Jesuitism, and Jansenism. Now, each one of these opposing conceptions is unintelligible without the two others. This
is what always happens in any case of close competition; only in
complete separation is there complete indifference.

It is therefore difficult to describe, even summarily, the outstanding features of this stage of the modern crisis. The subject
becomes further complicated when, instead of remaining in the
field of ideas, we try to call attention to the social and economic
events of the period, and in particular to the role played by the
different national communities. Consider the differences between
England or Holland, and France—and still more Spain—in the
development of a common modern spirit. Even during the
seventeenth century, if not in thought at least in action, the two
former countries had already entered the climate that gave rise
to the great controversies of the century following. They became
even places of refuge for an aspect of European thought and
life which we will call—ambiguously and inexactly, since we give
it a broader sense than is usual—"nonconformity." In England,

especially, the fact of becoming a place of refuge was one of the ways in which that country's characteristic "tutelage" of the European peoples was manifested. Ortega y Gasset said on various occasions that England has always been half a century ahead of the Continent. It has also frequently been recognized that England has been a country that could silently accomplish certain revolutions which, on the Continent, often produce sanguinary upheavals. There have been several reasons for England's exceptional historical development. One has been England's "good sense," coupled with a moderate distrust of "ideas." Another has been the skillful advantage that England has taken of "nonconformity," especially in respect to economic development. We are not competent to decide how much truth there is in the well-known thesis of the relation between Protestantism and the "spirit of capitalism." Yet it seems to be an undeniable fact that in England and in a few other countries certain modes of religious feeling were dominant which stressed the value of economic property acquired by one's own efforts and which consequently channeled individual and collective human energies in that direction. Unfortunately, both our point of view and the lack of space at our command oblige us to disregard these differences. This is comparatively feasible since in the course of the eighteenth century very different currents succeeded in coinciding at many points: the English "liberals"; the French Encyclopaedists; the Spanish, Italian, and German scholars; in short, all the "free spirits" of Europe and, very soon, of America. Let us give them a common name: the "new rationalists."

They were not, of course, the only "intellectuals" active during this period. In another of his books on Europe in crisis, Hazard pointed out that the reign of mocking criticism in the eighteenth century did not prevent many other kinds of men (the extreme apologist for tradition, the disconsolate sceptic, the "man of feeling") to be active and influential. In point of controversial activity, these other men were not at all behind the rationalists. Both possessed a characteristic that had already appeared in the seventeenth century, but which in the eighteenth reached astonishing proportions—they were indefatigable. Now, the fact that our image of the eighteenth century is still *predominantly* the image put into circulation by the men of the Enlightenment is not the result of a conscious falsification of historical reality. It seems as if, despite the first stirrings of Romanticism, the great weight of tradition, the frequent distrust of reason, the popular-traditional wave that soon flowed over Europe, and many other similar factors, the new rationalists proved to be the victors. This fact is easy to explain. The defenders of tradition, of orthodoxy, were strong and numerous. But let us look at the weapons with which they defended their positions. They were exactly the same weapons as those wielded by their adversaries. Again, as in the seventeenth century, it was the way of thinking, and not what was thought, which proved historically significant. The controversy between "reason" and "revelation," then, blinded the eighteenth-century intellectuals to the fact that the partisans of the latter used the same *type* of reasoning as the defenders of the former. Both employed the same type of arguments, spoke the same type of language. They even had the same divided consciousness. In short, they met in common ground.

Nevertheless, the new rationalists were the true representatives of the century. They had the inside track; the interests of the rising classes coincided with their mental modes. In addition, despite their strong dislike of tradition, they were the true traditionalists of the period; they brought together all the scattered threads prepared by the immediately preceding centuries. They were, as Hazard said, the successors to the men of the seventeenth century, the winners in the debate that ended about the year 1714 (the year of the treaty of Rastatt), to resume, although in a very different form, from the first quarter of the eighteenth century. They represented the "new European equilibrium." They were the "emancipated." In this they were at one with those who, though not concerned with intellectual problems, represented the same attitude in their lives.

For, at bottom, what was the difference between those who tried to overthrow tradition and those who continued to respect it but, basically, were indifferent to it? Perhaps there was one difference—the latter were even more "radical." The belligerent attitude of the former showed that they had not entirely gotten rid of the enemy; he remained hanging on their flank, contending with them in a constant struggle interrupted by occasional truces. For here, too, the condition was fulfilled which we have pointed out as common to all periods of modern history—the fact that when some men claim to have found a total solution for a state of historical crisis, this very same crisis has already spread to other men and raises new problems. The "many" who hammered out a solution for the crisis still, as in previous centuries, opposed an idea to an idea. The "many more" who represented the social subsoil of the crisis opposed, as Groethuysen well saw, a way of life to a way of life.

It was here that the peculiar condition of this new phase of the great "stable crisis" of the modern West was best revealed. To understand the eighteenth century, it is usual to turn to its ideas, as if only they reflected it adequately. Actually, the best mirror of the period was its life patterns. In all periods it is important to know what society does or does not permit men to become. A period in which it is "permitted" to become a "courtier" is not the same as one in which there is opportunity to become a "hero" or a "wit" or a "philosopher." But in the eighteenth century these possibilities or impossibilities were decisive. For a moment had arrived when the social class to which one belonged (provided, of course, that it lay within certain ranks), or one's belief (provided that it was in harmony with certain rather broad patterns), was of less moment than the life pattern that one had chosen. One could, then, be a king, or a minister, or a member of the ecclesiastical hierarchy, or an aristocrat, or a wealthy bourgeois, or an industrialist, or a thinker—in each case one had to mold oneself to a particular type of life, for whose manifestation certain ideas were necessary—and not vice versa. It could even be said that the famous ideas of the Enlightenment were fostered because people lived in a time when it was no longer fashionable to be a courtier or a hero, in which one had to be "tolerant" or "anti-enthusiastic," or "cultivated." We cannot here treat of this aspect in the requisite detail, because, once again, it is not our task to write history. But the foregoing indications were necessary in order to make clear that when in the following pages we speak of ideas, we are, strictly, referring to a reality that includes forms of life. We are dealing, in short, with "mental styles" in which modes of life and ideologies interpenetrate almost completely.

This is what took place with one of the fundamental traits of the period—"rationalism." Cassirer has very rightly remarked that when the eighteenth century wanted to designate "the original intellectual force which guides the discovery and determination of truth," it used the noun "reason." But "reason" is a concept whose content changes with changing periods. The seventeenth century—especially through the voice of its great philosophers—understood it as a body of principles. The eighteenth understood it as a series of results. Hence in the latter century "phenomena" were "the data, and *principles* the goal of investigation," whereas in the seventeenth the data *par excellence,* the basic points of departure, were principles. The conclusion is obvious. In the eighteenth century "reason" did no longer designate the "innate ideas" that were supposed to be deposited by God in the minds of men. "Reason" designated a method of acquisition of knowledge. Hence the eighteenth century did not conceive of reason "as a sound body of knowledge, principles, and truths, but as a kind of *energy,* a force which is fully comprehensible only in its *agency* and *effects.*" All this is very true. But Cassirer, who saw with such clarity the difference between the conception of reason prevailing in the seventeenth century and the conception of reason fostered by the enlightened men of the eighteenth century, did not grasp the meaning of this difference. Such a meaning becomes clear only when we consider the type of men who fomented rationalism, and the people for whom they did so. The rationalism of the seventeenth century, in short, proved unsatisfactory for most of the intellectuals of the eighteenth century. Too majestic, too static, it was in addition excessively centralizing. Rather than a human activity, it seemed to the men of the 1700's—and indeed it has been for its proponents—a kind of divine activity. The men of the eighteenth century, then, did to reason what Aristotle had done to the Platonic ideas: they brought it down from heaven to earth. This is a most significant fact. For only on the basis of the new turn taken by rationalism was it possible for the enlightened men of the eighteenth century to perform the operation in which they were held to be masters: the enthronement of nature. It is an enthronement clearly different from the one that took place at various times during the Renaissance period, when the term "nature" designated the *physis* (or "basic principle") in the sense of the ancients rather than the "material universe" in the sense of the moderns. In this enthronement, almost all men agreed—lovers of novelty and haters of novelty alike. "Look into the wilderness of forgotten books and pamphlets dealing with religion and morality; interminable arguments, clashing opinions, different and seemingly irreconcilable conclusions you will find, and yet strangely enough controversialists of every party unite in calling upon nature as the sovereign arbiter of all their quarrels." So wrote Carl A. Becker in his book on the Heavenly City of the eighteenth-century philosophers. All men of the period, then, recognized the authority of nature; the only thing in which they differed was, according to Becker, "the scope of its authority," as to whether it merely confirmed or wholly supplanted "the authority of the old revelation." A less important difference than it appears, however, if we think less of ideas than of the way in which ideas are manifested. Therefore, whatever philosophic system they proposed, the men of the eighteenth century took this world and nature as points of departure. They could *think* what they would of this world, but they *felt* that they were not mere visitors, but permanent residents of it.

Here we find the master key that may serve to unlock the door of eighteenth-century ideology. It was not even requisite that many men in the eighteenth century should reach the above conclusions. In order to live in a certain way, it is not always necessary to adhere to a particular philosophic system. It is quite possible to speak sincerely in favor of certain ideas and to live in accordance with some other, very different ideas. Let us examine, for example, the idea of death, so subtly studied by Groethuysen. All men recognize that they must die. How, then, is it possible that some—and they were already many—consider this world a permanent residence? *First,* because accepting an idea is not the same as realizing it. Even as early as the Middle Ages and in the modern period down to the sixteenth century at least, this discrepancy was frequent. Many acted *as if* they would never die; or, what comes to the same, as if they would do so in a very indeterminate future. But the idea of death was always present in them; all religious ceremonies, into which the principal events of life entered, emphasized it. This could even

produce a "familiarity" with death that today we find disconcerting. Nothing could be more different, then, from what takes
place in our time, in which the idea of death is disguised and in
some countries even suppressed. *Secondly*, because, even with
the idea of death constantly in mind, there were various ways
in which the void caused by not thinking of it as an impending
event could be filled. "I shall die, but my children will continue
me." Or: "They will not only continue me, they will inherit
my work, my enterprise." If one did not think of or believe in
one's own enterprise, other elements were there to replace it—
pride in one's estate, in the national community, perhaps in mankind. In thought, or at least in action, the links with the trans-
mundane, the transcendent, were everywhere cut. There were,
of course, exceptions. Within Catholicism the Jansenists constantly emphasized the *memento mori*. There were similar manifestations in the other Christian Churches, even among some
freethinkers. But very soon the great coalitions armed against
them—the Jesuits, heedful of the world; the bourgeoisie, hungry
for prosperity; the aristocrats, intent on preserving their honors;
the libertines, deists, and atheists, wanting once again to prove
the soundness of the old Lucretian ideas. Side by side with these
men there were some austere, somber people—Puritans, defenders of economic freedom, directors of great commercial and industrial enterprises. Why these too? Because in order to become
"this-worldly" it is not necessary to be a lover of life, a sensual,
unprejudiced, human being. This world and this life have
many aspects; among them we can mention those emphasized
by the "austere" of the period—hard work, sobriety, a sense of
duty, a rigid pietism.

Now, the truly representative type of the eighteenth century
was the man who not only acted and thought in a "this-worldly"
way, but who, in addition, frequently gave the key-note for the
period: the "philosopher." Following established usage, "philosophers" (in quotation marks) designate the men of the eighteenth
century who sought to establish the City of God on this earth.

The city of God, or the city of men? Both—for it was to be
the city of God *among* men. For all men? Here lies a great
problem. In principle, this "city of God" was supposed to be

built for all men. When Voltaire, Rousseau, D'Alembert, William Butler, Adam Smith, or Lessing speak of human beings, they do not make exceptions. They assume that all men are born equal. All men are equal in two respects: in their ultimate goodness, once they were freed from the bonds of false traditions (or, as in Rousseau, of civilization itself), and in their incurable imbecility. Many of the pages written by the "philosophers" could be brought together under the title of a book published at the end of the First World War: *Man is Good*. But as many more could stand under the title that has been given to another book: *Man, the Imbecile*. Man seems, then, to have two natures. In fact, he has only one. For various reasons, never made clear by the "philosophers," the "true reality" of man has always been hidden, eclipsed, perverted by other men. Hence the peculiar impression produced by human history: it is a conglomeration of stupidities, which we do not know whether to take comically or tragically. Probably in both ways, for history seems to be a tragicomedy. In what, then, is the city of God on earth to consist? In the better among men working to dissipate the surrounding darkness. These better men are the enemies of superstition, the enlightened. But enlightenment alone is not a sufficient condition for the betterment of the human race. Enlightenment must be backed by strength. Hence the famous theory of "enlightened despotism," which, with dozens of variations, dominated the thinking of the "philosophers," the scholars, the "free men" of the eighteenth century. Hence, although they talked of "men," the partisans of Enlightenment were thinking of "some"—and, of course, "enough"—men. These select individuals, able to understand the importance of literature, but above all of the sciences and the mechanical arts, were the salt—better, the axis —of history. Without their intervention, history would be nothing but a pitiful succession of villainies. The cream of society, then, was the nucleus of the powerful who were willing to become enlightened, and the whole body of the enlightened, who were actually under the orders of the powerful but who claimed to serve the rest of mankind. If one of the most significant elements in a period is the idea held in it about who is the "best ruler," the eighteenth century is fertile in instruction. It was a century that disliked gradations, that delighted in dilemmas. One was either for "light" or against it. In the former case, even

tyranny could be forgiven. In the latter case, not the lordliest
of gestures, not the most densely branched genealogical tree,
could make up for it.

But is not this analysis going too far? After all, not every man
of the Enlightenment swore by the despots. Some preferred to
find solutions that did not depend on the changing humor of a
few men. Side by side with the "despotic" tendencies, flowed
the "liberal." These consisted in advocating an increased flexibility in human society. Here we have the thesis of the "balance between forces." This thesis was an expression of the "spirit
of the laws"; better, of the "spirit of society." Its ideal was England; its leading representative, Montesquieu. This thesis is not
negligible. When in the nineteenth century many men once more
set about the eternal task of finding a solution, the balance doctrine—even among those who rejected it—proved to be a
permanent obsession. Thus, the eighteenth century forged
many of the mental instruments with which the best minds of
the following century labored to remake society. The one, and
the essential, difference lay in the fact that during the nineteenth
century the aforementioned problems no longer arose only for
the "many"—those whose position lay between nobility and
"canaille"—but for all. If some did not think so, revolutions—
or their consequences—undertook to disabuse them. But this
fact again confirms that the new *raison d'être* for reality proved
impotent at the very moment that it was first clearly formulated.
The concept of reason elaborated by the "few" did not suffice
for the "many"; the latter had to distort it in order to fit the new
rising social groups into its frame. But the concept of reason
elaborated by the "many" in its turn proved inadequate for "all."
Already in the last decades of the eighteenth century, the "discrepancy," the "dislocation," was clearly perceptible. Even from
the social point of view, the feelings during the period of the so-
called "Proto-Romanticism" are illuminating. It was no mere
access of melancholy that made Rousseau say, at the beginning
of his *Rêveries d'un promeneur solitaire,* that he had been left
alone upon earth with no society but "himself" and that he
"would have loved men, despite themselves." It was no mere
perfervid imagination that caused Young and Cadalso to write

their somber and meditative *Nights*. The growing "dislocation" expressed itself as an "inexplicable" uneasiness. And the three great historical events to which we shall refer at the beginning of the next chapter were the signal that the great modern symphony was about to enter upon its last and most grandiose movement.

The knot that the men of the Enlightenment had tied with such ardor took in only a part of society. But worse than that, it left out a considerable part of the century's ideas. Even in this respect they stopped half way. Men as different as Hume, Kant, and Robespierre undertook to point out the omissions of the Enlightenment period, not because they were all extremists (no one was ever more cautious, moderate, and intent on keeping his balance than Kant), but because they were at one in a stern conviction against which the pointed, ironic weapon of eighteenth-century optimism shattered to bits. Robespierre said that the Encyclopaedists disregarded the rights of the people—they had prepared the Revolution, but that was all. Hume, with his acute, dry, disillusioned mind, showed that not only the concept of reason elaborated during the seventeenth century, but also the one fostered by the eighteenth-century philosophers was full of flaws. Kant wrote that severe criticism was the sign of profound thought, that "our age is the age of criticism, to which everything must submit." *Everything.* Nothing was to escape it —neither "religion because of its sanctity," nor "law-giving because of its majesty." Half measures were an illusion that cost dearly. Perhaps a time would come when reason should step back "to yield precedence to faith." But such a moment must not come at the beginning but at the end, when the traditional beliefs would become postulates of "practical reason" instead of being the results of unsupported speculation.

Thus the cycle begun with the philosophers of the seventeenth century seemed to have reached its close. And indeed the two stages of the crisis were two aspects of a single phase. Hence the difference between the crisis of "all" and the crisis of the "many" is greater than the difference between the latter and the crisis of the "few." This is true not only in respect to social changes, but also in respect to intellectual assumptions. The crises of the "few" and of the "many" could still be described in terms of the formula "growth of rationalism." We can scarcely continue to apply the same formula to the nineteenth- and twentieth-century ideologies. If, as always in the West, there was still a rationalism, its intellectual foundations had a different character. One of these foundations was the idea of evolutionism. To be sure, "evolution" meant at the beginning "the development of Reason." But very soon Reason itself was regarded as a moment—important, but not unique—in a great evolutionary scheme. Many new things began when the *"ancien régime"* fell. The Holy Alliance could not hold them back. To a certain extent, what actually happened was the very opposite—the great reaction against the ideals of the Enlightenment opened the dikes that let in the flood of a new world. In the midst of the post-Napoleonic reactionary peace, European and American life, economy, and ideology set out on the great flight that carried them to the threshold of contemporary society.

Notes

The first writer who clearly defined the relation between religious affiliation and the development of modern capitalism was Max Weber in his famous essay "Die protestantische Ethik und der Geist des Kapitalismus," *Archiv für Sozialwissenschaft und Sozialpolitik,* Vols. XX and XXI (1904-5), later included in Vol. I of his *Gesammelte Aufsätze zur Religionssoziologie,* Tübingen (1920). English translation of Weber's essay, *The Protestant Ethic and the Spirit of Capitalism,* London (1930). Weber dealt especially with what he called the "worldly asceticism" of Calvinists, Pietists, Methodists, and Baptist sects (particularly the Quakers). Since then, the subject has been frequently discussed. We will also mention Ernst Troeltsch's important study, *Die Soziallehren der christlichen Kirchen und Gruppen,* Tübingen (1912), translated into English, *The Social Teaching of the Christian Churches,* London (1931); and the book by R. H. Tawney, *Religion and the Rise of Capitalism,* New York (1926), cheaper edition (1929). Also important is Werner Sombart's classic book (1902) on the general development of capitalism. Though all of these studies criticize Marx's ideas, they would not have been possible but for his work. Hence they often stress "real factors"—whatever be the role that they accord to them—in contradistinction to the "Geisteswissenschaf-ten" approach taken by Groethuysen after his master Dilthey.

The objections raised immediately after the publication of Max Weber's book—especially those that show the existence of capitalism in historical periods and communities not affected by "worldly asceticism," and those that point out that modern capitalist enterprise was born in Italy as early as the twelfth century—are lessened if it is borne in mind that Weber himself gave the term "capitalism" not only the meaning of a will to acquire economic means but also that of a full-scale rationali-zation of that will. Weber especially stressed the fact of the rational organization of free labor as a fundamental characteristic of modern capitalism. He also dwelt on the influence exercised by modern technique, especially from the first decades of the nineteenth century. Paradoxically, modern technique, which contributed to the rationalization of capitalist enterprise in England, Holland, and the United States, tends to produce an increasing leveling among the various countries of the globe, so that it can help to lessen the influence of specific religious af-filiations and their corresponding "ethics."

Hegel's notion of the unhappy consciousness (*unglückliches Bewusstsein*) is found in his *Phenomenology of Mind* (IV. B. 3). It is a divided consciousness (*in sich entzweites, gedoppeltes, Bewusstsein*).–Cardinal Newman's distinction between the two forms of assent is made in *An Essay in Aid of a Grammar of Assent*, New York (1870), 34-93.–The two books by Paul Hazard are: (1) For the period 1680-1715, *La crise de la conscience européenne*, Paris (1935); English translation by J. Lewis May, *The European Mind (1680-1715)*, London (1953); (2) for the eighteenth century, *La pensée européenne au XVIIIe siècle, de Montesquieu à Lessing*, Paris, 3 vols. (1946); English translation also by J. Lewis May, *European Thought in the Eighteenth Century from Montesquieu to Lessing*, London (1954).–The book by Bernhard Groethuysen is *Die Entstehung der bürgerlichen Welt- und Lebensanschauung in Frankreich*, Halle/Saale, 2 vols. (1927-1930). This book deals only with France, but many of its ideas for the interpretation of the eighteenth century are applicable, *mutatis mutandis*, to other countries.–Among the various passages in which Ortega y Gasset discussed England's being "ahead" of the Continent is his "Epílogo para ingleses," included in the first "Colección Austral" edition of *La rebelión de las masas*, Buenos Aires

(1937). The original English translation of this work, *The Revolt of the Masses*, New York (1932), does not contain the "Epilogue," but the most recent reprints of Ortega's book do.–The quotation from Cassirer is from his *Die Philosophie der Aufklärung*, Tübingen (1934). English translation by Fritz C. A. Koeller and J. P. Pettegrove, *The Philosophy of the Enlightenment*, Princeton (1951). Paperback edition, Boston, The Beacon Press (1955).– The book by Carl L. Becker is *The Heavenly City of the Eighteenth Century Philosophers*, New Haven (1932). The sentence quoted occurs on p. 52.–The reference to the idea of death is largely taken from the book by Groethuysen cited above. For a sardonic description of the modern "disguising" of death, see Evelyn Waugh's novel *The Loved One, An Anglo-American Tragedy.–L'Homme, cet imbécile* is the title of a book by M. Guibert (Paris, 1950). It is obviously another form of Alexis Carrel's famous title, *Man, the Unknown* (1st English edition, 1935; 1st French edition, 1937), which was followed by books by various writers: *Man, the Too-well Known; Man, the Unknown Neurotic*, etc.–*Man is Good* is the title of a book by Leonhard Frank (*Der Mensch is gut*), first published in 1918.–The quotation from Rousseau is from the "Première Promenade" in *Rêveries d'un promeneur solitaire.–*The sentence from Robespierre is from a speech given 8 Floreal, year II (May 8, 1794).–The passage from Kant is a note to the preface of the first edition (1781) of the *Critique of Pure Reason.*

10. The Crisis of "All"

The crisis of "all," our crisis.–Geographical and social expansion of the West.–Acceleration in history.–The nineteenth century, prelude to contemporary society.

The three great Revolutions and their aftereffects.–Preponderant role of the Industrial Revolution.–Nationalism and its meaning.–Nationalism and social structure. –European and extra-European nationalism.–Colonization and its consequences.–The recoil of colonization on the colonizing countries.

The reflection of the crisis in ideologies.–Ideology and power.–The "century of the bourgeoisie."–Bourgeoisie and proletariat in the nineteenth century.

The great historical theses.–Pessimism and optimism. –Justification of the past: Hegel and Spencer.–Statism and individualism.

The "social question," problem of the century.–Science and society.–Material technique and human technique.

The problem of equality.–The two consequences of naturalism.–Equality and the "struggle for existence."– The proposed solutions.–Once again, "many" and "all." –Reason and the human masses.–The ambivalence of the "revolt of the masses."–Incorporation of the masses, and dynamism of the West.–Necessity for a new adjustment.

The crisis of "all" is our crisis. Hence it includes the problems of contemporary society. It is only for the sake of greater clarity that we shall treat the two subjects separately.

For contemporary society would remain opaque without its immediate historical background. This in its turn is the product of the entire modern Western development, which has been described in the foregoing chapters. In them, we have seen that the West was "unfolding" in two senses: on the one hand, with its geographical expansion; on the other, with its social, technical, and political expansion. New territories and new groups of men were one by one incorporated into a world that in the beginning had only been the dream of a few minority groups. Obviously this incorporation could not have taken place without casting some stain on the purity of such dreams. This fact must be faced without mournful backward glances. The one thing we need to know is whether the greater size of the new historical picture will not shatter the old frame; whether the rise of the masses, by distorting the "projects" of the minorities, will not finally destroy them. We have every hope that this will not occur. The process so far described did not seem to have taken us too far from the original bases. But there appears to be a big "jump" from the Western world of the end of the eighteenth century, still almost entirely concentrated in Europe, to the world of today, conscious that the least pressure at any point of the globe has violent repercussions all over the planet. We are witnessing an extremely rapid process, which confirms various recent views regarding the acceleration of historical evolution and even a general evolutionary acceleration. The process filled the entire nineteenth century. That century, then, prefigures many of the present-day attitudes and ideas.

Three great historical events mark the transition from the second to the third and last stage of the crisis: the American Revolution, the French Revolution, and the Industrial Revolution. With each of them we include its aftereffects. With the first, that is, we include the formation of a new economically powerful State which cleared, sowed, and settled the lands that later linked the West of Europe to the Far East. With the second, we include the Napoleonic wars and their impact on Europe and on Latin America. With the third—the most pregnant with consequences—we include the increasing application of technique to mass industrial production. The interplay between the three processes confirms a fact that we have constantly emphasized: the fact that social, political, and economic factors must always be taken into account together with intellectual or spiritual factors. If we dwell on the Industrial Revolution, however, it is because, under the conditions created in the West, economico-industrial development has exerted constantly increasing pressures. The detonator has been technique, and so we shall presently discuss the problem of technique at some length. But since technique in its turn would be incomprehensible without the development of modern natural science, it may be said that the great transformations in modern society have been possible by virtue of one of the greatest creations of the human mind, a creation that came out of the intellectual climate generated in the first modern centuries. It is common knowledge that without technique at least half of our society would be paralyzed (if not destroyed), and that the paralysis would affect the development of ideas no less than it would economic and social processes. But it is equally true that without both an economic and an intellectual foundation, technical evolution would be impossible. Human history is an immense animal gnawing on its tail.

As in the preceding chapters, we shall be sparing of references to historical facts. But we cannot help mentioning two other great events: nationalism and colonization. By the first, we understand not only certain struggles between the national European states, but also the participation of great masses of men in these struggles. From the wars of the sixteenth century to the Napoleonic wars, armies constantly increased their manpower. But only from the end of the eighteenth century were there true national armies. The changes introduced by the new type of warfare need hardly be stressed; not only did mercenaries prove inadequate, but the services required by the troops began to reach considerable proportions. Now, war was only one aspect in the development of nationalism. Another aspect was the "hardening" and "solidification" of some great powers. We will not say, with a French General, that, "after intense eruptions, the world has crystallized." The last decades above all have shown what such "crystallizations" amount to. But we will recognize that up to the beginning of the Second World War, universal history seemed to be ruled by the mutual conflicts among a few great European powers, and the intervention—which for a time still appeared to be only occasional—of Russia and the United States. This was due to the fact that it was primarily in the European countries that the highest point was reached both in "nationalism" and in the intervention of practically the entire population in military conflicts—or in the armed peace that preceded and followed them. As usual, the end of one evolution coincides with the beginning of another. Never was there so much nationalism; yet never was there such a strong desire to change the native tradition for an extraneous one. This paradoxical attitude was shared by great and small powers alike; both exalted what they at the same time destroyed. But this process interests us only in so far as it brings out one of the chief conditions of nationalism: its close relation to social movements and to the resulting political consciousness of great masses of men. Thus the nationalism to which we refer plays above all a social and political role; it is a movement that emerges whenever, in a given geographical area, vast multitudes take part in public life. The meaning of "nationalism" in our context is therefore not merely "the historical development of a nation." For "nation" is an ambiguous word; what it meant in the seventeenth century has not too much in common with what it meant in the nineteenth century. In our own time nationalism plays a role similar to the one already played in the nineteenth century, through the "awakening" of large and small communities outside of Europe, especially in Asia and Africa. Here too we have a social process—so closely connected with political developments that often we do not know which causes which. Possibly they condition each other mutually, and it is as right to say that we are witnessing a national awakening manifested through a social revolution as to say that we are witnessing a social process that takes the form of a political development.

Thus contemporary extra-European nationalism is a repetition, under different circumstances, of the very process that developed in Europe during the nineteenth century. Technical progress contributes to the spread of certain attitudes and ideologies, which, starting from Europe, have served outside of Europe to return the blow with the same arms. The recoil has taken place in various ways. In Japan there has seemed to be an adaptation to modern techniques without any great change in the traditional structure of the old Empire. Elsewhere—as in China—the recoil has seemed to set off a far-reaching revolutionary process. Yet the unexpected may still happen—Japan may have felt its traditional structure shaken more than it appears to have been, and the wrench that China has given to the immense carapace of its traditions may, among other consequences, have that of reviving the most living of them. In any case, the shock from the West has not been in vain. We shall return to this subject in our final chapter. We must now describe another fundamental fact of the period—colonization.

The term "colonization" designates a great many different phenomena. For our purpose the most important among them is European establishment in very different and sometimes very distant territories. Spain and Portugal had opened the way. But here we must be on our guard; the Hispano-Portuguese colonization, which circumnavigated the globe, was of a very different nature from that which began approximately with the British occupation of India. Hispano-Portuguese colonization was not only a result of an economic or economico-military enterprise; it was also the unfolding of a military-political and politico-religious plan. We must, then, exclude it from our picture, just as, for other reasons, we must exclude the settling of North America. Hence we differ from those who see in the present influence of America on Europe the reflux of an earlier flux, a kind of counterblow. What we call "the Western world," then, includes America also, especially those parts of it which have most completely assimilated the forms of European civilization. For similar reasons, European Russia cannot be considered as an entirely extra-European area. If the idea that European Russia is completely un-European seems plausible at times, it is because it is believed that Russia's extra-European enterprises—chiefly Siberia—have carried Russia too far from its modern European orbit. What we must emphasize then is that nineteenth-century Europe was involved in the prosecution of a colonial expansion which had already begun in the eighteenth but which was only adequately systematized and rationalized in the nineteenth. In the course of this expansion the European powers succeeded in setting foot on almost every littoral of the globe. The coasts of the world received the impact of new ways of life and of new techniques. From the economic point of view, the main cause of this expansion was the necessity, basic for every highly industrialized area, of obtaining raw materials. But in addition questions of military strategy, of cultural penetration, of political prestige were involved. The old Oriental empires were penetrated; areas which, like the Arabic world, were living in lethargy after having almost overrun Europe, were shaken to their foundations. Extraterritorial rights were established, as in China. New waves of humanity flowed to places practically uninhabited before, as in Siberia. Without colonization, then, the new stage of the modern world would be unintelligible. It would be even more so at the present time, when we clearly realize that European questions—which only twenty years ago completely absorbed the attention of the modern historian—must always be understood in their relation to world questions. We will not say, with many: "Europe has vanished; with the loss of its political and economic power, it has nothing left but a vague 'cultural' influence." History takes many turns, and there is reason to think that if technique can change the strategic situation of countries hitherto little favored from the point of view of the values of industrial civilization, it can again change what it has already modified. But even if Europe overcomes its present crisis and recovers possession of enough political and moral power to make its weight felt on the whole planet, it will have to reckon with the new world situation. The same can be said of the other zones that are now "awakening," and among which we must count not only Asia, but also Africa, and not only those parts of it—such as North Africa and South Africa—which are already playing a role in world politics, but also certain territories (such as the present protectorates) which are entering the whirlpool of industrial revolution with ever increasing speed. All of them must make their plans in view of the new world situation. Here we have one of the results of the process of colonization. Hence it is one of the fundamental facts of the period, one of the essential elements of our great crisis.

This crisis is, once again, the crisis of "all." According to our schema, it should be reflected in some of the intellectual productions of the period. The particular solution given by the Enlightenment to its own problems was obviously inadequate to solve the problems that soon arose all over Europe and America. The bourgeoisie succeeded in fitting itself more or less comfortably into an apparently rigid frame. But the resulting social and spiritual equilibrium, like all those reached during the modern period, was precarious. New disequilibriums soon appeared. First, new human groups emerged into public light. Second, the recently incorporated and assimilated social classes began to experience the dissatisfactions that come to one who, having found a new dwelling-place, sets about enlarging and improving it. The first type of disequilibrium showed itself in the various forms of "Jacobinism" that—not in France only—went far beyond the "bourgeois positions." The "Jacobins" were not satisfied with getting rid of economic bondage; they wanted to destroy social and spiritual bondage as well. The second type of disequilibrium was reflected in the thought of "Romanticism." The picture of society and the world painted by the eighteenth-century Enlightenment had, despite Rousseau's crude brushstrokes, come out too "bright." At first this picture had produced an impression of satisfaction and even of enthusiasm. But man is a restless animal, and in the modern age a *bestia cupidissima rerum novarum.* Too much light, like too much shadow, wearies him. He loves constant change. Now, the new historical developments were set in motion primarily by the bourgeoisie. Continuing his conquest of economic and social power, the bourgeois fulfilled the conditions indicated by Groethuysen—to impose forms of life upon thought; to sacrifice even thought to attain one's own ends. Hence the bourgeois was at once more and less radical-minded than the philosophers of the Enlightenment. From the intellectual point of view, he was often timid. It was better to *seem* to con-

form to tradition; after all, the aristocracy still held many of the
reins of power all over Europe and could pull hard on the bit.
But from the point of view of social life, the bourgeois feared
much less; he clearly understood that he could already impose his
views through action, although for the moment he was deficient
on the side of thought. Thus if in the end he recognized his own
ideology in the thought of the Enlightenment, it was only because that thought had come to be accepted by many as the
"spirit of the century."

Thus a process set in that repeats itself as if in obedience to a
law. At the moment when the modes of life of the socially and
economically dominant groups coincided with the forms of
thought of the victorious intellectual strata, the former felt that
the coincidence must be temporary. It became necessary to seek
the form of thought that would really be adequate to the new
historical situation. What had been gained must be preserved;
it was the moment of "equilibrium." When such a situation appears, the conservative always give the impression of being reactionary. Yet, it would be wrong to think of the bourgeois
classes as wanting to turn the clock back. The brake is necessary.
But it must not be allowed to stop us. It must only make our
journey safer. "Let us, then, praise whatever sets bounds. The
'canaille' have gone too far; if the old aristocracies—which have
also been 'incorporated'—are able to re-stabilize the situation, so
much the better. After all, it is we who in fact hold the reins."
So—sometimes secretly, sometimes at the top of his voice—
thought the "bourgeois." He was not only the "businessman,"
the "peasant grown rich," the "incipient industrialist." The economic activity of these *parvenus* set up fields of force that drew
more and more men. The specialized industrial worker was, of
course, not yet among them. But the increasing number of "man-
agers" of all sorts responded to the attraction. Public officials too
entered the new classes. These classes were not yet fully powerful. They were not solidly united. But for many of their members, the situation had markedly changed. "Let us"—they seemed
to say—"respect the forms of the *'ancien régime,'* since the Holy
Alliance forces us to do so. But no one can deceive us. The revo-

lutions have not taken place for nothing. There is no way of turning the stream back into its old channel. The one thing that must be done is to keep it from overflowing." We are not simply piling up metaphors. Many historians today recognize that without the period of peace inaugurated by the Holy Alliance—politically reactionary and *"ancien régime"* though it was—the economic evolution of the Western world would have been greatly hindered. Now, this evolution continued in favor of the new classes that had emerged to power and influence, and of the men who joined these classes or served them. Thus the nineteenth century continues to produce the impression that, even more than the eighteenth, it was the great century of the bourgeoisie. But no sooner do we state this formula than we realize its one-sidedness. For the nineteenth century was not only the century in which the injunction "Get rich!" rang far and wide, but also the century that heard the slogan "Workers of all countries, unite!" "Jacobinism" had not been a momentary eruption. As usual, the "pure" were swept away. But under the flotsam from the shipwreck, the tide rose.

It rose to such a height that, from the third decade of the century, we cannot distinguish between bourgeois reactionaries and "Jacobin" progressives. The confusion occurred on the European continent—and in many parts of America—simply because the groups had intermingled. In England, it was because they had never been separate; as has often been remarked, English political moderation produced revolutions without upheavals. Indeed, as newer and newer groups rose to public life, it became more and more difficult to determine which side each was on. But were there really sides? We are describing the crisis of "all." All, then, must take part in it and undergo its assaults. When we turn our attention to the Industrial Revolution, this fact becomes even more obvious. The changes introduced usually react on the "bosses" *and* on the "workers." They occupy different positions; entrenched in them, they are engaged in violent warfare. If they could, they would annihilate each other. But they live on a common soil; when a storm breaks loose, it makes no distinctions. In the beginning, the upheavals affected only a few individuals; some fell, others took their places, but the classes remained. Next the classes themselves entered the struggle. At different times, one or another appeared to hold power. But this soon turned out to be illusion. As at the end of the ancient world, power had seemed to belong to everyone and to no one. It had seemed to have no face, which is why it tried so hard to show one.

But let us not anticipate; the last lines already refer to the twentieth century—better, to the last three decades. But we were still describing a moment when none of all this was clearly perceptible. A storm of progressivism was still abroad, agitating men's hearts. To be accurate, we should say that this wind began to blow strongly only from the third or fourth decade of the last century. Until then, there had been too much instability to allow much hope. From the French Revolution to the defeat of Napoleon, the European world had been under unremitting tension. Then, for a number of years, threatening winds blew—reaction after reaction, to strangle freedom or to proclaim it. As if this were not enough, the first consequences of the Industrial Revolution in England gave no great cause for rejoicing. Such consequences seemed disastrous—the exploitation of human labor reached unthinkable proportions. Why, then, give hope the reins if the very machine that was to save labor produced unheard-of cruelties? Yet the storm gradually subsided. Not because people saw a golden age opening before them. That age was still in the future—sometimes in the very distant future. But there *was* hope of a golden age. Those "on top" believed that, once they had reached port, the refuge would be not only impregnable, but increasingly comfortable. Some even thought that its comfort depended on the well-being of those who were out in the storm; these must, then, be "protected"—at least those who were subjected to the storms of the West; the rest did not yet count. In their turn, the underprivileged began to conceive their own hopes. They indulged themselves in a luxury until then forbidden to the great masses of population. Instead of living for the day or for eternity (or for both together), they lived for a historical future—a future not only of their names or their families, but of their nation or their class. To be sure, the nineteenth century, even after its third decade, was also the century of pessimism. Have there ever been in history pessimists so thoroughly systematic, so consistent, as Schopenhauer, as Eduard von Hartman? But this pessimism had two functions—above all, one that is frequent in history: it served as counterpoint. With respect to the progressives, the pessimists performed, then, a function similar to that which, in the eighteenth century, the primitivists had performed in respect to the followers of Reason. But they also performed a function of escape—like Stoicism, metaphysical pessimism was a way of withdrawal adopted by certain minds, perhaps to show that historical pictures cannot be painted with one color. This pessimism has nothing in common with that of Nietzsche, who, though he wrote in the nineteenth century, anticipated many of our own fears and anxieties. Thus nineteenth-century optimism found itself framed between two pessimisms —one that looked toward the past, another that looked toward the future. Between the two, hope flourished. It was not the vague hope of eighteenth-century progressivism; not the hope based on the declaration that all men are born equal, but the hope that lay in seeing in what concrete ways men could become so. It was, then, a hope founded on sound possibilities. Some based their hopes on economic expansion; others on an increasing use of machines, once the earlier cruelty and suffering should have been eliminated; others on the rise and consolidation of the revolutionary spirit, increasingly incarnated in the dispossessed classes and especially in the working classes. In one way or another, the bulk of Western humanity jumped a horse that had its first serious fall in the second decade of our century, when pessimism no longer appeared as a form of withdrawal but as a form of combat—when instead of the metaphysical pessimism of Schopenhauer or the desolate pessimism of Nietzsche, prevailed the "realistic pessimism" of Spengler.

In steadily increasing numbers and with steadily increasing enthusiasm, Western humanity got aboard the same vehicle. The inhabitants of the West might have different and even contrary interests, but all took part in public life. Hence if there was to be a solution, it must be for all. This the leading intellectual figures of the century understood quite well. The first of them was Hegel. Whatever we may think of him as a metaphysician, there is little doubt that, in his meditations on history, he put his finger on very sore spots in human society. He undertook to explain history— *all of history*. But not in the manner of Voltaire, as a struggle between Good and Evil, Enlightenment and Ignorance. Evil and Ignorance played their roles too; they were necessary conditions

for evolution, stages in the great march; and that not in the manner of Vico, as a repetition of the same cycles. Of course, Hegel
was no radical innovator. He was preceded—and accompanied
—by many "Romantics" (a Herder, a Fichte, a Friedrich Schlegel) as well as by those who, like Goethe, tried, in Nietzsche's
words, to "overcome the Eighteenth Century," whose aspiration
was to "totality," to "complete freedom" of spirit. It is true that
many Christian philosophers had also contributed to outlining a
great philosophy of history. But although this philosophy still
remained in force, it was in force in a very peculiar way—as a
conception that had to fit into the frame of a great evolutionist
scheme. Thus Hegel's philosophy of history closed a whole
period. The philosopher himself believed that he had closed it
for good and all; history was supposed by him to have come to
a standstill from the moment when a system—his own system—
had appeared which accounted for history entirely. The fact that
this assumption proved to be an illusion—history not only did
not come to a standstill, but seemed to be going on at top speed
—did not prevent its being recognized that, in some respects,
Hegel's vision of history was singularly penetrating. One of the
nineteenth-century thinkers whose influence has persisted longest,
Marx, was intellectually rooted in the soil of Hegelianism. It will
be said that we are presenting only one side of the intellectual
picture of the past century, and that with it, and even in opposition to it, there was another side that stubbornly made a way for
itself—the "liberal," individualistic conception of history. Its
chief exponent was Spencer. Now, Spencer's social philosophy
marked also the culmination of an intellectual trend—a trend
that went hand in hand with the ways of life that were then prevailing in the country that seemed to have struck out on the decisive course. This was Victorian England, where the Industrial
Revolution had just completed its first great cycle, and where,
too, the bases had been laid for what appeared to be the relentless and systematic westernization of the planet: the British Empire. In any case, it would be unfair not to take into account the
immense differences that separate Hegelianism—or Marxism—
from Spencerianism and its affiliates. It would be equally unfair
to omit mentioning the political, social, and historico-philo

sophical doctrines which were formulated in various continental countries and which oscillated between these two. Among them were doctrinaire liberalism, the reformulation of traditionalism, and politico-religious positivism. Nevertheless, when we look at them from a sufficient distance, we see that they were all solutions for the same problem. It was a different problem from that raised by the eighteenth-century philosophers, and therefore had to be attacked with different intellectual weapons. Hence whatever the solution proposed—from extreme liberal individualism, even bordering on anarchism, to complete statism—the same data were taken into account and the solution was to apply to all men. Even the intermediate solutions—such as that of doctrinaire liberalism—which seemed to be constructed for certain groups, were based on the underlying conviction that through these groups society could be stabilized completely. For, of course, it was *again* the stabilization of society which was sought—some way of closing an excessive and dangerous opening, of finding another *modus vivendi*. After the ephemeral "stability" of the last moments of the *"ancien régime,"* society had once again "opened." But it could not remain open indefinitely, for many sensed that its maximum opening would coincide with its complete dissolution. It "must," then, close. When? How? In these two questions lies the axis of the problem—the famous "social problem"; for the period, it was the entire human problem—of the nineteenth century.

Many things revolve around it. Science itself, which should have seemed inalterable and aloof from such questions, constantly changed its appearance. For men see very different realities in science in different periods. The people of the seventeenth century saw above all its theoretical structure. Although it had practical applications of great scope, and sometimes even developed out of practice, modern science was then regarded as fundamentally a pure, "disinterested," theoretical activity. It has been said that its purity did not prevent it from influencing the lives of men; the Copernican theory, historians of science show, changed the image of the world; men ceased to regard themselves as the center of the universe; the idea of infinity banished all localism; mechanism relegated the ideas of finality, purpose, Providence, to the lumber room. But as a point of fact it was not these ideas that changed the world of men, but the way in which men used and interpreted them. With the same ideas, men can create very different "images of the world." If already in the seventeenth century modern Western life was inseparable from science, this was not due only to science. For science itself was possible only because of "modern life." Now, unlike the preceding centuries, the nineteenth thought of science—even of the "purest" and most "disinterested" kind—in intimate relation to society and its organization. Science was asked to solve the "social problem." Science was to organize the "city of men"—a different city, of course, from that of the eighteenth-century "philosophers." For now it was not only a question of freedom *versus* tyranny, of light *versus* ignorance. "All men are created equal, that they are endowed by their Creator with certain unalienable Rights." True enough—but, where does that get us? What good are rights without the possibility of exercising them? The pursuit of happiness is all very well, but the great problem is *how* to procure happiness. In addition, some people began to wonder whether the problems of society could be solved by means of such glittering proclamations. There were even some writers, like Dostoevski, who conjectured that perhaps man did not want to be happy. But this type of conjecture belongs rather to our century; it is one ingredient of its "irrationalism" and one more proof that Dostoevski, like Nietzsche, was a thinker ahead of his time. The bulk of the men during the nineteenth century did not stray far from the opinion that a concrete way of attaining happiness must be sought and that science could considerably contribute to attaining it. Thus "science" and "society" were presented as terms in the same equation. For the first time social problems began to be submitted to a scientific treatment which was often conceived after the pattern of the natural sciences but which still lacked what our century has abundantly supplied: highly developed techniques.

For here begins a change which we must explore, because on this change depends much of the difference to be established between the last century and ours. In the nineteenth century, scientifico-natural technique was already on the whole at men's disposition. But it was so rather as a store of possibilities than as something that concretely shaped the structure of daily life. This latter development has taken place everywhere—in West *and* East, in city *and* country—only during the present century. However, there is little doubt that in the nineteenth century men already lived in a world very different from the world of their fathers. Already a technique which, contrary to the strictly "individual-absolute" technique of the East, could be rapidly applied to great masses of men, was beginning to make its presence felt. Much of the science of the last decades of the nineteenth century went into elaborating it.

The first modern centuries had laid the foundations for the reaffirmation of a doctrine that, basically, was a sub-product of the Christian conception—the doctrine according to which all men are created equal. The difference is that, while in the Christian conception men's equality is measured by their presence before God, in the modern conception it is also measured by a human or natural standard—men, it has been said, are equal before God, but also before society, before the universe. It was, then, the idea of an equality in this world which predominated in the modern age. The best minds of the nineteenth century set to work to provide scientific, and not only moral or religious, bases for this doctrine. Now, the systematic elaboration of the bases of "this-worldliness" led to disconcerting conclusions. To be sure, already in the sixteenth century, but especially in the seventeenth and the eighteenth, the majority of the solutions proposed by minorities and majorities were based on the concept of nature. Natural equity, natural law, natural religion—these are some of the manifestations of the naturalistic thought of the period. But this "naturalism" was ambiguous. Either it was a manifestation of the traditional modes of religious feeling, or it resulted from the well-known claim to human autonomy which flourished in the modern period. The idea of nature and the corresponding naturalistic conceptions drifted in this ambiguity for three centuries. But the nineteenth century set itself to establish "naturalness" on other grounds. It succeeded when it firmly introduced naturalism into the science of living beings. Darwinism (by which we mean the impact produced by Darwin's ideas rather than these ideas themselves) was the most influential representative of this tendency. In the course of its elaboration, a fact previously unsuspected was discovered: the fact that man, as a "purely natural being," could not aspire to equality; that biological inequality— and "therefore" intellectual, moral, social, and political inequality

—constituted the foundation of the human being. This was a very startling discovery. Did it not sweep away all the politico-social ideas that had been laboriously worked out during the preceding centuries? Did not man now revert to the point at which his "natural history" had been "interrupted"—and even "deflected"—by Christianity? There were many who thought so. Nietzsche was one of them. Seduced by the idea of the "potency of life," he came to believe that this potency had been destroyed by the Christian spirit of humility, and that it could only be recovered by the affirmation of man's basic "nature." Now, this seemed to conflict with another great trend in modern thought, which we have called "liberalism." But the conflict was not total. For, if political liberalism can escape from naturalism, a similar escape is almost impossible for economic liberalism understood in its most radical sense as a perpetual, unwearying, and cruel "struggle for existence." There are, of course, profound psychological motives for maintaining this last conception; when new fields are to be explored, the "pioneering spirit" is needed. But this spirit has often two great drawbacks; it exalts inequality for inequality's sake and it forgets that a time arrives when it becomes necessary to organize not only a particular enterprise but the whole of human society. We will return to this problem. For the moment it will suffice to show that one of the typical doctrines of the last decades of the nineteenth century produced a terrifying impact only during the twentieth century, when some decided to preach the necessity—or perhaps the inevitability—of brutality for its own sake. In any case, as soon as we approach the end of the last century, we observe a recrudescence of the same problem that arose at its beginning—the great problem of human society. Can society be organized? How? Can it be happy? Should it be happy? Yet from roughly 1830 to 1870 it was believed that a solution had been found. "Let us accept the inheritance of modern times; the Enlightenment was naif; besides, it thought in terms of the 'many' but not of 'all.' Yet something can be salvaged from it. Science can help us to find a solution, since it is not merely a contemplation or a pure manipulation of nature, but implies the existence of an intimate relation between the exploitation of nature and the organization of human society. In this way all—at least the 'all' of the West—can adopt new forms of life and thought which are the culmination of a very long process, since all earlier evolution has been only a preparation for the present moment. We are not, like the Romanticists, trying to put the clock back; we are simply explaining what has happened. Every period plays its role in history; the role of our period consists in bringing together the various threads of Western history and weaving them into a strong fabric that can protect us against future storms."

So thought many. It was not only a solution; it was a series of solutions. All of them presented a considerable advantage—a great part of the members of the Western community were given a place in them. Then too, in their moderate forms they did not exclude earlier traditions, for those who wished to cling to them; after all, tradition has a strange knack of finding the right opening and introducing itself into the new forms of life and thought that at first had seemed to shun tradition. In this sense, these solutions accomplished the end proposed. Some of the essential modes of Western life were enlarged to the point where they could take in not only the "few" or the "many," but "all"—or "almost all." To be sure, they had to be somewhat distorted in the process. But there was always the consolation that the distortion would be only temporary. And indeed, down to the present, it has been so. But the problem that faces our period is more serious, for now it is not a matter of Western assimilation but of "planetary" integration.

Here there is no final answer; there is only a hope. Indeed, the great masses debase and vulgarize everything; their rise to public life often looks more like the "vertical invasion of the barbarians" of which Ortega y Gasset spoke than like a genuine incorporation. But we must not become discouraged too quickly and conclude that nothing can be done for "man," for when he congregates with his fellows in great numbers he becomes vulgar or brutal. Bitter as our experiences in this field have been up to now, it should not be forgotten that they are limited in scope and that, in any case, it is not sensible to sever oneself from the majority when the questions that must be confronted concern the majority. We must courageously face the dangers implicit in any great process of incorporation. Otherwise no real incorporation will take place. This courage can easily be coupled with hope.

For the history of the modern age has shown that incorporation is feasible and that, once the first dangerous moments have been got through—those in which everything seems to sink into degradation, into a downward leveling—there is an increased enrichment of human society. These warnings are especially pertinent to the present moment, and should properly appear in the next chapter. But since these problems arose in most serious form for the West already in the nineteenth century, we may be forgiven this anticipation.

An example will clarify our thought in this connection. To combat illiteracy seems, at first sight, to invite a cheapening of culture. Once the majority can read, people say, they fling themselves voraciously on all kinds of literary garbage, and, as if that were not enough, allow themselves to be swayed by all kinds of propaganda. In the end, they may even break the heads of those who were "naif" enough to propose such a wild idea. They may, indeed. But there is another side in our picture—by learning to read, people will enjoy possibilities previously denied to them. Hence it would be unjust, in the name of a reality that may be transitory, to abolish the possibility of a genuine betterment of human society. All human problems have the form of a two-edged sword. We must see to it that only the better edge cuts into the future. This seemed to be actually happening for Western society in the last years of the past century. It confirmed the persistence of that peculiar characteristic of our society which we have called "dynamism." To this characteristic we should add another, already defined by Guizot—the fact that the tendency to unity in Western civilization has never been detrimental to its variety. But as soon as this conviction was reached, the same process that we have so often mentioned repeated itself—the equilibrium that had been attained lasted hardly longer than the moment in which it was observed. A break then occurred which, with the utmost vigor and clarity, divided the past century from ours. It consisted in two facts. The first was the consciousness that it was by no means certain that all men had been incorporated into the essential modes of Western civilization, and that therefore new adjustments were necessary. As a consequence of such a consciousness a new wave of pessimism broke, this time of pessimism over reason, learning, and science. It was the signal for the appearance of innumerable lamentations over the "bankruptcy of science," the "breakdown of culture." A major event, the First World War, marked the dividing line chronologically. The second fact was the "new awakening" of the East, symbolized by the Chinese revolution of 1911, to which we might add another "awakening," that symbolized by the Mexican revolution of 1910. New voices, then, entered the symphony; so it is not at all surprising that the orchestra suddenly seemed out of tune, and that a huge, terrifying, irresistible wave suddenly broke—this time not over Europe and America or the more or less Westernized areas of the world, but over the entire planet.

But the history of this last process is already our own history. The new situation demands a new clarification. To conclude, then, we shall formulate some reflections on it.

Notes

The problem of the progressive acceleration in history has lately been discussed by several writers. In his *Essai sur l'accélération dans l'histoire,* Paris (1948), Daniel Halévy mentions a text of Michelet's which supports what we said earlier. Neither this text nor Halévy's book itself, however, consider the question broadly enough. In his *L'accélération évolutive,* Paris-Santiago de Chile (1947), and in his more complete *Problématique de l'évolution,* Paris (1954), François Meyer undertook an interesting, and daring, investigation into the cosmic foundations of historical acceleration. The question will probably attract the attention of future philosophers and historians. In our opinion, the process of historical acceleration cannot be separated from the process that we have analyzed in Part II of the present book —the incorporation of constantly increasing masses of people into public life. The acceleration of the historical rhythm is the more noteworthy in that it would seem that what ought to happen would be the reverse—the progressive incorporation of the masses ought to set up a resistance difficult to overcome. Nevertheless, what actually happens in history can be formulated as follows: the greater the mass, the greater the acceleration. The ancient empires endured for hundreds of years. Of course, political events did not leave their peoples' forms of life untouched; changes sometimes consisted in one people's supplanting another by exterminating the former inhabitants. Normally, however, political changes taking place in the dominating strata simply passed over the surface of the dominated mass; the depths were not wholly untouched, but evolution there was slow. So it is no matter of chance that the modern historical rhythm has progressively accelerated and that in our period it has reached its maximum tempo.

The image of the world provided by science—especially by physics and astronomy—makes a great impact on society. But such an impact is less profound than is commonly supposed. It is often said that when men have a clearer idea of their place in the cosmos, many of the rivalries that embitter their relationships will disappear. However, if this were true, there would be no reason why the discovery of the "infinity of worlds" should not have produced more radical changes in men's minds. Certainly, it produced some. No less certainly, the changes were the greater as more and more men shared in the various kinds of knowledge deriving from the "scientific image of the world." But the human being can also shut himself up in his little burrow with all the tenderness and all the ferocity of which he is capable, and quite independently of what science may have to say about the cosmos. No amount of daily listening to the information broadcast and televised over the four quarters of the globe prevents a man from continuing to feel spiteful—or loving—toward his neighbors. To believe that our vision of the cosmos affects our way of life entirely or fundamentally is the same as to suppose that the idea that this world is but a vale of tears prevented anyone from being concerned with worldly things. But the human mind is flexible enough to harbor different, and even contradictory, ideas and feelings.

In mentioning the application of scientifico-naturalistic techniques to the social problems we have described only one aspect of the question. Dozens of angry voices have been raised against scientifico-naturalistic positivism in our century, and were raised even in the century before ours. In many cases a strict separation between the human-historical-social realm and the realm of natural phenomena was advocated. In others it was observed that man is not only a natural being and that hence the techniques of natural science are not properly applicable to human problems. If the proposition that man is not only a natural being is understood in the sense that his forms of behavior are constantly changing, we agree with it. For this is only to claim that man's peculiar dynamism must be approached by various methods, not exclusively those of natural science. And this applies to the individual no less than to society. But if the statement in question is understood as advocating a complete epistemological separation between two scientific fields, we reject it. The so-called "analysis of human existence" is not incompatible with the epistemological connection between the natural and the "spiritual"; such an analysis may even give the connection its philosophical foundation.

We are not unaware of the many negative aspects presented by the moments in which new masses are incorporated; even to enumerate them would fill a large book. They can all be concentrated in the phrase "temperamental democracy" (*humorale Demokratie*), which Max Scheler coined in a moment of irritation against the frequently disastrous consequences that result when constantly increasing numbers of people intervene—whether actively or through the sounding board of public opinion—in certain functions previously reserved for minorities or for restricted groups. Almost the whole of Ortega y Gasset's book, *The Revolt of the Masses,* is devoted to delineating these negative aspects, which are evident, but which must be viewed as temporary, as springs of possibility rather than as immutable realities. To be sure, at the moment of transition to an incorporation of great masses these "usurp" functions that belong to particular groups. We shall consider two examples. Diplomacy, formerly reserved for certain specialists or for certain dominant minorities, today largely depends upon public reactions. This is not the best way to ensure the adoption of solutions that are good for the public itself; as has often been said, in the absence of the necessary rationality in reaching the decision, the result is often an irrational response, a kicking against the pricks. But this will not necessarily be the case always. *The great question is whether, once the new masses have been assimilated, the necessary rational element can be injected into them.* To entrust the administration of justice entirely to a specialized body has serious disadvantages; the most obvious among them being the arbitrariness often engendered by the private interests of such specialized body. Naturally, these disadvantages vanish when the persons charged with administering justice possess, in addition to the necessary ability to judge rightly, the necessary independence. But let us suppose that those who administer justice do not possess such an ability or such an independence; the general public must then intervene. Now, this can be done in two ways. One consists in introducing certain "devices" ("neutralization" of the prosecutor by the defending lawyer; intervention of a jury, where a group chosen from the entire public decides the guilt or innocence of the defendant). Despite possible arbitrary miscarriages of justice through prejudice or ignorance, these means are salutary and can correct the aforementioned disadvantages. But let us suppose that the "neutralization" disappears or is reduced to a minimum and that, in addition, the intervention of the public in a judgment is "massive." Will not the result then be purely temperamental, arbitrary, and frequently cruel? If it is not to be so, rationality will have to be introduced into the decisions of great masses. There are several ways of doing this. In some cases, the introduction of rationality can be complete; under these circumstances, when problems affecting the great majority are at issue, it is right that the now incorporated and comparatively rationalized majority should decide. But as it would be utopian to insist that the great majority should decide directly in all matters, we have to fall back on other methods which are partial and auxiliary—specialized functions; minorities that assume different charges; representation, and so on.

Naturally the most important of the negative aspects presented by the incorporation of masses is the one that has manifested itself often enough in history—the situation in which, instead of leading to greater freedom, the process of incorporation, undertaken to avoid the danger of anarchy, leads to the most ferocious despotism. Our own time affords many examples of this. Compared with this danger, all others—even the temporary cheapening of forms of life and thought—become inconsequential. For in our day tyranny, with the technical means at its command, can produce very much greater effects than any that have been seen before; it can even change (temporarily, we think) the psychological structure of the individual. Instead of becoming a reservoir of fruitful possibilities, the renewed society can become a formless, malleable mass, not only vulgarized but degraded. And not even this would necessarily obviate material upheavals. On the contrary—in order to keep a society in a state of permanent malleability, its psychological tensions would have to be diverted in various ways. One of these might be cruelty. Indeed, it has been said that the satisfaction of humanity's aggressive impulses is more dangerous today than at any other period. A man who in normal circumstances is satisfied with slamming a door, can today, by making use of the means put at his command by one or another ideology, completely destroy a city, a province. Man is not more cruel today than before, but he possesses greater technical means for exercising cruelty. Individual action—whether for good or for evil—can reach farther, just as publicity in the functions of government, with the vast sounding-box of public opinion behind it, can—likewise for good or for evil—produce a great disproportion between action and result; the echo of an immense public forces the adoption of slogans, attitudes, decisions aimed at satisfying its momentary whims and not directed to solving the situation under consideration. Jean Paulhan once wrote: "Men can experience an intense pleasure in cutting other men to pieces, and hence—or perhaps—in realizing that they are actually cutting them to pieces. I do not know what sort of cowardice it is that commonly leads us to conceal such an obvious fact." This is an observation that can be made in all periods, although possibly the passage cited is guilty of being one-sided; it would be equally right to say: "Men can experience intense pleasure in sacrificing themselves for others, etc." There is need here for a series of distinctions. The aggressive impulses can be considered from three points of view—psychological, technical, and historico-social. The last two are those that concern us here. Thus, we regard collective massacres, mass barbarism, as a social phenomenon, conditioned by history. This clarifies facts that are otherwise opaque—for example that certain political methods of unparalleled cruelty have been adopted or put into execution by psychologically sensitive people. And, inversely, that humanitarian policies have been directed by psychologically brutal men.

The step from the "few" to the "many" and from the "many" to "all" has not only sociological implications, but also (and increasingly) demographic implications. The population of the planet—which had not risen above twenty millions six millennia before our era—reached scarcely half a billion in the middle of the seventeenth century, rose above a billion in the middle of the nineteenth century, above a billion and a half at the beginning of the present century, and above two and a half billion in the middle of it. This rhythm of growth shows no sign of diminishing, for the rate of increase is itself increasing. In view of this, the figures should soon attain staggering proportions—it is expected that by 1980 the world population will be four billions. Particularly spectacular increases are expected in India and China—the latter is to rise rapidly from its present population of six hundred millions to a billion.

The massive application of curative and preventive medicine, the rise in the standard of living in ever wider areas, go far to explain this increase, which coincides with an increase in normal life expectancy. But the former increase would be inconceivable were it not also furthered by the dissemination of all the techniques that result from the expansion of "industrial society"—the same "industrial society" which, as Raymond Aron (*Preuves*, 63, May 1956, p. 16) points out, has also fathered socialism and capitalism, state intervention and free enterprise, the great human concentrations of Detroit and Billancourt, of Moscow and Coventry. Now, all this raises two serious problems. One is the problem of the "natural" limitations that can be imposed on this growth. The other is that of the "spiritual" limitations. The two problems are, of course, intimately connected.

The "natural" limitations derive from the fact that the resources now available (area of cultivated or cultivable ground, sources of energy in course of exploitation) are inadequate for a population that is increasing in geometrical proportion. In addition, some of the sources of energy—and not the least important ones for the present structure of industrial civilization, such as coal and oil—are already showing signs of becoming exhausted. To meet this problem, two types of measures have been suggested. One type operates through diminution or "malthusianism" (birth control or planned parenthood; a more careful exploitation or use of raw materials). The other operates through expansion (continuation of the increase in population; search for new sources of food—cultivation of certain species of algae, production of synthetic foods for direct or indirect consumption; search for new sources of energy—solar, nuclear, etc.; attempts to find less wasteful conversions—direct conversion of radiation to electricity). The proponents of the first type of solutions believe that there are limits beyond which the growth of the world population cannot go, and further, that such limits have nearly been reached. The proponents of the second type of solutions assert that there is no limit in sight, since the technical possibilities for discoveries and exploitation are practically infinite. In our opinion, both schools err, the one by not going far enough, the other by going too far. The upholders of "malthusianism" neglect the fact that increases in population are not in themselves catastrophic and that, on the contrary, they can in many cases develop possibilities thus far unsuspected (one of the sources of energy being, without any doubt, "human energy"). The fanatics of expansion fail to understand that the process of expansion does not obey the law "the more, the better," and that an expansion that does not frequently and prudently pause to restore its own equilibrium is simply cutting its own throat. Self-restorations of equilibrium are, fortunately, not mere wishful thinking. It has been noticed that the most economically developed and technically capable human groups are those that most easily self-regulate their demographic growth, yet without necessarily initiating descending curves. "Self-regulation" consists, therefore, in a constantly flexible equilibrium between possibilities and realities (thus, the United States today self-regulates its demographic process through a decided "expansionist" tendency). There are plenty of examples; northern Italy maintains a demographic equilibrium that southern Italy lacks and will lack for some time; the United States, Western Europe, and the Soviet Union exhibit an equilibrium—which is actually expansive—that is not to be found in many areas of South America, in North Africa, or in India.

The solution of the problem of the "spiritual" limitations is, in part, dependent upon geographical conditions; not only is population density very unevenly distributed over the surface of the planet, but the great demographic explosions are also very unevenly distributed. On the one hand, as has frequently been observed (see, for example, André Siegfried, *Aspects du vingtième siècle*, Paris, 1955), this can produce dangerous "pressures," political crises that constantly threaten to engender conflicts which may be localizable but which may become general. On the other hand, it produces "cultural crises" that give rise to innumerable phenomena of fanaticism, or, as the case may be, of eradication. From this point of view too, the problem is to discover how and in what proportion "all" can, as we hope, rise to the level long reserved for the "many" or the "few."

The so greatly deplored popularization of culture that occurs in the moments of transition described in the text is not confined to literary-humanistic culture. In our period we can observe an

alarming debasement in the popularization of science. It appears
in two forms. The first is a superstition of science, to which all
kinds of possibilities are attributed, even those that are contrary
to scientific language and take no account of the "postulates of
impotence" or the "principles of impotence" of which several
scientists have written (see Edmund Whittaker, *From Euclid to
Eddington,* Cambridge [1949]; George Thomson, *The Foreseeable Future,* Cambridge [1955]). The second takes the form of
the science fiction. Under the term "science fiction," we do not,
however, refer to the type of literature that Jules Verne exemplified in his day, nor even to the scientifico-social anticipations of
H. G. Wells. Verne and Wells worked in the nineteenth-century
atmosphere of "healthy progress"; only in the latter of the two
(for example, in *The Island of Dr. Moreau*) are there some
touches of "decadence," of the mixing of human with subhuman.
The science fiction of today, on the other hand, save for some
honorable exceptions (Ray Bradbury, Robert Heinlein, and a few
others), is only a caricature of the "scientific imagination"; it is a
peculiar mixture of perversity and ingenuousness. Thus it represents the "scientific" counterpart to "literary garbage." In it we
see the most banal love adventures taking place between beings
who spend their time traveling from planet to planet; in it we
discover the existence of fantastic underground races who come
up at night to suck the blood of the humans (Wells had something of the sort in his *Time Machine,* but he still managed to
keep his book an instrument of "social criticism"). Some of the
current science fiction writers are careful to conform to so-called
"scientific probability," but this does not prevent them from con-
structing any and every human improbability on the basis of it.
Others mix together all kinds of improbabilities, and add large
amounts of bad taste—and we get "Superman." In addition,
movies and television multiply these images. Thus science—
perfectly healthy in itself—can be turned into a poison. The
dozens of pseudo-scientific magazines that flourish throughout
the world, and the hundreds of no less pseudo-scientific films
that are shown everywhere, contribute to the above process.

The interdependence of every point on the planet in respect to
every other has often been emphasized in recent times. Three
quotations will serve as examples. In his *Regards sur le monde
actuel,* Paris (1931; English translation by Francis Scarfe, *Reflec-*

tions on the World Today, London [1951]), Paul Valéry wrote: "Until now, all policies used to speculate on *the isolation of events.* History used to consist of events which could be *localized.* Any disturbance at a particular point of the globe used to develop as though in unbounded space; at a sufficient distance it was devoid of effects. . . . That age is drawing to an end." In his *Ursprung und Ziel der Geschichte,* Zürich (1949; English translation by Michael Bullock, *The Origin and Goal of History,* New Haven [1953]), Karl Jaspers wrote: "Technology has brought about the unification of the globe by making possible a hitherto unheard of speed of communications." Hence "the history of the one humanity has begun." In his *La generación del noventa y ocho,* Madrid (1945), Pedro Laín Entralgo writes: "For my part, I believe that a truly universal history did not begin to exist before the World Wars of 1914 and 1939; and above all until, for the purposes of the latter, the fate of the inhabitants of Tibet or of Timbuctoo depended on a military action carried out on the Elbe or the Oder."–The quotation concerning the "crystallization" of the historical European "eruption" into nations comes from General Charles de Gaulle's book, *Vers l'armée de métier,* Paris (1934), 80; English translation: *The Army of the Future,* New York (1941). A. Weber also discusses "national crystallizations" (*Nationale Kristallisationen*), pp. 344-355, in the book mentioned in the note at the end of Chapter 8.– For the reference to Groethuysen, see the book by him cited in the notes to the preceding chapter.–The idea of "overcoming the Enlightenment" by "complete freedom of spirit" comes from Nietzsche, *Götzendämmerung* (*The Twilight of the Idols*), sect. 49.–The book of Spencer's to which we have chiefly referred is *The Man versus the State,* New York (1884), often reprinted.– For the reference to Guizot, see his *Histoire de la civilization en Europe, depuis la chute de l'empire romain, jusqu'à la révolution française,* Paris (1828), frequently reprinted. This work was translated into English as early as 1837, with the title, *The History of Civilization from the Fall of the Roman Empire to the French Revolution,* and has also been often reprinted.

11. Contemporary Society

Difficulty of the subject.–Possible questions.–Our choice: I. The problem of technique; II. The problem of the organization of society; III. The problem of the salvation of the individual and the search for an absolute.

I

Technique: its role in modern society.–Technique as the "Spirit of the Age."
Intellection and manipulation of reality: mysticism and mechanism.–The problem of the invasion of techniques. –Criticism of technique: sound and unsound arguments.
Technique and society.–Manipulation of machines and manipulation of men.–"Human Technique" in East and West.–The ultimate justification for technique.

II

Organization of society and renewal of the individual: their mutual implication.–Present problems of social organization: their urgency and magnitude.
The possibilities for organization.–False solutions.– From laissez-faire to planning: the various meanings of the latter.–The essential conditions for the coexistence of planning and freedom.–Economic problems: capital-

ism and communism.–Profound freedoms and peripheral freedoms.

Individual and society.–The function of "Nonconformity": individual thought and social structure.–Individual, mass, and group.–The internally differentiated society.–Possibilities and realities in human society.

The role of the "intelligentsia" in society: struggle or adaptation.–Greatness and servitude of the "intelligentsia."

III

The individual problem: the individual and the absolute.–The question of loss of faith: faith, scepticism, and "the divided consciousness."

Genuine faith and spurious faith.–Faith and fanaticism.–Faith and arguments.–Faith, belief, and truth.

The question of faith in contemporary man.–Absence of faith: reasons for it.–Insecurity and rootlessness.–The world of the absurd.–Rationality and irrationality.–Incongruity between belief and experience.

Presence of faith: reasons for it.–Ambivalence of the absolute.–From rootlessness to hope.

The solutions proposed: false solutions and genuine solutions.–Conditions for genuineness: universality, truth, humanity.–Transcendence and immanence of the absolute.–The four absolutes and the necessity for balance between them.–The basic question: the renewal of the individual man and of all men.–Conditions for renewal. –The forging of the future society, an infinite task.

Unfortunately, the reflections promised at the end of the previous chapter cannot be very orderly. In order to sketch the outlines of a historical period, various conditions are requisite: that the period be ended; that it be far enough from us for the details to have become blurred, the contradictions softened. . . . None of these conditions are fulfilled in the world in which we live. What can we say about this world that will not prove to be vague generalizations or commonplace recordings of fact? And yet we must orient ourselves to some extent in the labyrinth of the present. Let us enter it then—but cautiously, conscious that we are walking on uncertain ground. Such is always the case when prophecy is not allowed to usurp the place of history.

The first difficulty that we encounter appears as soon as we try to circumscribe the problems to be raised. What are we to discuss? Shall it be the formation of the contemporary super-States, products of a vast industrial, military, and political revolution, in the course of which certain empires fall and others rise, yet not without the victors being forced to adopt many characteristics of the vanquished? Shall it be the continuous social upheavals that are the result not only of the important historical role played by the proletariat but also of the "proletarization" of vast groups of humanity? Shall it be the steadily increasing influence of new techniques on the organization of human societies? Or the discrepancy, so often remarked, between material progress and moral progress, or between technical developments and political organization? Shall it be the different ways of life? Shall it be the death struggle, and sometimes the interpenetration, between different ideologies? Or perhaps the resounding explosions of all kinds of irrationalistic tendencies? Any of these subjects would suffice for an entire book. What, then, might not be the result if we tried to bring them all together into a systematic outline? We could attempt it, but we fear that it would be at the sacrifice of essential aspects; an investigation into the "foundations" of contemporary man and contemporary society would probably lead to a series of vague statements. No doubt the use of certain key terms—such as "individualism" or "collectivism," "intellectualism" or "voluntarism," "immanentism" or "transcendentalism"—would help us to some extent. But we distrust these terms, waiting for the time when they will become fully meaningful. For the moment, it will suffice to attack the problem raised by contemporary society by choosing certain themes which leave the reader's mind open to subsequent reflections.

We shall choose three themes: technique, the organization of society, and the search for an "absolute." The examination of these themes will imply an analysis of the most important material, social, and human problems raised during the twentieth century. The analysis of the "human problems" will, in addition, give us the opportunity to say something about a fact that many "progressives" have neglected and that many "traditionalists" have misinterpreted: the fact that the individual man is not a self-contained entity, and that it is only when he sets out to conceive of himself in terms of another and higher reality, that he can fulfil his mission *as an individual*.

I

In the preceding chapter we have already emphasized the impact of technique on modern society. What is happening today in the field of technique is, after all, the result of the technical developments which have taken place during the last two centuries. But here, too, the quantitative factor is so basic that an examination of the technical progress experienced by men during the last fifty years gives the impression that there has been a sudden "leap." Particularly during the last decade technical developments have reached such a height that some people think that present-day technique will never be surpassed. In any case, even if in future nothing further were done than to exploit the technical possibilities now open, technical progress today would be beyond comparison with that of any other period of Western history. This fact has made room for the usual mixture of hopes and fears, with the latter notoriously predominating. In exceeding all measures, does not technique exceed the measure of humanity? This is the first and most serious problem raised by contemporary technique. The role played by technique in our every day life seems to obscure all other issues; technique appears to have become the *Zeitgeist* itself, the "spirit of the age."

Nor is this all. The astonishing development of technique has fundamentally changed the very structure and function of science. One of the characteristics of Western society has been said to be its "activism." This "activism" is probably deep-rooted; it has been maintained that it is chiefly derived from the ideals fostered by Christianity, and that, in any case, it has largely contributed to distinguishing Western man at all periods from "Eastern man." Even if we accept this view, we must not forget the goals usually set by Western man when he has cultivated science. Thus during the seventeenth century pure theoretical aims still predominated in scientific activity. Practice was not overlooked: Galileo learned a great deal from walking about among pulleys; Francis Bacon insisted upon the urgency of building machines; all the European scientists of the same period devoted a great part of their time to experimentation, to building new instruments, to solving practical problems. But, compared with our period, the seventeenth century gives the impression of being outstandingly "theoretical." Hence at the present time scientific activity seems to have ceased to be a *modus intelligendi* and to have become instead a *modus operandi*. The decisive step has been taken—to contemporary man, science appears to be primarily a set of prodigious technical achievements.

To understand how great the above difference is, let us compare the present idea of knowledge with the idea of knowledge that reached its fullest development in the twelfth century, at the height of the Middle Ages. "The first light, then, since it enlightens the mind for an appreciation of the *arts and crafts*, which are, as it were, exterior to man and intended to supply the needs of the body, is called the light of *mechanical skill*. Being, in a certain sense, servile and of a lower nature than philosophical knowledge, this light can rightly be termed *external*." Thus St. Bonaventura, in his *De reductione artium ad theologiam*. We could cite many other examples. All would confirm our ideas. Certainly St. Bonaventura's ideals have not entirely vanished. Some people still think that it would be proper to follow the medieval ideals about the degrees of knowledge: First, theology; second, philosophy; last, technique. In addition, pure science today still manifests itself vigorously. But it does so only among minorities; it is not the *aspect* that science presents to the ordinary man, as, in the Middle Ages, knowledge appeared to him under the form of theology. The medieval common man did not know what theology was about, but he regarded it with reverence. Therefore, there has been a "leap" not only from the predominance of contemplation to that of action, but also from the predominance of inward action to that of outward action. The latter is no longer conceived as a manifestation of the former. Thus, to use Bergson's terminology, mechanism now predominates over mysticism. Instead of the combination of higher and inner light, there is a combination of lower and outer light, of sensory knowledge and technique. We are not making value judgments here; we confine ourselves to description. Thus technique today has changed in two ways. First, technique has changed in quantity. Second, it has changed in function. What we are left with, then, is the problem of the human attitude toward technique, which has truly become an essential factor in our life.

Is this a gain? Is it a loss? Again hundreds of voices are prepared to discuss the subject. We say "again"; for even before the Industrial Revolution began, there was a great deal of argument for and against technique. The question of mechanization became a great question. The almost unshakable optimism and confidence in the benefits of applied science which predominated through a considerable part of the eighteenth century, was replaced by a spirit of pessimism and revulsion. This raised many problems. "Should production be regulated from within?" "Should it be left to its own devices?" "Should agriculture have the first claim on our attention?" "Should free trade between colonies be stimulated?" All these questions soon affected large numbers of men, and considerable areas of everyday life. In the nineteenth century especially, the debates over the problems raised by mechanization were extremely lively. All sorts of solutions were proposed; to encourage, to abolish, to regulate mechanization were some of the proposals made in this respect. It soon became apparent that the "problem of the machine" implied the "problem of society"; both "humanistic" economists, such as Le Play, and revolutionary economists, such as Marx, agreed upon the fact that the meaning of the terms "mechanization" and "society" could not be analyzed separately. In short, it was agreed that the problem of mechanization could not be solved merely in its own terms; it was the very structure of society which must change in some fashion, whether peacefully or violently. Thenceforth the problem of technique remained bound up with the problem that we shall soon treat under the name of "organization."

The above discussions still go on in our time. A very common attitude is one of pessimism. Thousands of pages have been devoted to demonstrating the evils of technique. Most authors differ from the criticisms voiced in the nineteenth century in that they no longer see a reform of society as a way out. In his book on "the failure of technology," Juenger suggests that it makes no difference whether a society is capitalistic or socialistic in structure. Both can be transformed into "technocratic" communities; hence both are powerless to rid themselves of the "evils of technique." For the true root of the evil, says Juenger, is not social but purely human. It is the recoil caused by a "purposeless perfection," which ends in a complete reduction of human beings to the status of mere "things." Carried away by techniques, we seem to have now become incapable of entering into direct relations not only with our fellow men but also with things themselves. Today this situation has even reached certain comic extremes. Many caricaturists are beginning to depict the new extravagances of our period—the man who, his eyes glued to his television set, sees on the screen the same spectacle that is taking place in the street outside his window. Impressions received from the outside world end by seeming vaguely fraudulent. We could go on in this vein and rehearse all the well-known commonplaces—the impossibility of withdrawing into privacy, the continual and insupportable pressures from our surroundings, and so on. Many of these observations describe very faithfully the facts. But we do not see any good reason for assuming that mechanization or technique is the only source of these "evils." To adopt this viewpoint would, in addition, be to fall into the paradoxical iconoclasm of those who, while they denounce technique, make all the use of it they can. Laundromats certainly prevent us from doing our washing at the riverside and enjoying the shade of the poplars. But washing at the riverside does not consist entirely in enjoying the delights of shade. The telephone invades the home. But the privacy of one's home is also made possible, thanks to the telephone. The radio and television disturb us. But no one is obliged to keep the switch on continuously. Advertisements, slogans, formulas repeated to satiety stupefy us, mechanize us, disgust us. It is no less true that many of our contemporaries profit from them. True, the proliferation of techniques can make it possible for man to live not only *among* things but *by* them. But there must be some ingrained tendency in man to succumb to "things," to account for the lightning rapidity with which mechanization has spread in human society. This fact links the problem of technique with those that are to be treated hereafter—with the question of the organization of society and of the "salvation" of the person.

It is not befitting to solve the problems raised by the predominance of technique in contemporary society by simply going back to a pre-technical past. As has often been said, technique, at the same time that it can "dehumanize" man can also offer the possibility for the attainment of a greater freedom in man's existence. As a result of technique, we can be hopeful that one day man will cease to be exploited by man. Now, to attain this end, we must clearly see that technique cannot be its own motive force. Human affairs cannot entirely be solved either by machines or by those who direct them—the "technocracy." For technocracy has a strong tendency to technicize not only the means of which man makes use, but also man himself. In sober truth, the dangers of mechanization are small, in comparison with those represented by the indiscriminate introduction of techniques into human affairs. Thus the real danger is not the misuse of machines, but misuse of the technical manipulation of men. We refer here to some of the "scientifico-social" artifices that are currently employed to organize society and justified by the frequently alleged comparison between the functioning of society and of the machine. In this respect, too, our own period is incommensurable with all others. It has been said that ours is the age of nuclear energy. It can also be said that it is the age of the electronic brain. And perhaps one day cybernetics will be even more omnipresent in human life than nuclear physics. We are then faced with a most serious problem. For here, too, no going back will help us. To make a clean sweep of technique for manipulating men would be no proper solution. Like mechanical technique, social technique becomes essential when society grows complex and presents problems incommensurable with those that arise when it is composed of only a few individuals. A French political scientist, Maurice Duverger, has said that the so-called advantage of Russia over the West does not lie in the fact that Soviet man has a faith and that Westerners have none. After all, this absence of all faith in the one camp—and the corresponding omnipresence of it in the other—is quite open to question. The advantage, if it exists, Duverger writes, lies in the fact that the Russians apply a technique of human manipulation from which the West for ethical reasons abstains. Now, the fact is that the West too employs many human techniques—and not only in the widely discussed proposals of the technocrats and in the process of "human engineering," which some interpret as the application of the scientific spirit to human society, and others as the last stronghold of capitalism. We can even say that the West has *always* employed techniques of human manipulation. Only those who have chosen to pass through the "strait gate," those who have lived in accordance with resistance to the State— the "monastics"—have partially escaped such techniques. But there is some truth in Duverger's thesis. How, then, are we to solve our problem without falling into an ineffectual nostalgia for an uncertain past, which—without anyone's bothering to go into details—is vaguely declared to have been paradisiacal?

There is only one solution. It consists in always connecting the problem of technique with the other problems mentioned, thus avoiding any one-sided solution. Above all, it consists in realizing that the right solution can never be given by devoting ourselves exclusively to manipulating things, and that any such manipulation will prove unfruitful unless we try at the same time to understand the nature and the meaning of the things we manipulate. Theory, in short, must never be replaced entirely by practice. In fact, the dehumanization of human existence through technique may arise only when technique has not the constant support of the objective intelligence that has produced science and philosophy. After all, this intelligence possesses a characteristic that makes it quite human: it can understand its own limitations. Thanks to this fact, man is able to use technique without misusing it. Which is another way of abiding by the ancient, and often neglected, rule: Render unto Caesar that which is Caesar's, and unto God that which is God's.

II

The problems raised by technique have led us to touch more than once upon the question of the organization of human society.

It appears to be *the* question of our age. It has sometimes been contended that an answer to this question must be found *either* through the renewal of the inner man *or* through a collective change. Those who favor the former solution are faced with serious obstacles. Unless they equate "human society" with "a community of saints," they have to pay attention to the relation, not only inner but outer, between different persons. In their turn, those who expect everything from a change in the structure of society forget that, if man is reduced entirely to his social function, there is no way of really improving the human condition. In view of all this, it must be admitted that the two solutions imply each other; no change in the structure of society is feasible without a change in the person, and vice versa. Hence, in investigating the theme of "organization," we shall also, by implication, treat that of the "salvation of the individual."

It is a commonplace to say that human society must be organized. The question, however, is *how* should it be organized. Now, just as in the matter of technique, our period differs from others in respect to the problem of the organization of society. The difference lies not in the nature of the problem itself, but in its magnitude: never before have so many problems of human organization arisen with such force. Obviously, it was no small matter to organize Egyptian society, or the Roman or the Inca empires, or, on another level, the empire of the "Golden Horde." But, within the arduous problems inherent in all these cultures, there were certain "advantages," which we lack or of which we cannot avail ourselves. Egyptian society or the Inca empire dealt with the matter of organization by almost completely closing their respective communities. Especially in the latter instance, the regimentation appeared to be complete. The Mongol empire solved the problem by allowing the greater part of its components—not only individuals but groups—to remain "loose." Both erred—the one through going too far, the other by not going far enough. The problem of the structure of the Roman empire was less easy to solve; perhaps this explains the fact that the solutions were extremely flexible and ingenious, to the extent that some of them have remained alive down to the present. But when we reach our own epoch, all earlier problems, serious though they were, lose some of their virulence. For we are called upon to organize a series of large societies, and, in addition, to do it in such a way that the organization of each of them represents the annihilation neither of its members nor of the remaining societies. It is a baffling problem. Our first reaction to it may well be: it is unsolvable.

The tendency to interdependence between all the countries of our planet is not one of the least embarrassing factors in our problem. How are orbits so complex to be harmonized? Let us not be seduced by the apocalyptic idea that everything will be solved when one society finally imposes itself on all the others, unifying the world by fire and sword. These more or less Spenglerian notions are merely the product of wrath, despair, and, of course, fanaticism. Germany dreamed of an *Imperium mundi*, but such an empire was supposed to be ruled by zoological laws rather than by historical laws. Whatever type of society in the long run imposes itself on great masses, it will have to do so, then, in the name of all human beings, not in that of some allegedly privileged race. Unspeakable designs can certainly be concealed under the expression "in the name of all human beings." It is none the less certain that even such designs must adopt today a "convincing" terminology. Hence the problem of organizing contemporary society cannot be solved through the formation of an *Imperium* of the traditional type. The answer to the problem is more complex. It demands the fulfilment of three conditions. First, the organization of society must set out from a certain clearly acknowledged tendency toward a world unification of such a nature that it does not prevent the survival of a great variety of ways of life. Second, if it is to achieve lasting success, organization cannot be understood one-sidedly, as a mere "mechanical" or "organic" arrangement. Third, however great and powerful the organization achieved, it must not destroy the very bases which make it possible. This last condition—which we have consciously expressed somewhat vaguely—presupposes that the problem of organization is always connected with the question of the "salvation of the individual." It is only in order to simplify the exposition that we treat the two subjects separately.

Everybody in this day and age agrees not only that society has to be organized but also that, for better or worse, it is already organized. Otherwise it could not survive even for an instant. It even appears that society organizes itself "naturally" and adapts itself, more or less efficiently, to the requirements imposed by its continual assimilation of new elements. It might, then, appear that the problem should not too greatly concern us; many changes can be made in details, but not in the whole. There is some truth in this assumption, so much as consists in admitting that society must either organize itself or perish. But let us not fall into the biologistic fallacy. Society *can* organize itself, but it *can* likewise let itself disintegrate. If it dies, it is not from "exhaustion," and if it survives, it is not always from "vitality." Its destiny depends greatly upon the actions of men. The modern period is in this respect very illuminating. It was not inevitable that Western society should have solved the vast problem of the ceaseless incorporation of new elements in the way it did. It could perfectly well have closed itself too soon—or it could close itself too late. In the first case, it would have paralyzed itself; in the second, it would dissolve. Down to the present, then, the modern period has solved the problem; it has understood that Western society could be neither a "community of saints" nor an "association of termites." It is the same problem that, greatly magnified, and including the entire world in its scope, confronts us today. Society cannot exist in a continual openness, ready to receive and assimilate *any* element. Nor yet can it exist entirely closed, ready to reject *any* element. Well and good, it will be said; there you have the solution—to live between open and closed, between mysticism and mechanics. We accept the solution. But even to do so, is to have said next to nothing. Unless it be filled with content, it is in danger of becoming a purely formal solution.

For what today makes the question of the organization of society more acute than ever before is not only the vast number of humans living in this society. We must also consider certain other factors—the accelerating tempo at which problems arise, the apparent inevitability of some of the solutions given. Besides, no one can deny that the anxieties of our period are largely due to the fact that, as Karl Mannheim pointed out, "we are living in a period of transition from laissez-faire to a planned society." The recognition of this fact leads many to a fatalistic attitude that is decidedly dangerous. Some, for example, think: Society has no way out but to organize itself; furthermore, it must organize itself solidly. Do what we will, we shall find ourselves saddled with types of society in which any organization will lead to a rigid social hierarchy. The name does not matter—perhaps these types of society will be called democratic, fascist, communist. Or perhaps they will have some other name; James Burnham, for example, has said that the world will not jump from capitalism to socialism but will arrive at a "managerial" regime, at a new form of technocracy. In consequence, freedom will disappear, crushed by what ought to support it: organization. The only thing to do is to find some individual solution—why not revive contempt or resignation or flight? Examination of the rhythm of history confirms these pessimistic views. Until now, we are told, Western society has found various ways of stabilizing itself without closing itself completely. So far it has avoided stagnation, that is, progressive paralysis of its members, and, finally, of the entire body social. This was because Western society "had time," so to speak; because though problems pressed upon it, they did not suffocate it. But the West has also been increasingly dynamic. It has continuously thrown off models of life. The desire for originality, the will to create, the urge to express individuality have been the blaze which has constantly kindled our civilization. Now, never before has it reached our frenzied, runaway speed. The tempo that governs the present historical rhythm is bound to increase to the point of delirium. Hence, in order to integrate itself with the entire planet, the West must find modes of stabilization that conform to the new situation. By the same token, those who hold this view conclude, there is nothing to do but to find—and find at once—a means of closing our society, *by whatever method*. It is impossible to continue in the "critical" process of unending "dissolution." Thus far the arguments, in which both "traditionalists" and many new "progressives" concur. In consequence, it is inferred, all the disadvantages that may arise for the individual in the future, and that we so greatly fear, are merely the result of a "natural" process. There is nothing we can do, we are told, but to make our choice—either in favor of continual novelty, perpetual stimulation, which lead to disintegration, or in favor of habit, discipline, repetition, which are the basis of stability. The latter choice is the one that the present situation "imposes." Hence there is a ceaseless search for different ways of stabilizing the restlessness of contemporary society. Stabilization, some people think, cannot be avoided or even modified.

True enough, the transition from laissez-faire to planning is inevitable, together with the fact that it must be understood in a broader sense than the purely economic. But it is not inevitable that the transition will bring about a complete closing of our society, with the consequent risk of a paralysis. Karl Mannheim made this point perfectly clear. To plan is not necessarily an evil. Everything depends on how and for what we plan—whether for variety or for monotony, for freedom or for slavery. It will seem a paradox to say that we can plan for freedom and variety. And, certainly, there are many incompatibilities between freedom and planning. But there are not as many as is supposed. In fact, planning *can* be the basis of freedom. We often take it for granted that planning strangles freedoms hitherto regarded as essential. But we must be cautious on this point. In the seventeenth century, Europe did not enjoy certain freedoms that later flourished. Yet it would have been considered a drastic attack on freedom to call up the men of the national community for compulsory military service—a service which it has since even been possible to regard as an evidence of a free society. Will not the same happen tomorrow in respect to certain "attacks on freedom" which today seem scandalous to us? So let us not confuse human freedom—the almost sacred freedom of the person—with changing and peripheral freedoms. The demands of organization—including "organization for freedom"—may require our setting aside some of these accidental freedoms, at the same time that we exercise the utmost care not to trample upon our essential freedoms—the "rights of man." The reader is asked to reflect for a moment on what would happen in the world today if an attempt were made to loosen the bonds of organization in too great measure. To say that disorder would ensue would be inadequate; what would descend upon us would be rather pure chaos. For when we are dealing with vast human masses, on whom it is wished—and rightly—to confer an acceptable minimum standard of living, the problems to be faced cannot be equated with those that arise in small societies. Let us take as an example an obvious and momentous problem: the economic question. How much planning will it require to attain some social justice—to attain, for example, an even comparatively just distribution of raw materials, an equilibrium in industrialization between different countries? Such a planning need not be based on inequality; no responsible economist today would affirm that the efficient operation of world economy demands the coexistence of privileged and underprivileged groups. Under the technical conditions of earlier periods, it was even possible to hold that the personal freedom of a few actually depended on the slavery of many. This was said, almost in so many words, by Aristotle. Similar views were urged by certain inhabitants of modern Europe when the process of colonization was set in motion. We reject these views. They are morally unacceptable and, in addition, they are today ineffectual. It is not necessary, for example, that the industrialization of the greater part of the globe (with a corresponding intensification of agriculture) should produce crises, struggles, upheavals, for the standard of living can still be greatly raised for all men. The great problem, then, is whether or not we really will know how to make proper use of the available resources and give the vast masses on this planet the standard of living that has until now been enjoyed only by minorities.

Planning cannot, therefore, be regarded as an end, but only as a means. When it is treated as an end, society appears to find stability, "salvation." But this proves to be an ephemeral illusion.

The mechanization of the individual, the identification of man with his social function destroy the possibilities for renewal without which society cannot long subsist. No society, in fact, can live if its possibilities are strangled. It can perhaps manage to function perfectly. But it will be functioning in a void. Planning for planning's sake—just as a total lack of planning—will bring chaos. At first it will not be an "external" chaos. But sooner or later, external chaos will come. Those who manage to delay its arrival will have to make all kinds of sacrifices in order to survive; they will have to close not only the present and the future but even the past; they will have to come to the point of "absolute totalitarianism." History itself, which is not only a force for stagnation but can also be a force for renewal, will have to be modified, if not destroyed. The resulting "perfect" but purposeless organization will, then, be organization for the absolute present. Mankind will live without future, because it will have previously eliminated all past.

We do not deny the fact that organization, and organization on a grand scale, is today more necessary than ever. Otherwise, how is man to be freed from countless servitudes? If everyone had to spend his life in insecurity, engrossed in solving all sorts of problems—material and spiritual—life would be unbearable. Absolute freedom would coincide with absolute slavery. "Society," through its organization, frees men from these servitudes. Thus we could draw the conclusion: the more planning, the more freedom. But, in doing so, we should disregard an important fact—the fact that when planning infiltrates the *entire* human being, the process of liberation is interrupted, changes direction, and goes into reverse. To express this—merely as an example —in figures: it is possible that, with 99% of human life subjected to planning, the remaining 1% will be liberated for a pure and concentrated freedom. Freedom will be reduced to a minimum. But at certain moments such a reduction is necessary in order that what remains free shall really be so. Now let us imagine that even this very small zone is in turn invaded by planning, that the entire 100% is now planned. Then not only is there no question of any planning for freedom, but all planning will be for slavery. In view of this consequence, some have thought that the best procedure would be to do away with all planning, all organization. This latter view is no less misleading than its opposite.

Since, however, it has few supporters, we shall continue turning our attention to the former. This is the view that has found expression in many social theories developed since the beginnings of the Industrial Revolution. Paradoxically, both communism and supercapitalism have been in agreement on this view of planning to the limit. Both have set out from the same supposition—that man and his social function are equivalent. Lenin once said that "socialism is the Soviets plus electrification." It is not long before action—and even thought—proceed as if only the latter of the two ingredients mattered. Technocrats of various schools all agree that there is no reason for leaving a single inch of human activity to chance. In principle, to be sure, this applies only to production. But very soon it is the turn of consumption, and of all the ways of life that consumption determines, from the most frivolous and peripheral to the deepest and most important. Thus a moment can arrive when the limit becomes blurred. But this is precisely the point that we wished to bring out, and that we shall express in the formula: "In planning there must always be a limit."

Thus the problem of the organization of society once again touches that of the individual or, better, that of the person. The person imposes the final limit. But, with this, we have introduced an ethical and even metaphysical concept, which perhaps not everybody will accept. Of what concern is the person to us, some will say, when all that we set out to achieve is the highest efficiency of human society? We accept the challenge and suppose for the moment that we should only be concerned with what advantages will accrue to the organization of society by carrying this organization to the extreme. Even then great caution is necessary. For let us imagine that we have actually solved all the problems of social organization, that all the members of the society are now perfectly adjusted to its structure. This means that all those who have resisted adjustment will have been considered either criminal or abnormal. They will have had either to cease to exist or to readjust to society. In the latter case, readjustment can have been effected in various ways: by "indoctrination," by the "liberation" of complexes that prevented complete adaptation to the social milieu, by "habituation" through a series of conditioned reflexes. All the psycho-social techniques will have contributed to the process. So here at last we have society, thoroughly organized. And it runs like clockwork. Well—but will this be good for society itself? Apparently, the answer is affirmative. By the terms of our hypothesis, solutions having been found for all the troublesome problems formerly raised by the existence of the individual, with his personal life and his sometimes "antisocial" leanings, what can stop us? But the matter is not so simple as is supposed. For the proposed solution would have been attained *only if society were exclusively* a reality and not also a certain number of possibilities. Now, the latter are essential to society if it is to continue functioning in the future. A society each of whose members was completely adjusted would be a society made up of pure "realities," a wholly closed society, valid for a particular historical moment, which would become an "eternity." To avoid consequence, it is necessary that the society contains a certain proportion of "nonconformity." This ingredient must not be abused, for nonconformity is in much the same case as freedom—too much of it or too little of it is dangerous. Naturally, the right proportion of nonconformity varies according to circumstances. No rigid doctrine can be proposed on this point. But the interesting thing about this aspect of the question is that it is not confined to the relation between the individual and society, but extends to the relation between groups inside of society. Until now we have constantly used such terms as "society," "incorporation of masses," etc. This does not imply that we have neglected the distinction—now classical in sociology—between "mass" and "group." We implicitly took it into account in our chapter on "The Powerful," when we brought out the difference between an amorphous society and a flexible society. The same thing holds true now. One of the problems raised by the necessity for organization consists precisely in the transformation of masses into groups, and, after this process is accomplished, in spiritual and material integration between groups. Now, these processes can be carried out in two very different ways. On the one hand, they can be realized in the service of a dominant group, or else for the entire collectivity, but regarded as an internally undifferentiated entity. On the other hand, they can be brought about for the entire collectivity considered as an internally differentiated society, not after the fashion of an organism, but in the way in which things occur, or should occur, in a "community of persons," in which each member is at once incommunicable and essentially communicative, is at the service of society and at the same time recognizes each person as an end in itself. The latter course is the one that we here propose as the most plausible one—*and even as the most efficient one.* In any case—provided there is any intention that society shall evolve, that is, "progress"—the integration of groups must leave a sufficient margin free for the future appearance of numerous, various, and unexpected combinations. And even when this freedom in association is, under the stress of certain periods, restricted to a minimum, it must never be totally abolished, it must be preserved as a possibility that will one day be put to use. Possibilities, indeed, must be emphasized, as much as realities. For, in the last analysis, only the possibility that a society will one day be different from what it is, allows us to term it a "human society" and not a mere grouping of social functions, which could, in principle, be performed by any kind of entities—by insects or by cogwheels.

There are, of course, certain moments of history in which a number of possibilities have to be sacrificed to unavoidable realities. The area of social possibilities and personal freedoms shrinks dangerously at these times; it even seems that it will vanish entirely. It is not surprising that, in such moments, the role played by the "intelligentsia" markedly diminishes. Indeed, much of the greatness and misery of these periods is reflected in the fate that befalls the "intelligentsia." It is also reflected in the types of relationships that are established between the "intelligentsia" and the society to which they belong. These relationships possess a curious character; they usually oscillate between complete agreement and violent hostility. It is the latter which seems to prevail in the world today. Under these circumstances, the intelligentsia must face the situation by adopting one of two attitudes.

First, they can resolve to fight. The intelligentsia then become reformist—they are prepared *either* to propitiate change *or* to encourage adaptation. In the former case, they can become martyrs; in the latter, despots. In both cases, however, they adapt themselves to society—present or future—in such a way that they end by perishing; either they are annihilated or they annihilate themselves. Certainly, some degree of adaptation to society is necessary to the intelligentsia if they are to survive. Dilthey has rightly said that subordination of individuality to the social system is the very thing that can sometimes make the *clerc* a power. But in this there are limits. To transgress them is to incur the death sentence: the limits become blurred, but, with them, he who disregarded them vanishes too.

The other course open to the intelligentsia is to withdraw. This is a case of strategic retreat. When, that is, the intelligentsia are summoned to adapt themselves totally—in any of the directions above mentioned—they can, in order to survive, adopt a twofold position. On the one hand (the intelligentsia are "objective") they can recognize the power of reality and, hence, the necessity for submitting to it. On the other hand (the intelligentsia are clever) they can retreat from it. In the latter case, many people commonly revile them—they have, it is said, committed an act of cowardice. Now, if in individual instances there may be cowardice, an attentive examination of the whole situation shows that such a retreat is often a skilful movement. In this way the intelligentsia can even split themselves in two. They can show, and indeed vociferate, their enthusiasm for adaptation. But, while they subsist *as an intelligentsia,* they will, at bottom, maintain a certain "reservation." This reservation will be in favor of possibility, in favor of the future. And it will be precisely because of it that the intelligentsia will one day be able to exercise a beneficial influence on society. For it must not be supposed that intelligence is effective only when its influence on society is direct and visible. There are many intellectuals who, led by such a belief, end by forgetting the complexity of the relations between the force of intelligence and the force of society. Anxious to exercise influence at all costs, they conclude that they can only do so when their adaptation—to whatever type of society it may be—reaches a maximum. They are even capable of calling this attitude "realistic," without taking into account that genuine realism must consider all factors, including those that still lie in the realm of possibility. But this is a subject that would take us too far, and that, in the end, would be only apposite to our theme. We have touched it up, however, because it provides a particularly illuminating example for understanding the relation between possibilities and realities in society. Furthermore, without having such an example in mind, it will be difficult to comprehend some of the reflections that are to follow on our final theme—the theme that we have alternatively termed the "salvation of the individual" and the "desire for an absolute." It is this that binds the individual—let us take this term in a meaning similar to "person"—in an indissoluble union with that which is "above" him. More, perhaps, than the problem of technique and of organization, it is *the* real problem.

III

We are dealing with a formidably complex question. In a certain sense, it is analogous to the one discussed in Part I, under the heading "The New Man." But the obvious similarities must not lead us to think that it is the same question, solvable by the same means. If this were the case, the problem would be comparatively easy. Man, it could be said, has lost all faith. Since he cannot live happily without a considerable amount of it, the thing to do is to find a faith, new or old (in principle, then, *any* faith), which will fill the void in his life and allow him to attend to his duties without too much perturbation. Once a faith is uncovered, all of man's anxieties will vanish; instead of hesitating before committing himself to affirming anything, he will pursue his road undeviatingly. Along the way he will perhaps liquidate those of his fellows who, either from error or obstinacy, block his path. It does not matter—these slight disturbances will not be enough to dim the limpid crystal of the new faith, or of the old faith made over.

The matter, however, is far less simple than it appears to be. Above all, it is not easy to answer the question, "Has *all* mankind lost faith, and therefore stands in need of a new faith or the renovation of *the* old faith?" The answer could, with equal justification, be affirmative or negative. First, because we do not know exactly what is meant by the word "faith"—still less by "*the* faith." Second, because—supposing that we are clear on the first point—it is quite possible to find vast masses of men who have lost all faith, *and* equally vast masses who have not lost it or who have acquired a new one. Third, because it is probable that both those who have faith and those who have none manifest their possession or their lack of it ambiguously, more after the fashion of the "divided consciousness" than of the "simple peasant" or the "fearless free-thinker." It will, then, be proper to refer to all these aspects of the question and to satisfy the desire, common to us all, to cast light on such intricate matters.

Let us take up the first point. It is an overwhelming question, if it is to be examined with any degree of thoroughness. Fortunately, such a detailed examination is not necessary. It is enough if we reach comparative clarity as to the meaning of the word "faith" and if we distinguish to some extent between its genuine and its spurious varieties. The latter operation is fundamental, in view of the frequency with which in our day genuine faith is confused with purely irrational exaltation and fanaticism. This is not to say that faith is always incompatible with fanaticism. History shows that the two have frequently gone hand in hand. But if faith can be coupled with fanaticism, the latter alone is insufficient to produce faith. When we put such questions as "Does man today have faith?" "Does he need it?" we have this distinction in mind. Let us now consider this last question, which is the easiest to connect with the first of the three above-mentioned aspects of the problem of faith—the meaning of the word "faith" for contemporary man.

It is probable that man—in whatever period and region—is not satisfied with purely "external" solutions, however brilliant. Let us suppose that men have externally adapted themselves to a particular mode of society. Unless the adaptation has been such that the term "human persons" has lost all meaning, there will always be a certain dissatisfaction in the members of the society. The main source of such a dissatisfaction will be the external nature of the adaptation, for if men are not convinced that they have adapted themselves inwardly, they will hardly speak of a faith by which they live. We must, then, exclude from the meaning of the word "faith" any concept that does not refer to the fact that faith springs from the depths of the human person directly and "spontaneously." This exclusion enables us to separate the concept of faith from that of fanaticism. For if fanaticism too is "spontaneous," it is a purely "automatic" spontaneity; often it is only an attempt to free the individual from inferiority complexes. Hence fanaticism usually appears at moments when the individual is blindly immersed in a collectivity and, in the company of other individuals, does what he would not dare to do alone. At such times the violent throwing off of personal responsibility gives pure fanaticism the characteristics that have become so familiar to most of us: unbridled violence, irrational dogmatism, complete alienation of the person. It follows from all this that genuine faith must be personal in nature. But it must be also social, since the person cannot conceive of himself without a community of which he is a full member—not only a part or a function. It also follows from this that genuine faith, although itself inexplicable, is constantly seeking reasons in its own support. To be sure, the will to reason about one's own faith must not be confused with a well-known phenomenon to which we shall soon allude: reason in the service of unreason. In the latter case, reason hardly examines the irrational elements; it contents itself with manipulating them. In the former case, it tends to dissipate useless doubts and troubling obscurities.

It will now already be clear that the question "Does man need a faith?" must be answered in the affirmative, if we accept the conception of "faith" just outlined. This conception is similar in many points to the conception of "belief" as it has been developed by Ortega y Gasset. Like "belief," "faith" designates a fact upon which we count in order to make life worth living. Hence Ortega y Gasset says that a belief is something by which one lives and, *therefore,* something for which one can die. Belief is "reality itself," and not a humbug forged by reason, imagination, or desire. The belief must, therefore, be "true," that is, refer to something real. This is, of course, a very delicate point, in view of the fact that belief is often taken as the measure of truth. Thus we appear to find ourselves in a vicious circle. Let us confine ourselves, then, to assuming that belief or faith must always be intimately connected with truth. Consequently, it is impossible to accept a very common contention: That since man needs a faith, *any* faith will do, because faith does nothing but fill the void of man's existence. Faith, of course, usually appears as a psychological attitude. But it is not sufficient for faith to be a psychological attitude; what is asserted in an act of faith is also an essential ingredient of faith. We do not imply that affirmations of faith must have a very specific content. It will suffice here if we point out that there are contents that are capable of providing the "objective" basis for a faith, and others that are not. Among the former, we count four: God, man, society, and nature. None of them excludes the others, possibly each implies the others. . . . But let us leave this for later. What is important now is that the following three points be made perfectly clear. First, that, in fact, men cannot live without faith. Second, that faith cannot be "any affirmation whatever." Third, that it cannot be reduced to a merely psychological attitude.

We are now in a position to attack the second aspect of our problem—that of discovering whether contemporary man is without faith or has already found it or regained it.

The first difficulty that we encounter lies in the very form of phrasing the question. Is it legitimate, in fact, to use the term "contemporary man"? No doubt, as a result of the process of expansion and integration discussed earlier, the majority of the inhabitants of this planet are today in a similar situation. The destiny of each of them depends to a great extent upon the destiny of all, and for this reason each feels the tremendous weight of all humanity bearing down upon him. Thus the term "contemporary man" can, *grosso modo*, mean each one of the present inhabitants of the globe and at the same time all of them. Furthermore, the great ambiguity of the term "contemporary man" becomes clear as soon as we examine the answers most frequently given to the question under consideration. They can be divided into two general groups. For some, contemporary man is completely devoid of faith. For others, he possesses faith to a superlative degree. Obviously, the two answers refer to different types of men, but at the same time each answer claims to be valid for all men. Before we enter into the controversy, let us see in what the two most generally maintained opinions consist.

1. Some maintain that faith or belief has completely vanished. In proof, they cite the typical phenomenon of "uprooting" undergone by so many. It is a rootlessness whose principal cause is the upheavals that have been occurring and are continuing to

occur in the world. As these upheavals show no signs of coming
to an end, the question "What is going to happen?" (inseparable
from the question "What is *really* happening?") has become
practically universal. The upheavals, moreover, are of such a
nature that, if not in quality at least in quantity, they appear to
exceed anything of the kind in previous periods of history. It
appears that in vast zones of our planet, and potentially in all of
them, the threats that we analyzed in our chapter on the Cynics
and Stoics—death, exile, loss of freedom—have again become
familiar. And to these we must add others: torture, mental or
physical, and the rise of all kinds of violence, from violence
enacted in frenzy to violence perpetrated in cold blood. We
have countless examples of all these threats; indeed, many of us
have experienced them directly. A considerable amount of contemporary literature—particularly in the field of the novel—
has been based on subjects that, implicitly or explicitly,
describe the situations to which we have referred. This literature
has even acquired a name—"the literature of extreme situations."
These can all be reduced to one terrifying feeling: lack of security, not only on the part of man in himself, but also of each man
in society. For society itself seems almost to be floating in a
void. The precision with which its functions are often performed
today is not reason enough for this feeling of insecurity to disappear. Society more and more gives the impression of being
an extremely fragile entity. And this impression is confirmed
each time one of its cogs fails to mesh—the immense machine
comes to a noisy stop, or else begins to operate for ends very
different from those for which it was set up. Then, too, in the
minds of the "uprooted," this kind of insecurity is almost always
accompanied by the impression that, do what we will, "the truth
is that by now nothing can be done." Thus the impression of
insecurity, together with that of impotence, combine to produce
the feeling of rootlessness. We have come, it would seem, to a
period in which Kafka's forebodings have been fulfilled to the
letter: There is a vast "castle," which finally becomes so familiar
to us that we canalize all our acts into channels marked out by
innumerable officials, but of which we know nothing; there is a
"Trial," which obliges us to go through all sorts of procedures,

each of which is perfectly rational in itself although as a whole these procedures are utterly unintelligible. It is the world of the absurd, which so many writers have tried to describe since Kafka and which, in fact, had begun to appear in European literature before him. Now, whereas works of this sort in the past dealt only with a foreboding, or with the description of a psychological temperament, today they refer to a very familiar reality. For Pío Baroja's Andrés Hurtado or César, the world was something ugly, dark, impure, and impossible to control. For Kafka's characters, it was something delirious and absurd. But for the characters in such a novel as *The Plague*, by Camus, it is the reflection of a situation that has *already* prevailed more than once in contemporary life and that threatens to repeat itself. In other words, the facts are as current as this morning's newspaper. Thus it would appear that we are becoming citizens of that world to which Mannheim referred when he set up his distinction between substantial and functional rationality—a world in which everything happens intelligibly . . . in the service of the absurd. Order works for destruction; faith, for nihilism. Is it at all surprising that many men feel helpless in the face of this situation? Let us suppose that they have a faith. What good will such a faith do to them if it can never be substantiated by current experience? The consequence of the above facts and arguments is simple—many men have no faith and feel uprooted; while others, who have a faith, are unsuccessfully probing at its foundations.

2. All this, or not very much less, is said by those who maintain that faith has disappeared. Nor are they at any loss for arguments, and especially for facts, which support their view. Thus their description is accurate. But it is faulty in two respects. First, because it fails to admit that, despite everything, there are men who *do* have a belief. Second, because it forgets that even the most uprooted of men are trying to find a belief. We shall treat the first point briefly. But, before doing so, we must determine the unknown quantity with which we have to deal in the expression "aspiration to a faith."

What kind of aspiration is this? There cannot be much doubt in this respect. Our age can be described by the title of a contemporary poem: *The Age of Anxiety*. Or, by that of a contemporary novel: *The Age of Longing*. The anxiety is not about anything in particular; it simply designates the pure uneasiness of disorientation. But the longing is longing for a belief that will once again give man his place in the universe—for an "absolute." It will be objected that these are mere metaphors, and that, in addition, aspiration to an absolute is suspiciously "metaphysical." Well, then, let us be cautious. Is it so certain that such an aspiration exists? What does the "absolute" matter to the average man of our industrial civilization, or to the Asiatic peasant? What does it matter to the modern Western bourgeois, to the contemporary proletarian? Why all this insistence on an absolute, instead of modestly confining ourselves to simple and solid realities: bread, a roof, and some degree of assurance that no one will come and torture us, no one enslave us, no one let loose fire and destruction upon us? Is not this concern with an absolute an idle preoccupation of intellectuals? Or is it not a longing that unfortunately prevails only among certain peoples (for example, the Slavs or the "Asiatics") but which among others is entirely without meaning? We do not deny that this is sometimes the case. Hence there is a certain preoccupation with the absolute which is specifically felt by some intellectuals and which does not appear in other people; a certain longing for unquestionable truths which we find clumsily but movingly expressed among some of the youth of the sovietized countries and which is all the more astonishing for being shared not only by many communists but also by many anticommunists—both agree in jettisoning all intellectual caution, all political realism. Thus, there are longings for an absolute which are characteristic of particular groups, of particular peoples, of particular historical situations. But the special forms that the longing for the absolute assumes at times cannot lead us to deny its presence among vast multitudes in all regions of the planet. Longing for an absolute is a universal phenomenon, and like all such phenomena, is at once encouraging and disheartening, since it can be the basis of liberation *and* the cause of authoritarian enslavement.

3. Hence, while lamentation over the lack of beliefs is widespread, there is everywhere a desire to find them. This fact gives rise to the production of innumerable "solutions." They are of all sorts—"genuine," "false," and sometimes a mixture of both.

Let us cite some at random. At times, our allegiance is demanded by the various forms of totalitarianism—some which advocate a "perfect society," others which, whether deliberately or not, are based on a pure will to power. Making no less claim on our attention are the "traditional forces," which appear to be growing steadily stronger and even to be corroborating the observation of Donoso Cortés: A day will come when, throughout Europe, there will remain only two phalanxes, the Catholics and the Socialists. Less obtrusive are the "solutions" that emanate from certain comparatively small circles based on various sorts of "initiations"—ideological, esthetic, or moral. We must also rank as a "solution" what at first sight appears only an exacerbation of the problem—unqualified affirmation of the complete helplessness of man, full consciousness that "man is alone," or that, as Nietzsche put it, "God is dead," with the consequence that each individual must assume entire responsibility for his own acts. In addition, the longing for an absolute does not always have to assume an ideological garb. It can be present under an invitation to adapt oneself completely to one of the existing societies, regarded as the sole viable society. It can sometimes assume forms that are scarcely severe, that are even "attractive." One of them is the abundance of "formulas for happiness." These have always existed, but never in such quantities as today. They are the very opposite of the doctrines of the "initiates." But the same purpose fosters them. Among these "formulas" there are certain tendencies that at times appear to be sheer idiocy but that are, rather, symbols of helplessness: psychoanalysis emptied of its scientific content; dianetics; semantics as a cure-all. There are thousands of these "formulas," above all widely circulated in the United States, because tendencies that arise all over the world (at least in Western civilization) can be carried to their extreme in this country, where they do not encounter as many traditional resistances as in Europe or Latin America. Such "formulas" appear to have no connection with any ideological absolute. But let us not be misled; the void left by ideology is immediately filled by another absolute—the "functional" and "technical" absolute, which absorbs, tears down, levels, with unequalled efficiency. Nevertheless, these "formulas" caricature certain serious, profound, and noble realities of West-

ern civilization, just as the totalitarian doctrines prevailing in
the Slavic and Asiatic worlds caricature other noble tendencies
toward the salvation of society and the renewal of man.

In short, there is no scarcity of "solutions." And indeed the
abundance of such "solutions" provides the principal argument
advanced by those who assert that today there is no lack of
faith. All these lamentations over man's rootlessness, over the
emptiness of human existence, are, they insist, characteristic only
of impotent minorities or of desperate groups. Beliefs, they
would have it, are vigorous; no one, for example, would try to
maintain that a communist could properly be described as an
"uprooted person," and (since for those who hold this opinion,
the content of belief is unimportant), no one would deny that
in recent times there has been a considerable increase in the
vigor and spread of the great positive religions. Thus, from the
four quarters of the globe, it will be proved to us that the majority of mankind is saturated with beliefs. And further, we are
told, the strength of these beliefs is demonstrated by something
that would have been inconceivable to a "liberal" of the past
century; many men, that is, are conscious that their belief commits not only their intelligence but also their entire being. This
is clearly shown by the answer Ignazio Silone received from an
Italian communist politician, Palmiro Togliatti: "If we were not
a serious movement, which implies a profound dedication both
of thought *and will.* . . ." It appears, then, that no more is required to prove that elegies on the absence of faith are merely
rhetorical. Nevertheless, the very exuberance with which these
"faiths" are manifested makes us doubt if this view is more plausible than the other. No sooner do we scratch the surface of contemporary man than we find that, just as what he calls "desperation" is to a great extent the search for a stable belief, so what
he calls "faith" is largely a mere reaction to the uncertainty in
which he feels himself submerged. The very fanaticism with
which he sometimes defends his "faith" shows that there must
be some flaw in it.

4. We should have said: "some *flaws* in it." There is no belief
that is actually held by all men, or that can be extended among
all men; instead of representing the possibility of agreement, the

existing beliefs are dangerously close to providing the foundation for every kind of disagreement; faith is tinged with anxiety, and not only with the "natural" anxiety characteristic of every human being, but with the exacerbated anxiety of critical periods. It would seem, then, that what is wanted is a belief that eliminates these defects and that could really become universal.

Is it possible to find such a belief? By "belief"—or by "faith" —we mean something that in principle does not need to manifest itself through outbursts of enthusiasm or explosions of fanaticism. "Belief," or "faith," in our sense, means, rather, the possession of a security, not based on self-complacency but on the simple fact that, without some assurance in regard to a few fundamental things, life becomes an intolerable burden. Thus faith presents itself as the salvation of the individual. Now, that by which the individual is saved must, so to speak, "subsist in itself"—must be something "absolute." We mean, of course, a "genuine absolute," that is, something that claims to be true instead of dissolving itself into a mere hallucination. Hence contemporary irrationalisms can only provide pseudo-absolutes. And, for the same reason, the numerous caricatures of beliefs which abound today do not provide true absolutes either. Genuine belief, or genuine faith, is revealed no less in what is affirmed than in the manner in which the affirmation is made. A partial absolute is not a true absolute. But neither should an absolute be a new Moloch, to which everything is sacrificed. For when, instead of our possessing an absolute, it is the absolute that possesses us, there is no possibility of foreseeing to what perversities we shall then be led. Thus the absolute must be both outside of us and inside of us. In this way, our life will be impregnated with something that is beyond it; but at the same time this "something" will be *humanized*. In an essay on irony, we have written that irony must be a serious attitude, born of a certain enthusiasm, but that enthusiasm must always be tempered by irony. Similarly, we will now say that the absolute will never be genuine if it is not to some extent "reasonable" and "ironic." At any rate, man has to maintain a delicate balance between the claims of the absolute and those of his own life. Thus the absolute for which we are speaking must be "objective" as well as "human." For, if it is the former, it cannot be arbitrary; if it is the latter, it cannot be implacable.

We have said that there are at least four beliefs capable of being transformed into absolutes: God, Man, Society, and Nature. Western man has dedicated a considerable portion of his life to each of them. Ancient man, in his "classic" period, could live confidently within the horizon of Nature—a "Nature" more embracing than the "Nature" of the moderns, for it included society as one of its "moments." Gradually a conception was arrived at, which found its culmination in Aristotle: Everything has its "natural" place, its allotted and well-defined position; the stone falls to the ground, smoke rises into the air, the body tends toward nourishment, the soul inclines toward good. What was not in harmony with this conception caused no uneasiness—either it was scarcely understood or it was understood as a deviation that should, and could, be corrected. The essence of every being, then, was its proper "good," in a changing hierarchy. And the supreme Good was only the last moment in the process of "Nature" conceived as the inexhaustible principle of all reality. Christian man of the Middle Ages could live confiding in a personal God, who provided for everything, who distributed reward and punishment in this world and the next, who sooner or later resolved all discords. Each thing had its "place" too, so that it had even been possible to find room in the new horizon of God for the ancient world of "Nature." The inclusion of the latter in the former maintained both in equilibrium. But when a supreme decision had to be made, Nature was suspended, in order that the divine omnipotence should shine through. Modern man—first, among the minorities of Europe; later, among the majorities of the entire globe—did not throw God overboard and replace him by Nature or Man. He continued to serve and speak of God, but it is doubtful if he delivered his entire being over to Him. As for Nature, modern man got rid of the belief that the Earth was the center of a comparatively fixed universe, he fought against anthropomorphism, and tried to objectify everything. But Nature was no longer (as it had been for the Greeks) the sustaining principle of all being; it was—and still to a great extent remains—a reality that can be manipulated, whether by our hands, our instruments, or our minds. Contrary to what occurred during the Renaissance, as a result of the recoil toward what some imagined to be the classic spirit, "Nature" was not anthropomorphized in the modern period. Neither was it deified. It became an instrument among others. After this period, and with daily increasing impetus, came belief in the power of Man. For the philosopher, it was belief in the individual man; for the masses, who were acting in history to a steadily increasing degree, it was belief in collective man, in Society. Thus the moment arrived when Society itself was transformed into an absolute. Now, the present crisis is the crisis of *each one* of these elements. Is not this, then, the moment to seek another "absolute"? We are incapable of such a task. Furthermore, it would be vain. In fact, we believe that, however much they may be sought, no other elements will be found than those we have named: God, Nature, Society, Man. Hence what would seem to hold the most promise would be to seek an equilibrium among them. It should be a dynamic equilibrium which will give none of the four principles an immutable place, to dislodge it from which would later require turning half the world upside down. It should, furthermore, be such an equilibrium as will recognize that, at certain moments, it is necessary to emphasize the significance of one of the elements to the apparent detriment of the others. Thus, when everything has been sacrificed to Nature, it is time to emphasize the "rights" of God, Man, and Society; when too much insistence is placed on Society, the importance of God, Man, and Nature needs to be stressed. . . . Obviously, this will not remedy all the evils that afflict our world. The real solutions must take into account many other factors, some of them of a very concrete nature. Hence, in the above abstractions, we do not undertake to propose any panacea. Quite the contrary—we undertake to say that to make any one particular thing a panacea is the speediest way to precipitate a general slaughter.

We are sure only of this: If there is to be a renewal—even limited and uncertain, after the manner of all human things—it must be a genuine renewal, not a partial reality raised to the status of the sole reality, not a caricature. In what such a renewal might consist, we cannot say. Will it be a renewal of Christianity on a global scale, a revivifying of the old tree, nourished, as so often before, by a new and powerful sap? Why not? Will it be a world revolution of the oppressed, borne on the tide of a new faith—faith in collective salvation? Why not? Will it be a "new rationalism"; a new awakening of the "liberal" and "enlightened" spirit, that enemy to all myth and folly, to any belief that is not tempered with common sense, compassion, irony? Why not? In any case, the form of life to come must fulfil some difficult conditions. It will have to assimilate, and to a certain degree level, the vast multitudes of the planet without degrading or debasing them in the process; it will have to make the human person an end, yet stop short of deifying man; it will have to maintain organization without completely destroying freedom; it will have to go on encouraging the development of technique without killing the spirit. It will, in short, have to take into account God, Society, Man, and Nature, without devoting itself entirely to any one of them, yet at the same time without immobilizing them in a static equilibrium. To do this successfully will certainly be a formidable task. Or rather, it will be an unending task. There is no danger, then, that this planet will one day find itself inhabited by a community of saints, instead of by our poor, our beloved society of human beings.

Notes

Some of our observations on technique are applicable to the problem of the organization of society. It can even be said that pessimism in respect to such an organization (an intellectual pessimism, which has not always affected concrete conduct) has followed the same rhythm as pessimism in respect to technique, at least during the last fifty years. Compare, for example, the optimism with which H. G. Wells, in *A Modern Utopia* (1905), foresaw a completely organized society and the pessimism that the same prospect aroused in a mid-twentieth-century writer, George Orwell, in his *1984* (1949). In both, identical social elements appear—the *samurai* or "voluntary nobility" in Wells, the members of the *Inner Party* in Orwell—but the judgment pronounced upon them is diametrically opposite. Chesterton, by the way, in *The Man Who Was Thursday* (1908), already distinguished between the "outer circle" and the "inner circle" of the revolutionary organization that he was depicting. And in the characters of his novel too there were those subtle dichotomies that are so frequent in contemporary analyses. The "outer circle" was composed of the ingenuous, those who believed that everything was being done for the sake of a better world. The members of the "inner circle" were those who had no illusions, those who were "too intellectual to think that man upon this earth can ever be quite free of original sin and the struggle." Hence "when they say that mankind shall be free at last, they mean that mankind shall commit suicide." In a later note we refer to the importance of the contemporary novel for an understanding of certain present-day problems. This novel of Chesterton's—like several others by the same writer—represents a remarkable anticipation of a number of characteristics that are widespread today. In Chapter IV, one of the characters says: "We discover from a book of sonnets that a crime will be committed." And another passage from the same chapter reads: "The moderns say we must not punish heretics. My only doubt is whether we have a right to punish anybody else."

Among the great hopes raised by the development of techniques is automation—the most typical manifestation of the "second industrial revolution." The vast amount of literature already produced on the subject is understandable, for the use of automation affects not only the methods of industrial production, but also the patterns of human consumption. Now, the forms of human consumption are not a strictly economic subject; the "figure" of human life in any given period of its history is largely dependent on them. To understand this, we may think of the changes already made in the "human landscape"— especially in the most highly developed countries economically —in consequence of the new types of consumption. It is already a commonplace to say that electricity and the radio have changed many structures of life in regions that were earlier practically "isolated." And so it is to point out the substantial changes produced by the introduction and increasing use of the automobile. But it should be noted that these changes go beyond a mere increase in the possibility of moving about; in the United States, for example, the automobile is literally producing an "explosion" of cities; the suburban type is increasingly supplanting both the rural and the urban types. Many more changes of the same nature can be expected when automation begins to affect consumption as a whole.

In the last two chapters the word "technique" often means "applied science," "applied natural science," "industrial science."

The word "technology" might have been used for this purpose. Nevertheless, we have used "technique" throughout the book in order to unify the vocabulary. It will be easy for the reader to give the word "technique" in each case its proper meaning.

The problem of the possible influence of the "intellectual" on society deserves a few further remarks.

In general, the modern intellectual has been the victim of two contrary illusions. The first consists in believing that the milieu in which he moves—the milieu of "ideas," of "intellectual problems," and of the means, including the material means, by which such a milieu is created (magazines, books, universities, etc.)—coincides with that of the majority of the population. At certain moments of success, he even reaches the point of thinking that his action and thought are "followed"—or at least discussed—by a considerable number of his fellow citizens. In consequence, he imagines that intellectual controversies are *directly* decisive.

The second illusion proceeds partly from a reaction against this tendency. By experience or reflection, the intellectual discovers that the majority of people do not even know the names that, for him, are the most outstanding, and (a fact of the utmost significance) that, when they do know them, it is only by virtue of a lamentable distortion. He thereupon resolves upon one of two courses of conduct—"intervention" or "contempt." If he chooses intervention, he finds himself in a situation where he is forced to give up being an "intellectual"—usually only in part, but sometimes entirely. If he chooses contempt, he undertakes a retreat—but it is not a "realistic" retreat (like that described in the chapter); instead, it is a retreat that, being merely disillusioned, is sterile not only for the present but also for the future.

The first decision is frequently taken today. Certainly, "intervention" is not always equivalent to "adaptation." But if the intellectual wants to act directly and profoundly on a large majority of the population, he must undertake a basic modification of his thought and of his way of expressing it. (To obviate an easy objection, we point out that in the "artist"—and especially in the "great artist"—no such modification is necessary; the "great artist" can be heard, read, followed, discussed by great masses of the population without having to adapt his language to them. But these great artists are exceptional, and we are here referring to the "ordinary" intellectual, and particularly to the intellectual whose instrument of expression is not artistic forms but ideas.) In addition, he must change even his usual media of communication and adopt those that promise a wider dissemination of his message—the radio, television, the film, the newspaper, and the mass-circulation periodical. This is the thesis maintained by Jean-Paul Sartre in his book *What is Literature?* (New York, 1949; English translation of *Situations*, II, Paris, [1948]). In adherence to this thesis, the intellectual will not confine himself to producing his work as well as he can; he will first of all consider to what groups of men his work can be addressed and in what form he must write it so that its influence will be "effective." Instead of aspiring to develop a rigorous, antirhetorical thought that tries to come to grips with reality, he will constantly seek the lines of least resistance by which he can reach the mass public.

It looks like an admirable solution. Actually, it is one more case of the classic procedure of putting the cart before the horse. For, with it, the intellectual forgets two facts.

The first is that influences are not always propagated in a simple way, as if ideas traveled directly from the mind of the intellectual to other minds. The intellectual forgets, then, that the influence of a work of intellect on society commonly follows tortuous paths. For example, it seems that the intellectual is revolutionary only when he attacks long-established powers whose sole interest is their own preservation, and enters the field in defense of a change. Yet not always the most "revolutionary" intellectuals have exercised the most influence on social transformations. An outstanding example is that of Descartes; it proves that sometimes the intellectual exercises influence all the more strongly, the more cautiously he proceeds and the less he undertakes to make a direct attack on the structure of society or its beliefs. In addition, the influences exercised by a work of intellect cannot be measured solely by the period in which it was produced or by the number of people it directly reached, either in its own time or later. We do not deny, then, the importance of the influence that a work of intellect may have upon society; we merely reject the means by which some believe that such influence should be exercised. Kant is not exactly an author who is read by the great masses of population, despite the "success" that he attained in his time among not inconsiderable circles. But his influence has been enormous. We are not unaware that the spread of education has caused an increasing number of people to come into contact with Kant's work. But this work had already influenced modes of thought among the Western peoples, long before any such pedagogical dissemination of it occurred. Thus the influence exercised by the *Critiques* cannot be measured only by the number of people who have actually read them or have received trustworthy accounts of them. Azorín must have had something of the sort in mind when he wrote, in *El Escritor,* that "there are two kinds of fame—horizontal and vertical"— which does not mean that the vertical type of fame is to last forever, nor that all of the horizontal examples are fated to vanish in an instant. An intellectual work that is difficult to comprehend can influence a human group, which, through other media, transmits it to another group, and so on, until finally it influences the ideas and attitudes of people who have never heard of the fountain from which they drink. On the other hand, a "popular" work can slip over the masses without leaving a trace. (This, be it said in passing, is one of the reasons why such powerful media as the film, the radio, the television, and the press often exercise less influence than is generally supposed.)

This brings us to the second fact that many of today's intellectuals forget. It is the fact that a great number of works have wholly failed to influence the masses *precisely because* their authors consciously and deliberately adopted the language that they considered most likely to make their books "popular." On the other hand, we find many cases in which a work, especially a work of art, which had at first appeared to be something "exquisite," "exclusive," suitable only for a minority, attains wide popularity. There have been so many instances of this type of sucess that one is sometimes tempted to believe that certain writers, in their fondness for unpopularity, secretly hope that this very fondness will in time turn out to be the most effective bait for conquering popularity. Naturally, no inviolable rules can be laid down in these matters. Hence we shall not attempt to decide the issue. We only affirm that the intellectual's intentions have a less decisive result on his possible influence than they would appear to have. The conclusion to be drawn is this: When the intellectual's work is genuine, without affected subtleties in the taste of a minority, but also without any deliberate intention of conquering the majority, it has a role—sometimes greater, sometimes less, but never valueless—in present or future society.

We have been unable to treat a subject that any fairly full analysis of our period should consider—the evolution of social mores.

It is not a minor subject. Sometimes it casts more light on history than the study of ideas or of social upheavals. In describing mid-nineteenth-century Madrid, in his *Fortunata y Jacinta,* Pérez Galdós wrote: "Clothing anticipated thought, and even before verse had been banished in favor of prose, wool had put an end to silk." It is a sentence worth pondering. For if mores, manners—and fashions—do not always "anticipate," they assign men to particular periods more accurately than many other factors. We see this clearly in such cases as the "anticipations of the future" in literature or the cinema. A novel or a film produced only a decade ago, and devoted to depicting a state of humanity supposedly greatly "advanced" in comparison with its own time, today gives the impression of something irrevocably "passé." The clothes, the furniture, the gestures, all seem to have become "dated." It would, then, be interesting to undertake a study of the evolution of mores in our own period. Probably it would reveal two complementary aspects—rapid transformation and increasing unification. What would have seemed utterly extravagant twenty years ago, is normal today. But, conversely, today there are strict taboos on a number of acts that, ten or fifteen years ago, would have seemed perfectly innocent.

We said that the person is not equivalent to his social function. At the same time we indicated that the person is social in nature. There is no contradiction here. We mean that neither pure society nor the pure individual is an actual reality. They are limiting concepts, between which the reality called "man" oscillates. Hence there is neither a purely individual ethics nor a purely social ethics; every moral imperative has its basis in society *and* in the person. Starting from different presuppositions, two contemporary thinkers have insisted upon this individual-social aspect of man—Ortega y Gasset, with his theory of inter-individuality, and Martin Buber, with his thesis of the "thou" as "mediator" between the "I" and the "we."

Some of the situations of contemporary existence have been extremely well described in the contemporary novel. Such novels are not mere copies of social and historical reality, nor are they mere artistic forms independent of time and space; they are a series of "existential schemas," which afford us a better understanding of actual human situations.

So Graham Greene must have thought when he wrote in *The Ministry of Fear:* " 'Let me lend you the *History of Contemporary Society.* It's in hundreds of volumes, but most of them are sold in cheap editions: *Death in Piccadilly, The Ambassador's Diamonds, The Theft of the Naval Papers, Diplomacy, Seven Days Leave, The Four Just Men. . . .'* " These all refer to "extreme situations," and in such a way that it is sometimes difficult to distinguish between reality and fantasy. In addition, all of them are imbued with a climate of *violence.* This climate has been analyzed in several well-known works. In some of them (Georges Sorel's *Reflections on Violence,* for example, or Ernst Jünger's *War, Our Mother*), the aim has been to exalt violence; in others (such as David Rousset's *The Universe of the Concentration Camps,* or Eugen Kogon's *The Theory and Practice of Hell*), it has been to denounce it. But there is nothing better than the novel to register the various forms of such a climate. The number of novels of this kind—we refer only to those worth mentioning as literature—is so great that a choice is embarrassing. We shall name a few of them:

On the one hand, there are books like those of André Malraux, from *Man's Fate* to *Man's Hope;* Ilya Ehrenburg's *The Storm,* Alexander Fadaev's *The Young Guard,* Louis Aragon's "river-novel" *The Communists.* On the other hand, there are books like Norman Mailer's *The Naked and the Dead,* Theodor Plivier's *Stalingrad,* John Hersey's *The Wall,* Arthur Koestler's *Scum of the Earth.* It does not matter that some of these writers have—or once had—a "faith," while others do not. For our purpose, they are all in the same boat. They have produced a kind of literature which began to appear in quantity as early as the end of the First World War. To it belong books relative to the war itself or to its consequences, from the most conscientiously "crude" examples (such as those by Dorgelès, Barbusse, Glaeser) to the most "humanitarian" (the widely read book of Remarque, for example). Included in it too is the interminable list of books that attempt to depict various political atmospheres, from Fedor Gladkov's *Cement*, or Ramón Sender's *Seven Red Sundays*, to Jan Valtin's *Out of the Night* (we are not concerned with whether the events related in these books have much or little basis in reality, still less with the doctrinal position of their authors; it suffices for us that the books are significant). Finally, the list must be extended to include the principal books produced by the so-called "lost generation" of North American writers (especially Hemingway)—with whose work we may to some extent connect (in reference to their meaning not their content) certain recent novels which abound in various forms of desolation—for example, Carmen Laforet's *Nothing*, Albert Camus' *The Stranger*, Camilo José Cela's *The Family of Pascual Duarte*, Elio Vittorini's *In Sicily*, Alberto Moravia's *Woman of Rome*, Françoise Sagan's *Bonjour Tristesse*, etc., and (though on an "ancient" but eternal theme) Pär Lagerkvist's *Barabbas*. All the books mentioned depict the atmosphere of "extreme situations" directly. But other works had foreshadowed them— those in which this atmosphere was "suggested" or "anticipated," as in Kafka; those that exploit the thesis of "gratuitous acts," as in André Gide or Aldous Huxley's *Point Counterpoint*. Continuing these, there were the novels in which the same atmosphere (especially its more violent aspects) was "sociologically" explained; this is the case with the milieu described in Volume XXIII of Jules Romains's *Men of Good Will* series, *The Gathering of the Gangs*, or with the similar but slightly more *unheimisch* milieu to which Thomas Mann referred in Chapter XXX of his *Doctor Faustus*. The culmination of all this literature seems to be the series of works in which the principal characters not only find themselves in an extreme situation but also theorize about it—this is the case with the lucid Igor in Charles Plissnier's *False Passports*, with the subtle Ivanov in Arthur Koestler's *Darkness at Noon*, with the implacable O'Brien in George Orwell's *1984*. . . . In all of them a phenomenon characteristic of our epoch is manifest—the appearance of the "logicians against logic." We will stop here. We only set out to give a few examples to confirm the truth of the quotation from Greene at the beginning of this note. He who would be thoroughly informed concerning contemporary man must not, then, confine himself to reading books about events that have actually occurred; for certain aspects of the present, imagination is more revealing than reality.

This book, although it touches upon sociological themes, is not a work of sociology. Hence we have not been able to refer in it to certain interesting social phenomena that do not fit into the traditional categories and that have already found their place in literature. For example, we have not been able to touch upon a question that is fundamental today—that of the role that the so-called white-collar worker (the clerk, the office-worker, the bureaucrat, the salesman, the professional, the average intellectual) plays in contemporary society. Those who are interested in the problems raised by this social class at a particular period and in a country where the question of the white-collar worker has reached overwhelming proportions (though not out of line with what is prevalent throughout the Western world) may consult C. Wright Mills' *White Collar*, New York (1951), the central theme of which is the study of the social—and human—consequences of the increasing "rationalization" and "industrialization" of office work. In his Introduction, Mills refers to some of the contemporary literature that has taken cognizance of the problem and is an aid to understanding aspects of contemporary man not always treated in the novels mentioned in the previous note. One example is the Johannes Pinneberg of Hans Fallada's *Little Man, What Now?* Another is the Willy Loman of Arthur Miller's dramatic *Death of a Salesman*. The two types are quite different in many ways (largely due to the fact that one belongs to the European society of about 1930 while the other is a North American of about 1947). But they have one common trait—that of reflecting, from a particularly unstable social situation, the same attitude of mingled uprootedness and hope, of fantasy and desperation, in which many men in vast areas of the globe have been living and still live.

The quotation from Saint Bonaventura is given in the translation by Sister Emma Thérèse Healy in her edition of the *De Reductione*, Saint Bonaventura College, Saint Bonaventure, N. Y. (1939).–For the difference between mysticism and mechanism in the sense in which we use the terms, see Bergson's book, previously cited, *The Two Sources*, etc.–The work of F. G. Juenger's is *Die Perfektion der Technik*, Frankfurt am M. (1946); English translation, *The Failure of Technology; Per-*

fection without Purpose, Hinsdale, Ill. (1949).–On the development of mechanization in the nineteenth and twentieth centuries there is an extensive bibliography. For the problem of pessimism and optimism during the growth of the Industrial Revolution in the past century, we recommend Chapter IV of P. M. Schuhl's *Machinisme et Philosophie*, 2nd ed., Paris (1947). Here the principal opinions on the subject are enumerated and discussed. Interesting data on increase of production through machines will be found in the Conclusion of the same book. They are sufficient for our purpose. For what has occurred since Schuhl terminated his investigation of the subject (1947) is merely a multiplication of the same data and an increasing application of techniques to man and to the organization of society. On the relation between society and mechanistico-industrial development, we mention especially Georges Friedmann's *Problèmes humains du machinisme industriel*, Paris (1946), and *Où va le travail humain?* Paris (1951). For the distribution of economic activities in accordance with technical progress, Jean Fourastié, *Le grand espoir du XXᵉ siècle*, Paris (1950), and *Machinisme et bien-être*, Paris (1951).–Two novels that contain, respectively, trenchant and cruel criticisms of techniques are: Pedro Salinas, *The Incredible Bomb*, and C. Virgil Gheorghiu, *The Twenty-fifth Hour*. We mention only the most recent works of this kind; the reader will remember, among others, Aldous Huxley's ironic criticism in his *Brave New World*.–Commonplaces on the modern world in F. Strowski, *L'homme moderne*, Paris (1931), and J. Huizinga, *In the Shadow of Tomorrow* (1935), a "diagnosis of the spiritual ills of our time." We mention them only to warn the reader against them—much to our regret in the case of Huizinga, whose other books are admirable. Something rather better on the subject in Manuel García Morente, *Ensayos sobre el progreso*, Madrid (1934), and "Ensayo sobre la vida privada," *Revista de Occidente*, XLVII (1935), 90-110 and 164-203, both reprinted in *Ensayos*, Madrid (1945), 89-199. Julián Marías presents an accurate "outline of our situation" in the chapter so titled in his *Reason and Life: The Introduction to Philosophy*, New Haven (1956), English translation of *Introducción a la filosofía*, Madrid (1947). For proof that some of the complaints against modern city life (copiously indulged in by Strowski, Huizinga, and even García Morente) are not peculiar to our time, the reader has only to refer to what Seneca wrote in his *Ep.* LVI, 1, where he complains that he was surrounded by every kind of noise (his house being near a public bath).–Maurice Duverger's article is entitled "Les mains propres" and appeared in *Le Monde,* Paris, Aug. 3, 1950.

The "premature closing" of the Inca Empire is clearly brought out in Ernst Samhaber's brief but acute description in his *South America* (written in German, but published only in a Spanish translation by Ramón de la Serna, Buenos Aires [1946]), 65 ff.– The German idea of the *imperium mundi* (without the National-Socialist zoology in the style of Alfred Rosenberg), in Oswald Spengler, *Jahre der Entscheidung. Erster Teil: Deutschland und die weltgeschichtliche Entwicklung,* München (1933).–The idea of the transition from laissez-faire to a planned society in Karl Mannheim, *Diagnosis of our Time,* Cambridge (1943), New York (1944), 3 ff. For the two meanings of planning, *op. cit,* 7 ff.–The book by James Burnham is *The Managerial Revolution; What is Happening in the World,* New York (1941).–On history as a power for renewal, see Orwell's novel mentioned in the preceding note and the same writer's book of essays, *Shooting an Elephant,* London (1950), 121, as well as the suggestive passage in the Diary of the Marquis de Custine, *La Russie en 1839* (English translation, *Journey for our Time; the Journals of Marquis de Custine,* New York [1951]), under date of July 8, 1939, where he writes that when power seeks to be absolute, it decides not only to make the future but also to "remake the past."–The reference to Dilthey in *Einleitung in die Geisteswissenschaften,* I, Leipzig (1883), *Gesammelte Schriften,* Leipzig and Berlin, I, 354.–On the role of the intellectual in modern European society since the Renaissance: Theodor Geiger, *Aufgaben und Stellung der Intelligenz in der Gesellschaft,* 1949. This book may serve to counterbalance certain exaggerations of Mannheim's on the subject, expressed in the books of his that we mentioned earlier and especially in his *Ideologie und Utopie,* Bonn (1929); English translation with new material, *Ideology and Utopia,* New York (1936), reprinted (1956).

For the idea of belief in Ortega y Gasset, *Ideas y creencias,* Buenos Aires (1940), 11-60 (*OC,* V [1947], 377-405). There is an English translation of a portion of this book: "Believing and Thinking," *Essays and Studies by Students of Simmons College,* Vol. XI, No. 1 November, 1952, pages 1-6.–The two novels by Kafka mentioned in the chapter are *The Castle* and *The*

Trial; the two novels by Baroja are *The Tree of Knowledge* and *Cesar or Nothing.*–Mannheim's distinction between "substantial rationality" and "functional rationality," in his *Mensch und Gesellschaft im Zeitalter des Umbaus,* Leyden (1935).–*The Age of Anxiety: A Baroque Eclogue* is the title of a poem by W. H. Auden.–*The Age of Longing* is the title of a novel by Arthur Koestler.–Donoso Cortés' observation occurs in Part I, Chapter VIII of his *Ensayo sobre el catolicismo, el liberalismo y el socialismo considerados en sus principios fundamentales,* 1st ed., Madrid (1851), often reprinted.–The quotation from an Italian politician comes from a letter to the newspaper *Unità,* January 6, 1950. The italics in the text are ours.–On the mass social upheavals to which we have referred in the last two chapters, as well as at various points in Part I of this book, see Pitirim A. Sorokin, *Man and Society in Calamity,* New York (1942).

Index

armies, 169; and the rise of nationalism, 170; in contemporary society, 208; and groups, 211-212; and the problem of faith, 214-226; the intellectuals and the, 229-230

Mates, Benson, 33

Matthew, Saint: words of, 87, 88

Mechanization, 199-201

Mediation: Stoic conception of, 24, 28, 31; Christian, 90; spirit of, in the Modern Age, 141-144

Mediterranean world, 10, 53, 123, 146

Messianism, 55, 57, 60-61

Mexican Revolution, 186

Meyer, Eduard, 64, 105; on Jesus Christ, 87

Meyer, Ernst, 83

Meyer, François: on acceleration in history, 185

Michelet, Jules, 185

Middle Ages, 80, 118-119, 123, 129, 132-133; and the Renaissance, 111; and the Modern Age, 113, 132; the so-called "new," 121, 126; waning of the, 132, 134; conception of power in the, 144; idea of human life in the, 159-160; conception of technique in the, 198-199; basic conceptions in the, 224

Middle Classes, 153-154

Milik, J. T., 102

Miller, Arthur, 234

Mills, Charles Wright, 234

Minorities: and masses, 115-118, 187-189, 230-231; in the crisis of the "Few," 133

Modern Age: meaning of the, 110-121, 123, 125; historical divisions in the, 110-111, 118-119, 123; and the Middle Ages, 113, 132; nature of the, 115; two conceptions of the, 120-122, 126-128; the great question of the, 122; ideas about death in the, 159-160; ideas about science in the, 179-180; assimilation in the, 114; activism in the, 153, 198, 206-207; basic conceptions in the, 224

Modern Man, 121; and the medieval man, 132-133; basic beliefs of the, 224-225. See also Modern Age

Molière, Jean-Baptiste Poquelin, 34

Monarchy: absolute, 111, 153; role of, in the crisis of the "Few," 142-145; and the modern conception of God, 144

Montaigne, Michel Eyquem, Seigneur de, 136, 137

Montesquieu, Charles de Secondat, Baron de, 162

Moravia, Alberto, 233

Mores, evolution of, 231

Moscati, S., 102

Murray, Gilbert, 9

Mysteries, Greek, 93, 103-104

Napoleon, 176

Napoleonic Wars, 168-169

Nation: an ambiguous word, 170; "crystallization" of a, 193

Nationalism: its development, 169-171; its meaning, 170; European and extra-European, 171

National States, 133

Naturalism: and supernaturalism, 96-97, 135, 137; in the Modern Age, 181-182

Natural law, 181

Natural religion, 181

Natural resources, 190-191

Nature: return to, 23, 24, 27; according to the Stoics, 24, 26, 27; Greek and Hebraic conceptions of, 50, 53; ancient and modern conceptions of, 158-159; idea of, in the Modern Age, 181; belief in, 217, 224-226

Near East, 110

Neoplatonism: reflects a historical situation, 40; represented by Plotinus, 40-46; a history of a retreat, 46. See also Platonists, Neoplatonists

Neoplatonists: school of, 40; conception of man, 40-42; "Olympian attitude" of, 41; indifference to government, 41-42; on liberation of the soul, 42; "isolation," and "immobility" in, 42; emphasis on the flight from the sensible world, 42, 46-47; true meaning of "flight" according to, 42-45; on the role of the body, 43; on suffering and evil, 44; on the "there above," 44-

Sender, Ramón J., 233
Seneca, 11, 33, 34, 35, 105, 235; on self-sufficiency, 23; on experience, 25; on return to nature, 27; on self-alienation, 29; on clemency, 30; on conventions, 31; on the insignificance of human life, 31; and Plotinism, 47; on transfiguration, 91
Septimius Severus, 81
Siberia, 171, 172
Siegfried, André: on demographic "explosions," 191
Silone, Ignazio, 222
Simmel, Georg: on "the intersection of social circles," 125
Smith, Adam, 161
Social anarchy, 77, 113, 188
Social circles, intersection of, 125
Socialism, 206, 221
Social problems: in the nineteenth century, 179-180; and science, 179, 180, 182-183; application of technique to, 186-187
Society: and the individual, 13, 178, 203, 210-212, 215-216; Cynic conception of, 14; Cynics against, 16; Stoic conception of, 21-22, 24-25, 28, 31; Platonist conception of, 38, 40-42; inertia of, 76; leveling of, 76, 78, 184; militarization of, 77; anarchic state of, 77; uniformity of, 78; collapse of, 78; survival of, 78; Hebrew conception of, 86; and man, 95, 97-98; and God, 98; stable and unstable, 113-115, 133, 137, 179, 206-208; and ideas, 116, 153-154; "opening" of, 119; feudal, 133; European, 128; rule in, 133; monarchic, 142, 144, 153; in the crisis of the "Few," 144; in the crisis of the "Many," 154; in the crisis of "All," 169; contemporary, 168, 196-222; and science, 180, 182-183; men equal before, 181; organization of, 182-183, 203-214; and technique, 186-187, 200-201; regimentation of, 203-204; types of, 203-204, 206; conditions for a good, 204-205; dissolution of, 206-207; structure of, 211-212; belief in, 217, 224-226; reflected in the novel, 218, 232-

233; adaptation to, 221; pessimism on, 226-227
Sociology of knowledge, 8, 9
Socrates, 3, 29, 86, 87, 139; "in a concentration camp," 5; on man, 13; committed his life to his philosophy, 91
Soden, Hans Freiherr von, 63
Solomon, 54
Sombart, Werner, 164
Somervell, D. C., 11
Sophists, 9
Sophocles, 9
Sorel, Georges, 232
Sorokin, Pitirim A., 129, 237
Soul, Platonic and Neoplatonic conception of the, 42, 44-45, 47
Sovereign arbiter, 96; reason as, 134, 139-140, 145
Soviet Union, 191, 202. See also Russia
Spain, 136, 146, 154, 171
Spencer, Herbert, 167, 178, 193
Spengler, Oswald, 82, 177, 236
Spinoza, B. de, 25; and Descartes, 141
Spirit of the Age; Hegelian conception of the, 147-148; technique as the, 197
Stability of society, 113-115, 133, 137, 179, 206-208
Standard of living, rise in the, 190, 208
State: Christian community and the, 96; and the individual, 178, 202
Stein, Ernst, 80
Stoicism: as a way of life, 17; failure of, 21, 26, 28; contradictions in, 22-23; and modern pessimism, 176. See also Stoics
Stoics, 79, 98; emphasize resistance, 17; school of, 17; on knowledge, 17-18, 25, 29; emphasis of, on ethics, 17, 29, 31; against despotism, 18; as mediators, 18, 20; imago mundi, 19; ethics of, 19-20, 31; take refuge in the inner self, 20, 24; confront the problem of happiness, 19-20; look for freedom to resist, 21; on society, 21-22, 24-25, 28, 31; indifference of, 22, 30; impassibility of, 22-23; withdraw from life, 23; avoid the

Weber, Max, 83, 129; on bureaucracy, 71; on Protestantism and the "spirit of capitalism," 164, 165
Weil, Simone, 83; on human history, 74
Wells, H. G., 192, 226
West: origins of the, 9; historical periods in the, 110-111, 123; expansion of the, 114, 147, 168, 171; de-westernization of the, 114; crises in the, 122; definition of the, 146-147; role of the, in the world, 147; dynamism of the, 153, 206-207; rationalism in the, 163; storms in the, 176; pessimism and optimism in the, 177-178; organization of the, 183, 205; beliefs in the, 224-225
West, Nathanael, 34
Western Christian world, 9
Western history. See West
Westernization of the world, 114
Whittaker, Edmund, 192

Wilder, Thornton: on Julius Caesar, 83
William of Occam. See Occam, William of
Wilson, Edmund, 102
Workers, 175, 177; white-collar, 234
World: this world and the other, 31-32, 95-97, 159-161, 181; unity of the, 172, 192-193; image of the, changed by science, 179-180, 186; unity and diversity of the, 184; interdependence in the, today, 168, 192-193, 204

Young, Edward, 162

Zambrano, María, 31
Zealots, 64; beliefs of, 61-62
Zeitlin, S., 102
Zeller, Eduard, 33; on the Stoics, 17
Zeno of Citium, 33, 86
Zorrilla, José, 34
Zubiri, Xavier, 63, 142, 149; on Hebrews, 53; on Descartes, 141